D1561680

Participatory and Workplace **Democracy**

A THEORETICAL DEVELOPMENT IN
CRITIQUE OF LIBERALISM

Ronald M. Mason

SOUTHERN ILLINOIS UNIVERSITY PRESS
Carbondale and Edwardsville

HD
5650
.M366

Copyright © 1982 by
the Board of Trustees, Southern Illinois University

ALL RIGHTS RESERVED

Printed in the United States of America
Edited by Dan Seiters
Production supervised by Kathleen Giencke
Designed by Bob Nance, Design for Publishing

Library of Congress Cataloging in Publication Data

Mason, Ronald M.
    Participatory and workplace democracy.

    Bibliography: p.
    Includes index.
    1. Employees' representation in management.
2. Liberalism. 3. Democracy. I. Title.
HD5650.M366   658.3'152   81-16687
ISBN 0-8093-0992-0   AACR2

AUG 27 1982

To *Rhonda* and *Jeffrey*

Contents

Preface

GOOD TIMES SELDOM INSPIRE THEORISTS TO WRITE. THERE IS nothing unusual in claiming that the United States is troubled by disorder, but contemporary problems seem so severe, we could be on the brink of truly hard times. The situation symbolically is captured by the Chrysler Corporation teetering on the edge of complete collapse. The times demand action and reaction, but not despair. They demand new views and new alternatives derived from them. Thus hope is symbolized by innovative forms of representation and ownership within the Chrysler Corporation.

This book is part of the search for new views and alternatives. It attempts to escape the confining views of the past, to look anew at life in the United States, and to recommend ways that we can pursue improvement. Though not polemical, this book does attempt to be persuasive by arguing that life in the United States can be improved by making more democratic the various communities of which we are a part. This is its central contention. In an effort to identify fully the processes through which humans develop and the changes in human communities that are necessary for people to develop, this work must confront the major factor that limits our ability to envision better worlds—our dominant system of thought, liberalism. It is difficult to move beyond liberalism, for so much of our vocabulary, including what is political, is derived from liberalism. Since so much of our society is built on liberal principles, a critique of liberalism is often a critique of our society, and that is not always easy. Moreover, liberalism makes it appear that all that is not liberal is by definition totalitarian. This false impression is difficult to surmount.

Nevertheless, once the classical liberal conceptualizations in the tradition of John Locke are abandoned, it is possible to construct a viable version of democracy as a participatory form of community rule. Such a view of democracy would be distinctively different from the classical liberal formulation of democracy, which is representative civil government in which the interests, especially the property interests, of citizens are protected. It would stress the involvement of men and women in making community decisions that affect their daily lives. Unlike liberal democracy, which directs attention to the state, participatory democracy broadens the perspective to include all communities as settings for political interaction and as possible locations of democratic rule. This does not mean that certain communities cannot be emphasized. In addition to the continually important national community and the formal government associated with it, the workplace community is among those that gain relief from the non-Lockean liberal view. Indeed, close association between experiences in the workplace and in government plays the central role in the discussion of participatory and workplace democracy.

The seven chapters of this work elaborate upon these general views. The first sets the theoretical background against which the arguments concerning participatory and workplace democracy develop. Establishing a nonliberal view of the political world is its most important objective. Based on that nonliberal view, the next chapter offers a participatory conception of democracy that rivals liberal democracy. If democracy qua participation is to be sought, a greater understanding of participation must be achieved. This is the charge of the third chapter. When participation research is restructured to a nonliberal basis, the community of the workplace emerges as the critical setting for effective training in participation, especially participation in government. The fourth chapter explores this "workplace connection." There are reasons to pursue participation in the workplace, other than its relationship to participation in government. Another compelling reason, as developed in the fifth chapter, relates to the importance of work in our lives. Work cannot be of intrinsic value to us unless we are able to participate in the decisions that govern our lives in the workplace. The sixth chapter explores the dimensions of workplace democracy. The book closes by considering the entire development of participatory and workplace democracy as a critique of liberalism. It also presents a glimpse into the participatory society and discusses participation as a primary value in life.

Along its way, *Participatory and Workplace Democracy* offers a number of contributions. Among them are a critique of liberalism and the tenets upon which it rests, a new conception of the political, an original blend of theoretical and empirical concerns, a normative theory of democracy buttressed by empirical research on participation, a version of democracy applicable to any community, a conceptual revision of political sociology and participation research based on the critique of liberalism, and an interdisciplinary study of work and worker participation, which is given order by political theory and intellectual

history. Though both the reformulation of the political and the construction of democracy are significant, neither necessarily must be accepted for the reader to appreciate the importance of participation
and the fecundity of the workplace connection. At the same time
there are limitations to the work. Though reference will be made to a
variety of Western political ideas and to the circumstances of a number of nations, the focus is primarily on the United States. This emphasis on the United States is not maintained in the discussion of
workplace participation examples, for that is the subject of another
work. Participation plays a central role in the development of the argument, but not all forms of participation are examined. The forms
of participation generated during revolutionary periods are largely
ignored. In addition, concepts such as non-decision making and mo-
bilization of bias are recognized, but not treated in depth.

The most critical limitation is more apparent than real. Nowhere in
Participatory and Workplace Democracy is the actual feasibility of workplace democracy examined. This may seem to be a critical absence because no matter how desirable workplace democracy appears, it is unlikely that high levels of workplace participation would be instituted
unless it were demonstrated to be economically viable, feasible in
terms of the social-psychological reaction of workers, and the like.
Such an examination has been reserved for the companion volume,
The Feasibility of Workplace Democracy in the United States.

Whenever the gestation period of a book is long, the number of
people who should be acknowledged grows as well. This is so true of
Participatory and Workplace Democracy that I cannot possibly name all
deserving mention. You must know how deeply I appreciate your
support. At the same time I cannot possibly think of releasing the
book without acknowledging those who have played the most special
roles.

Early encouragement came from my colleagues at The University
of Iowa: Lane Davis, John McClusky, and John Nelson. Each provided
critical readings of the manuscript and improved it significantly.
Charles Drekmeier, John Foster, Rhonda Vinson, and Carole Pateman
also offered most helpful reviews, as did many of my democratic theory class students. Those who invited me to speak on the topic of
workplace democracy added to the encouragement; they include Don
Ratcheter of Central College, the National Endowment for the Hu-
manities summer group at Vanderbilt University, and Alden Williams
of Kansas State University. My home institution extended similar en-

couragement. Michael Dingerson and the Office of Research Development and Administration offered necessary financial assistance, while John Baker and the Political Science Department provided support for research and typing. Ron Teng, Sangsop Park, Tina Smucz and especially Jeffrey Gleeson offered superb research assistance, while Charlotte Keller, Mary Butts and Sandy Hickam ably handled the typing.

I wish to thank the people of Southern Illinois University Press for their constant support. The late Vernon Sternberg "discovered" the idea for the press, Jim Simmons and Walter Kent ran with it, and Kenney Withers ultimately placed it on the publication listing. Dan Seiters deserves praise for making my prose flow more smoothly.

A truly special thanks is due to Rhonda Vinson and Jeffrey Gleeson, both of whom never stopped believing in the project or working to realize it. The book is dedicated to them.

Carterville, Illinois   RONALD M. MASON
August 1981

Introduction

By Carole Pateman

FOR MANY PEOPLE in the 1980s "participation" and "participatory democracy" are merely echoes of a time past. These ideas appear to be nothing more than relics of the 1960s, with little or no relevance to the harsher realities of the present. Other slogans and concerns are promoted in the mass media, and commentators have shifted their attention to the "new right." But changing political fashions and economic depression do not mean that the problems encapsulated in the demand for participation are now unimportant. The hierarchical and undemocratic structure of our social institutions that was criticized and challenged through the slogan of participatory democracy remains fundamentally unchanged. Nor has the social pattern of political participation, as this is conventionally measured in empirical investigations, been greatly altered over the past two decades. It is still a largely white, male, middle-class activity and, as Verba and Nie concluded in *Participation in America*, its outcome reinforces the socially advantaged position of the participants. Nevertheless, our social world has changed since the days of the heady call for the long march through the institutions. Not only have the capitalist economies moved from boom to crisis, but the 1960s have left an important legacy of political movements and political consciousness. There is now, for example, widespread interest, both at grass roots and official levels, in workplace participation and industrial democracy, and numerous experiments (of varying significance for democratization) are taking place in the Western countries. There is also a vigorous women's movement which provides examples of participatory democratic organization and extends the question of democracy to the patriarchal as well as the class ordering of liberal institutions, including the workplace.

In most academic and popular discussions, liberal representative government plus universal suffrage has become accepted as "democracy," and political participation is conventionally defined in terms of electoral and associated activities. People often overlook how recent an achievement this "democracy" is. Blacks in the United States were effectively enfranchised only in the 1960s, and women won the vote in

Switzerland in 1971. An important consequence of the incorporation
of all adults as formally equal citizens is also seldom recognized; this
new status serves to highlight the contrast between formal political
equality and the substantive inequalities that structure social institutions. The liberal view of "democracy" holds that social inequalities
are irrelevant to political life; the rights of citizens should stop at the
gate to the factory, the office, the university, and the home. The current attempts to return to laissez-faire economics and hence to increase inequality show how entrenched this view is. But, as Ron Mason's study shows, even though the liberal view of the world is now
widely diffused among all sections of the population, it is not, and
never has been, unchallenged. Despite the disappearance of "participation" as a popular slogan, the increasing interest in workplace
participation today provides the basis for a practical and incisive challenge to the liberal separation of democracy from the institutions of
everyday life.

The major contribution of *Participatory and Workplace Democracy* is to
show why a democratic form of sociopolitical organization requires a
decisive break with the hegemony of the liberal theoretical perspective. In particular, it demands a break with the liberal view of the "political" and "political participation," which underlies the assimilation
of "democracy" to a particular form of government. Liberalism identifies the political with the government of the state and insists that it is
a sphere separate from the rest of social life. The alternative, democratic conception sees the political as one dimension of social life, the
collective dimension that is distinct, but not separate, from our personal lives; the political is not remote and special but a familiar part of
the everyday lives of citizens. The political will form an integral part
of the multiplicity of democratic communities that will constitute a
participatory democracy of the future. It is from such a perspective
on the political that Ron Mason defines democracy as a "type of community rule in which the process of decision making generally entails
widespread and effective participation of community members."
Once the liberal, and apparently "commonsense," view of the political
is called into question, the vital problem of the relation between liberalism and democracy can no longer be glossed over, or avoided by theorists who have rarely pursued the implications of the wide conceptions of the political to be found in some standard works of political
science.

In the past, the usual response to a nonliberal view of the political was that it led to totalitarianism. Ron Mason convincingly deals with this charge, arguing that because totalitarianism attempts to destroy, not to create, communities within which citizens can be politically active, it eliminates rather than enlarges the political. Another more recent, but related, criticism of participatory democratic arguments is that by extending the political they are ultimately unable to distinguish the particular from the general in social life. There is no good reason to go on assuming uncritically, however, that a distinction between the particular and general can be made only if the liberal separation of the political (or the state) from the rest of social life (or civil society) is maintained. There are ways in political theory to make distinctions other than through separation and abstraction. Participatory democrats are also told that their reconceptualization of the political merely trivializes political participation. It remains unclear why the problems and concerns of everyday life should be regarded as essentially trivial. They appear so only from the assumption that political activity takes place solely in the present-day equivalent of the liberal state that Marx once called a "heaven," and that it is, except on officially designated occasions, the preserve of the few. The conception of the political and democracy developed in *Participatory and Workplace Democracy* directs us to matters of fundamental importance in human life, to economic production, to our political education and development, and to the structure of the neighborhoods and households in which we live.

The critics of participatory democracy have usually rested their case on the unrealistic character of participationist arguments. The lack of realism is held to be confirmed by the findings of empirical investigations of political participation, but the critics' interpretation of the empirical findings has tended to go unchallenged. I have commented elsewhere on the failure—or rather, given their individualist liberal assumptions, the inability—of empirical or revisionist theorists of democracy to recognize the class and sex pattern of participation, clearly revealed in their own evidence, as a *problem*. This is, however, not the only way in which liberal perspectives color the discussion of and interpretation of evidence about political participation. Ron Mason shows how this is also true of the conventional empirical division between "social" and "political" participation. Empirical investigators usually correlate the former with the latter, and the result is a "schizophrenia concerning the political." The correlations can be made only if numerous activities and spheres of life that share the characteristics

of political participation and political life are defined as social rather
than political. Empirical investigators have actually been matching
different forms and expressions of political participation with each
other, so the consistently firm relationship between "social" and "political" participation is hardly surprising. A nonliberal conception of
the political, that sees all participation in group decision making as
political in whatever context it occurs, points the way through the confusion and promises major developments in research.

Conceptions of political participation are crucial for the question of
how much participation actually takes place and the extent and forms
of participation that might be possible in the future. The well-known
argument about the functional necessity of political apathy for democracy depends on the claim that most citizens are, and will remain,
politically inactive and disinterested. The groups presented as "naturally" inactive certainly appear to be nonparticipant when political
participation is measured in conventional electoral terms. Voting and
its associated activities, however, are typically discussed in the abstract,
unrelated to political consequences or to other forms of participation.
If electoral activities were critically examined in a wider political context the social pattern, level, and meaning of participation might look
very different. Empirical investigators have now begun to turn their
attention to "unorthodox" (or "protest") forms of activity, but their
liberal assumptions cannot, for example, include strikes as political
participation. If conventional estimates of the present level and social
distribution of participation are open to question, this is even more
true of future possibilities. There is nothing "natural" about the existing social pattern and form of participation.

The liberal view of political participation is static, ahistorical and
nondevelopmental. Participation is seen as instrumental (protection
of self-interest), or as a "protest" against instrumental ineffectiveness.
This one-dimensional conception cannot encompass forms of participation that enlarge the capacities of those involved or that create
new, democratic forms of organization and social structure; it ignores
the educative dimensions of participation as well as the way in which
participation in one political context can lead to further activity in a
different political arena. Ron Mason argues that to understand participation, it is necessary to look beyond the correlation of individual
attributes with modes of (electoral) participation to an investigation in
different communities of the forms of participation that contribute to
the development of an active, democratic citizenry. His "proximity hy-

pothesis" suggests that the more two experiences of participation approximate each other, the more likely it is that what is learned in one political context will be transferred to another. Participation in the workplace is crucial from this perspective, and the mass of empirical evidence gathered over the past two or more decades confirms that it can be expected to have a far-reaching effect on the capacities of individuals and the form and extent of political participation. Or, to put this the other way round, the guild socialists were right to argue that democracy remains a mockery while servility is demanded in the workplace. Democratic, unlike liberal, participation is not merely instrumental; nor (as is sometimes suggested) is it essentially expressive or noninstrumental. It is a multidimensional form of action that includes voting (of various kinds) but as only one of a range of forms of participation open to democratic citizens. From a *democratic* perspective political participation does not merely await the attention of empirical investigators but remains to be created.

From the same perspective it becomes clear that intrinsically satisfying and socially meaningful work is also lacking. The conventional liberal understanding of the "political" is widely taken for granted and, similarly, the meaning and locus of work tends to be uncritically accepted. In particular, the work of married women in their homes is not regarded as "work"; all work, it is widely assumed, takes place in a "workplace," not hidden in the home. Ron Mason shows how a conception of work as having only extrinsic value, a view that reduces work to mere labor, is part of the historical legacy of liberalism and capitalism and central to the question of democracy and participation. There is a close parallel between the liberal conceptions of political participation and work. Both are seen as nothing more than external means through which *homo civicus* or his other self, *homo economicus*, can further his interests; both are seen as costs which, rationally, it is advantageous not to pay. Again, the social pattern of dissatisfaction with work closely resembles the social distribution of political participation; those who are most likely to be dissatisfied with their work tend to come from the same groups who are least likely to be (conventional) political participants. Only when liberal assumptions are cast aside can this empirical data and the prevailing conception of work be seen as problems or, rather, as aspects of the same problem—the problem of democratization. Work and participation go hand in hand. Work is the means through which the material needs of the community are met, but at the same time it is "the means by which we create ourselves." Political participation is intrinsically valuable, for it is through participation that a democratic community is created and maintained and the capacities of its members enlarged. The democratized workplace is a central locus of political participation and of education through participation; democratization of the workplace is also necessary if intrinsically satisfying and meaningful work is to be created. The question of workplace participation and democracy is thus not, as is frequently implied, only a matter of electing workers' councils to manage enterprises—although that would be an enormous change—but is fundamentally bound up with the meaning and everyday organization of work. Worklife will not be intrinsically satisfying or an integral part of democratic political life until new modes of cooperation are created to replace the present hierarchical, competitive, and sexually divided organization of economic production.

The enthusiasm with which some managements have embraced workplace participation and, for example, its endorsement as official EEC policy, has led to charges that participation (instead of workers' control) is merely another means of incorporating the working class more securely into the structure of advanced capitalism. It is true that experiments are often introduced by managements concerned by low productivity rates, absenteeism, and general problems of morale, and that pseudoparticipation is more likely to be encountered than workplace democracy. But nothing is without its unintended consequences. Management-sponsored experiments in participation can lead to a legitimation of the status quo, but they can also—to use an old-fashioned phrase—be used as a means to encroaching control and so form the basis for democratization. Whether legitimation or democratization is the eventual outcome depends a good deal on the attitude of the labor movement. It is significant that, in a time of unemployment, inflation, and attacks on union rights, many union leaders are reexamining the potential of participation (and are also turning their attention to the use of their pension funds), while at shop-steward level, at Lucas Aerospace, in Britain, workers are showing how technology now used to further militarism can be turned to socially valuable purposes. Over a decade has passed since I did my own research into democracy and participation, and it is clear that since then real changes have occurred in the general level of awareness that a feasible democratic alternative to the existing organization of production is possible.

A break with the liberal past is necessary for the creation of a theory of a *democratic* practice, but this does not mean that it will be constructed in an historical void. Democratic theory may still be linked to liberalism, but there is also another past, "forgotten" by most theorists of democracy, that is recalled in *Participatory and Workplace Democracy*. This is the past of the "utopian" socialists, the guild socialists, the anarchists, and the council communists; it is the past of all the women and men who fought against capitalism and hierarchical, authoritarian, patriarchal institutions, who argued for the educative effect of participation, and who emphasized what Ron Mason calls the "workplace connection." To retrieve the democratic past and to transcend liberalism in the future is an exciting and difficult, complex task—but not an impossible one. In his companion volume Ron Mason shows in detail that the introduction of workplace democracy is feasible in the United States. The final chapter of the present study provides a nonliberal defense of the philosophy of participation, a defense that is urgently required at the present time when "participation" is no longer fashionable, and when right-wing forces appear to be gaining ground in most western countries. Though understandable, neither advocacy of apocalyptic revolution nor despair at the extent of the social changes required are the appropriate response to our present sociopolitical circumstances. Mason's argument offers us a theoretical defense of political action that can build on changes already taking place within the meaningless labor, the inequalities, and the depoliticized citizenship of liberalism to create a democratic community. He has thus made a major contribution to the task of transforming liberalism into democracy. Times of crisis are upsetting and uneasy, but they can be times in which the movement for democracy is able to recover and consolidate its past and advance to the future.

Participatory and Workplace Democracy

1

Theoretical Background

Critique of the Liberal Conception of the Political

THE WORLD DOES NOT APPEAR TO US IN FOCUS; WE MUST ORDER THE confusion with our minds. Yet things such as the political are not even given in the world. They are taken. The political always has been more created than discovered, and as such, a fundamental part of any political study is the construction of what is political. Although there are those such as Dahl, Easton, Frohock, Sartori, Schmitt and Strauss[1] who provide thoughtful contributions to the discussion of what may be considered political in our contemporary world, the normal practice among students of politics is to give this little explicit consideration. At best, they put forth some conventional statement of definition as if it were a votive offering and then proceed in complete ignorance of its implication. This must change for the advancement of our discipline depends on careful, phenomenological consideration of the political.

Although the political is always created, it appears "unnecessary" for us individually to create it, since a standard version is always present. In our world that version is based on the perspective of liberalism. Liberalism is the tradition of thought into which most of us are born. As political socialization affects our everyday thoughts and actions, so does liberalism affect our theoretical political thinking—in ways that are unrecognized. When we assume "no particular" perspective on the political world we observe and study, we all too often are assuming the perspective liberalism has proffered. To establish the theoretical perspective most relevant to participatory and workplace democracy, it is necessary to begin with the political as seen through liberal lenses.

Ironically, establishing the basic principles of liberalism is more diffi-

3

cult than it may appear. Not only is liberalism a fairly complex system of thought, but it is also "imperialistic." Liberal thought has a tendency to expand by absorbing opposing views. Thus a particular proposition and its antithesis may both be considered part of liberal thought: liberal emphasis on liberty may be extended to equality by making them mutually dependent; liberal conceptualizations in terms of the individual may be altered into group conceptualizations by subsuming individual interest into group or class interest; liberal aversion to the state may be transformed by removing the impediments to liberty and other liberal values. The difficulties can be reduced to manageable proportions by seeking the "main body" of liberal thought—sometimes called classical liberalism—and leaving the off-shoots to other discussions.

Many of the basic tenets of liberalism are to be found in the psychology of man as Hobbes described him. In his acquisitive egoism, Hobbesian man displays the utility satisfaction of self-interest that will come to be a hallmark of man in the liberal view. But it is John Locke and not Thomas Hobbes who first paints the full picture, and so it is to him that we shall turn for the details of liberalism, especially the liberal view of the political. This focus on Locke is made all the more relevant by the greater overt (but perhaps not covert) acceptance of him in America.

The key to unlocking the basic political tenets of liberalism is understanding the state of nature as Locke describes it. Unlike the state of nature Hobbes portrays in which men are isolated in a continuous struggle of all against all, man in Locke's state of nature is much more social. In fact, despite Locke's statement that men are driven into society by the "inconveniences" and dangers of the state of nature,[2] mankind already has formed society and community within the state of nature. Although this claim is supported wherever Locke discusses the state of nature, it appears most clearly in his discussion of individual powers within the state of nature.

The first is to do whatsoever he thinks fit for the preservation of himself and others within the permission of the law of nature, by which law, common to them all, he and all the rest of mankind are one community and make up one society, distinct from all other creatures. And were it not for the corruption and viciousness of degenerate men, there would be no need of any other, no necessity that men should separate from this great and natural community and by positive agreements combine into smaller and divided associations.

The other power a man has in the state of nature is the power to punish the crimes committed against that law. Both these he gives up when he joins in a private, if I may so call it, or particular politic society and incorporates into any commonwealth separate from the rest of mankind.[3]

If the readers will fashion the manifestation of these two powers into a full description of the state of nature, they can readily appreciate how elaborate was Locke's state of nature. It was little short of a fully operative society. Virtually all of life's values—life, liberty, and estate—are to be found in the state of nature together with ample opportunity to satisfy them. The state of nature is not lawless, for natural law, which is available for all to know unambiguously through their reason, instructs man as to how he should behave. For those who transgress the natural law and interfere with another's life, liberty, or estate, an individual has the right to seek punishment, and through natural law, has the ability to prescribe proper retribution. All of this occurs within the state of nature.

With such an elaborate system one may question what is left for the political. The answer is to be found in the movement out of the state of nature. Since there is the perpetual risk that the "inconveniences" of the state of nature could digress into a state of war, it is important that some mechanism be devised by which "the viciousness of degenerate men" can be controlled effectively. This mechanism is representative institutions that create public-interested laws and enforce them, thereby evoking justice; this mechanism is government. In John Locke's view the political is equated with civil government.

Classical liberalism, as it is derived from John Locke, thus asserts a radical division of life into social and political components. The political (or public) sphere pertains to government; the social (or private) sphere relates to all of the remaining interrelationships of men and women. Most people have little or no concern for the political because their desire is to maximize values; the political contains little value to the classical liberal. With all of life's values located in the social sphere, no one should expect rational, utility-seeking individuals to become involved politically. The role of government is to protect the life, liberty, and property of citizens and to provide a common judge against those who would make illegitimate claim to those values. Yet given the power of government to coerce, it is government itself that forms the greatest ultimate threat of life, liberty, and property. It is an important liberal principle that government be restricted as far as possible without hampering its ability to perform the protective function ascribed to it. From this view familiar slogans such as "government which governs least governs best" are produced.

Not only may the state of nature be seen as social, it may be viewed as political in scope as well. Activities typically related to the political were intimate to the lives of Lockean man. Each individual had the responsibility to interpret the natural laws in terms of their implication for proper conduct, each had an obligation to be obedient to those laws, and each had the right to administer justice if others did not abide by the same mandates. All were forced to relinquish the right to such political activities, however, when society emerged from the state of nature. Henceforth representatives were to be chosen as political agents, representatives who would formulate positive laws to govern and protect the represented. In this manner Lockean liberalism abstracted the political from everyday life, attenuating its importance. The political came to be what was governmental and government became the province of the few encharged with civil responsibilities. Government was formed originally by the consent of all, but thereafter government operated on the narrow basis of "tacit consent." It is upon this curtailed view of the political that liberalism constructs its version of democracy. Liberal democracy is characterized by government that is limited, constitutional, and representative. Although the liberal democratic government is derived of the citizens (government of the people) and claims to serve in their best interest (government for the people), there is very little opportunity for direct citizen involvement in government (government by the people). This probably is as it should be, for such involvement is largely unnecessary and very well could be dangerous. After all, the Lockean view of human nature is not much less tainted than is Hobbes's; the classical liberal view of man's fallen nature would not recommend the active involvement of men and women in government, especially when such involvement would likely lead to a more encompassing government.

It is this view of the political—a view that constitutes the political in terms of what is public and the public in terms of what is governmental—that has dominated modern and contemporary thinking on the subject. Since the inception of the modern age, nearly all political writing of a theoretical nature has concerned the state. Not only is the liberal banner contemporarily carried by those such as the "demo-cratic revisionists" (Schumpeter, Berelson, Dahl and others), who follow directly in the liberal tradition, but the major perspective is shared even by critics of liberalism. Marxists, for example, stand in opposition to the liberal view of the proper political order, but they do not generally oppose the manner in which liberal thought conceives of the political. In mainstream Marxist analysis, the political is often taken to be government, abstracted from the daily existence and di-minished in importance. Conceiving of the social/economic sphere as the substructure and the political sphere as merely superstructure is as much a liberal inheritance as are the assumptions Marx borrowed from classical economics. This accounts for the perfectly correct per-ceptions that despite the intensity of their disagreement, liberals and Marxists have little difficulty understanding each other. They share many of the same basic conceptualizations, especially as they concern the political.

Several contemporary theorists including Arendt, Sartori and Sen-nett[4] sense the decline of the political in our contemporary world and attribute the loss in one form or another to liberalism. It is diffi-cult, however, to construct a *bona fide* alternative to liberalism while operating within the basic framework provided by liberalism. Lib-eral assumptions naturally lead to liberal conclusions, and in this manner liberalism absorbs and neutralizes what were intended to be devastating critiques. Take for example Sheldon Wolin and his last-ingly important book, *Politics and Vision.*[5] Wolin is among those who lament most the loss of the sense of the political. This loss of *the sense* of the political does not mean the loss of the political itself within liberal thought. To the contrary, Wolin believes that liberalism, which blurs the political's distinctiveness with the social, has led modern analysts to project the political to all sorts of phenomena that do not warrant the denotation of being political. It is Wolin's hope that we might be able to create again a sphere of the political as distinct and as majestic as the one created by the Greeks. Inherent in Wolin's writing is the inclination to use the Greek view that politics relates to the public sphere as a modern model, but his inclination must be resisted. The outcome, if Wolin's inclination is followed, will not be an Hellenic, but another liberal formulation of the political. The seeds of the contradiction lie in the adherence to the view that the political is what is public. The solution to the dilemma is to embrace what Wolin found so difficult to accept: the designation as political some phenomena that hitherto had not been viewed as part of the public realm. Only in this manner can the political be made immediate to the everyday lives of individuals—as it once was to the lives of the citizens of Greek city-states. The logic of this position will be developed through an examination of the Greek construction of the political. During the investigation it will become apparent that Wolin misinterprets the influence of liberalism upon the political to be one of diffusion.

The political always has been created; the Greeks were the first to do so, for the Greeks were the first to devise a vocabulary that allowed discussion of the political. In their original formulation the Greeks divided life into two broad spheres: private and public. The private sphere encompassed life within the household and life related to the material maintenance of existence. It belonged foremost to those without status—women, children and slaves—but it belonged also to citizens who needed the necessary reprieve from the strain of public life. Since the private sphere did not provide the opportunity for development, those free men who clung to it were less than poor citizens, they were viewed as basically idiotic (*ídion*).

In opposition stood the public sphere, the exclusive realm of citizen action. Man is political (*zoon politikón*) and needs the public realm to develop fully; men become men among other men. For the Greeks the political was represented in the public, and the public was what related to the polis. Our modern difficulty translating the term *polis* is indicative of how very different life was for the ancient Greeks. The polis certainly was a political order, but it also was a religious and cultural ordering of men as well. In short, the polis was the entire network of factors connecting all who were not confined to the private realm. From such a view derives an image of the political that is intimate to the lives of Greek citizens. The political was as immediate as leaving the household and joining in the company of other men as they discussed among themselves the common factors of their lives. Life in the polis was life in common, that is, life in community (*koinonía*). Although the actual involvement of citizens in the public realm may have declined in the Greek polis, the political by construction was an integral part of the lives of all citizens.

With the collapse of the polis came a diminution in the clarity and importance of the political. The Greek notion of the political (*polítes*) could not be translated faithfully even to the Romans a few centuries later. Their closest approximation was *rēs pūblica*, a construction that did not carry much of the power associated with the Greek view of the political. The diminution is even greater in modern times. As with the Greeks, liberals refer the political to that which is public, but something vastly different is meant. For one thing the private sphere (time apart from general interaction with others) is no longer the imprisonment of those condemned not to mature and grow, as it was for the Greeks. There are positive values associated with it. More importantly, between the private and public spheres a third sphere has emerged in liberalism. It is the social sphere and contains within it most of the values of modern human existence. The social sphere is pervasive and expanding; it constantly assaults the boundaries of both the private and the public.

What then is the modern version of the public? With such an expansive social realm, what is left for the political? The answer was offered when we examined the writings of John Locke in the *Second Treatise*. The political is civil government, the formal representation of the nation's interest by those encharged with the responsibility of creating laws that promote everyone's interest.

In many ways this view merely reflects the changes that have occurred since the 5th century B.C. When we speak of what is common to all in the most inclusive community, we refer not to the *city*-state, but to the *nation*-state. The largest encompassing community is not counted in the hundreds of thousands, but in the hundreds of millions. The important conclusion to draw is that if the political is tied to the public, and if the public refers to what is common to all in the most extensive community, then the political must be abstracted from the daily existence of people. Liberalism, relating as it does to the emergence of nations, did little more than apply the Greek notion of the political as a public sphere to circumstances that have changed.

Sheldon Wolin's failure to recognize this particular feature of the liberal view of the public (and therefore of the political) is the fundamental source of problem in his recommendations concerning the political. Although he earnestly yearns for a political reminiscent of that which the Greeks created and enjoyed, his very presuppositions lead to the opposite—a political largely devoid of relevance to the average citizen. The following three statements related to the political indicate the reason that Wolin falls into the liberal trap: he defines the political as that which is related to the regulation of the most inclusive community.

At the same time, one of the essential qualities of what is political, and one that has powerfully shaped the view of political theorists about their subject-matter, is its relationship with what is "public."[6] . . . I shall take "politics" to include the following: (a) a form of activity centering around the quest for competitive advantage between groups, individuals, societies; (b) a form of activity conditioned by the fact that it occurs within a situation of change and relative scarcity; (c) a form of activity in which the pursuit of advantage produces consequences of such a magnitude that they affect in a significant way the whole society or a substantial portion of it.[7] . . . The "public" quality of a judgment has had two senses: a judgment, a policy, or a decision has been considered as truly public when expressed by an authoritative person or persons, that is by an authority recognized by the community; secondly, a judgment has been accepted as genuinely public when it appears to possess a general character, for only what is general is capable of application to the society as a whole.[8]

In constantly and consistently relating the political to the largest and most encompassing of communities, Wolin has insured that the political could not be intimate to the lives of citizens. How can the political be immediate when the relevant communities are often communities of millions? Though Wolin seeks the political of the Greeks because it is important, majestic, and a positive part of a person's development, he actually achieves the political of John Locke, which is removed from the lives of citizens and restricted in its developmental import. The political as a public sphere significantly affecting all or a substantial part of the society can be no other way.

Wolin's particular perspective on the political allows him to observe correctly that liberalism deprecates the political, but it misleads him into believing that the mode of deprecation is diffusion. It is true that liberalism sometimes blurs the distinctiveness of the political, but the major problem never has been the wanton spread of the political into all sorts of patently unpolitical areas. What liberalism has done instead is diminish the importance of the political by making it largely irrelevant to the lives of citizens in the routine affairs of their daily existence. The political is less relevant in terms of the individual's impact on it, rather than its impact on the individual. Thus in the words of Carole Pateman, liberalism "reified" the political; it made it seem as if citizenship were real, when in fact it was only apparent. The political long since had been removed from the lives of almost everyone.[9]

The disagreement in interpretation of politics is not simply a matter of "academic" interest; the differing positions lead to alternative approaches to solving the problems associated with the liberal view of the political. Wolin would have the political relate exclusively to our common life at the societal level. This certainly makes the political important, but it removes the political so effectively from the lives of individuals that they do not and cannot receive the developmental benefits from involvement in it. A new view of the political, one including phenomena usually thought to be outside the public realm, must be sought. Although the political will include factors seen as mundane, the political becomes important by gaining relevance. For the political to regain its immediacy in the lives of individuals and thus be the potential developmental force that it was for 5th century Athenians, it must be viewed as something other than an abstracted sphere that operates almost exclusively at the societal level. It must be re-created to exist in the daily lives of individuals, as it did for Greek citizens enjoying their community life. Otherwise we will continue to miss much of what ought to be included in the political landscape.

Reconceptualization of the Political

For too long we have taken liberal assumptions as if they were unassailable truths. Once accepted, we then looked at the world through liberal lenses and indeed discovered it to be tailored to the proportions of liberalism. For too long liberalism has restricted our view of the political by presenting it as an abstraction divorced from the everyday life of human beings. Many things that could be considered political could not be seen through the filter of liberalism; many things that were seen as political in form and content could not be considered political because they were at variance with the liberal view of the political. We have reached the limits of what the basic liberal view of politics has to offer. It is time that we move beyond liberalism and the depoliticization associated with its distinctions.

Before attempting to reconsider the political and restructure a suitable conception, it would be wise to take note of other attempts to offer significantly broader perspectives on the political. Most notable among them are David Easton's view of the political as that which relates to the "authoritative allocation of values for a society," [10] and Robert Dahl's construction of the political in terms of a political system that is "any persistent pattern of human relationships that involves, to any significant extent, control, influence, power or authority." [11] Both formulations have been absorbed into liberal conceptions of the political, for both suffer from the same malady. Their views of the political are abstracted from the world of experience, and therefore are difficult to translate. In the absence of a clear reference to what authoritative allocations of values are and what constitutes a political system, there is a tendency for these broad conceptions to be taken to relate to nothing more than formal government. Thus despite the explicit statement of Dahl that perhaps even families could be seen as political systems,[12] those who adopt Dahl's notion of a political system often take it to mean nothing other than formal government, excluding, for example, the politics of all nongovernmental organizations. Even Robert Dahl himself is not consistent with this broad view in his own analysis. As Peter Bachrach has claimed: "under this definition it would appear reasonable to assume that political elites would include heads of corporate giants who make decisions regularly on a myriad of issues . . . [but] on the basis of [Dahl's] theoretical and empirical studies on elites, we find this not the case." [13]

The core problem is that these broad views of the political are based on "macro-level" distinctions; the political exists some distance from the actions of individuals. Once the political is abstracted from the actions of individuals, it is easy to slip back into liberal preconceptions. The "political" system can be distinguished from the "social" system, and in fact made a subsystem of the social system. Likewise, authoritative allocations of values for a society (the political) can be contrasted easily with other institutional decision making, which may not be authoritative and binding for all of society (the nonpolitical). In neither case are we all that far from equating the political with what is governmental. These formulations in fact are quite consistent with the views of the political expressed by Sheldon Wolin earlier in this chapter.

Liberalism proffers such a dominating view of the political that it tends to absorb and convert other potentially nonliberal formulations of the political. The safest way to proceed beyond liberal preconceptions is to establish the necessary distinctions at the level of the individual. We must come to view certain types of individual actions as

participation in ————→ participatory ————→ participation in
the workplace   persuasion   government

cannot move beyond the possessive individualism of liberal man and cannot relate to other human beings except as they are instrumental to achieving his values. With that involvement, the individual develops an outlook and sentiments in ways that make possible the achievement of community and community values. The benefits of participation apply to all communities, including the most encompassing.

Participatory Democracy Challenged

Though we live in an age that embraces democracy as the paramount political good, the democratic ideal is by no means unchallenged. Any challenge to an ideal may result in a diminution of that ideal, but it may also serve as an impetus to its continued development. The critic thus plays an indispensable role in the rejuvenation of ideals. By confronting standard ideals with new arguments and new evidence in support of those arguments, the critic stimulates new strains of synthetic thought in defense of the ideal. The polylogue that ensues serves to update and renew the ideal by having a new generation of thinkers apply the ideal to their contemporary world. Should the ideal withstand attack, it develops; should it not, it atrophies.

One major impediment to a discussion of democracy's critics is the actual identification of those critics. Surely a theorist can be considered democratic or not by the works he produces; but there are many democratic theories and even more that incorrectly purport to be democratic. How can one tell? For our purpose, it is not simply the nature of the questions addressed by a theory, but rather its evaluations and recommendations that denote it as democratic. A theory should be termed democratic when the prescriptions it offers are democratic. Participation is the fundamental element of democracy. In reference to a given period of time, a theory can be considered democratic if it prescribes the extension of participation in community decision making (along the five dimensions) beyond the status quo. In opposition, a theory recommending the restriction of participation to present or lower levels will be considered undemocratic. Ordinarily, the further the theory deviates from the status quo, the stronger the proponent or antagonist of democracy its author is.

These simple principles assume substance by reference to several theorists in the democratic tradition. In one of his earlier political writings, *The Theory of Legislation*,[43] Jeremy Bentham recommended the extension of voting privileges, but he limited the franchise to include only independent, self-supporting, educated men. James Mill advocated universal suffrage, but his preoccupation with the representation of interests led him in such works as *An Essay on Government* to consider less participatory and more convenient ways to adequately reflect personal interests.[44] Finally, John Stuart Mill recommended universal suffrage combined with plural voting, which allowed some individuals' voting decision to carry more weight.[45] In addition, John Stuart Mill recommended increasing worker participation in industry as well.[46] A more complete examination of these proposals might produce the impression that each is "undemocratic" by contemporary standards. It is true that Bentham and the two Mills were more interested in the representation of interest than in participation, but they did offer a true extension of participation in terms of the times in which they lived. Each may properly be described as "democratic" and as part of the democratic tradition. Among the three, it is clear that John Stuart Mill would increase most the relative amount of participation, and so he should be judged the most democratic. Contemporary liberals who make the same types of recommendations, however, would not have their works considered democratic.

Having established a democratic touchstone, it is possible to proceed with an examination of democracy's contemporary critics. Because of the importance and originality of their contributions, special emphasis will be given to Joseph Schumpeter and Bernard Berelson.

Unlike the challenges of the past, a plethora of empirical findings have confronted democratic ideals in recent decades. Utilizing a more scientific methodology and a stockpile of survey research, the work of Berelson, Lipset, Dahl and others have tended in the eyes of many to undermine those ideals. From demonstration that the average American citizen is unaware of the mechanics of the political system, is uninformed about the major political actors, and is uninterested in political participation, it could be concluded that the democratic ideal as expressed in "traditional" or "classical" democratic theory no longer applied to the modern industrial world, but was only relevant to pre-Periclean Athens or eighteenth-century New England townships (and not even to those, given a careful scrutiny of history). Prior to much of the empirical research, an iconoclastic peak was reached by Joseph Schumpeter when he redefined democracy as a method of selecting decision makers.

In reaction to traditional democratic theory's inadequacies and the failure of its critics such as Graham Wallas to complete their task, Schumpeter defines the "democratic method" as that "institutional arrangement for arriving at political decisions in which individuals acquire the power to decide by means of a competitive struggle for the people's vote."[47] With his empirical and narrow-process definition of democracy, Schumpeter not only has exorcized such spirits as the "General Will" and the "Common Good," but has restated the democratic ideal as well. No longer would democracy signify or be associated with anything more loftly than can be derived from democracy meaning "only that the people have the opportunity of accepting or refusing the men who are to rule them."[48] As the following passage quoted in length makes clear, there is no room in the political arena for the average citizen except for the meager opportunity to vote.

The voters outside of parliament must respect the division of labor between themselves and the politicians they elect. They must not withdraw confidence too easily between elections and they must understand that, once they have elected an individual, *political action is his business and not theirs.* This means that they must refrain from instructing him about what he is to do—a principle that has indeed been universally recognized by constitutions and political theory ever since Edmund Burke's time. But its implications are not generally understood. On one hand, few people realize that this principle clashes with the classical doctrine of democracy and really spells its abandonment. For if the people are to rule in the sense of deciding individual issues, what would be more natural for them to do than to issue instructions to their representatives, as the voters for the French States-General did in and before 1789? On the other hand, it is still less recognized that if the principle be accepted, not only instructions as formal as those French *cahiers* but also less formal attempts at restricting the freedom of action of members of parliament—the practice of bombarding them with letters and telegrams for instance—ought to come under the same ban.[49]

If to be considered democratic a work must recommend the extension of effective participation beyond the boundaries of contemporary limits, there can be no other conclusion but that *Capitalism, Socialism and Democracy* is an antidemocratic work. After an election, Schumpeter actually would ban even the most simple input activities in order to reinforce the (liberal) notion that political activity is the proper province of representative and office holders, not ordinary citizens. Although many analysts may find merit in Schumpeter's prescriptions, by this standard, it cannot be valued on the grounds that it is democratic. It would seem to require an imaginative feat of apology, Herculean in proportion, to portray such a position as compatible with democracy. Ironically, Schumpeter's undemocratic conception of democracy may be the predominate contemporary conceptualization of all—so confused has "democracy" become.

Joseph Schumpeter's efforts are illustrative of the manner in which valuable concepts can have their meanings obscured and their potency adulterated. Democracy, a system in which the people rule, is a concept that possessed revolutionary import throughout much of its history. Under Schumpeter's hand it is reduced to the opportunity to vote in relatively free elections. Even Robert Dahl, who once advocated a similar conceptualization, but who specified many more preconditions for its viability and desirability, did not call that system "democracy"; instead he termed it "polyarchy."[50]

Schumpeter's legacy is not limited to the weakening of democracy's meaning. By establishing the nation as the sole community of importance, Schumpeter focused nearly exclusive attention upon the national government. In a nation exceeding two hundred million people, who of necessity are limited in political participation at the national level, it was not a large leap to identify representative government as the most pure democratic expression. With representative government's primacy established, it became progressively more futile to advocate expanding and enhancing participation in nongovernmental communities as well as at other governmental levels. How convenient it became to assume that participation would be limited to voting—so convenient in fact, that participation and voting nearly became interchangeable in our lexicon.

The most significant and disturbing effect of Schumpeter's work is the revision (destruction?) of the democratic ideal. It will be remembered that democracy is nothing more to Schumpeter than that "the people have the opportunity of accepting or refusing the men who rule them." In most cases this is realized nicely by holding periodic and relatively free elections. If the opportunity to vote in relatively free elections is taken as the measure of democracy, and if democracy means nothing more than this, many modern nations will compare very well with the standard; democracy is achieved. It will no longer be necessary to seek democracy, but to maintain it. (In the process democracy as an ideal enervates, the unavoidable fate of ideals achieved.)

This emphasis upon maintenance, more specifically translated as a preoccupation with political stability, has become a major characteristic of those who have come to be known as "democratic revisionists."[51]

Bernard Berelson and his associates were among the very first of the democratic revisionists to confront "traditional" democratic theory with empirical evidence gleaned from survey research. In *Voting*,[52] they report that the average citizen is indeed unaware of the mechanics of the political system, is uninformed concerning the major political actors, and is uninterested in participation. Such evidence contradicts what they call "traditional" democratic theory, which allegedly posits an active, intelligent, and rational citizenry. The miracle is that despite the populace's disturbing characteristics, the system works (we need not ask for whom it works, let its longevity suffice). Taking a moment to prescind, this situation may not be so miraculous after all. Could it be that the system works not despite but because of individual inadequacies? According to the authors, a political system requires a distribution of individual political attributes among the population in order for it to achieve equilibrium from which stability is derived. "What seems to be required of the electorate as a whole is a distribution of qualities along important dimensions. We need some people who are active in a certain respect, others in the middle and still others passive."[53] Fortunately for the system, the American citizenry is distributed along just such a continuum, replete with a sufficient number of apathetics to foster stability (Berelson et al. estimate that 40 percent of the American public fall into the apathetic category).[54] "True, the highly interested voters vote more and know more about campaigning, and read and listen more, and participate more; however, they are also less likely to change. Extreme interest goes with extreme partisanship and might culminate in rigid fanaticism that could destroy democratic processes if generalized throughout the community. Low affect toward the election—not caring much—underlies the solution of many political problems."[55]

What had previously appeared to be an inadequacy at the individual level now has been transformed into the saving grace at the systemic level. An ample number of apathetics is necessary to buffer the untoward effects of the more involved segments of the citizenry. Without those who do not know or care, rampant partisanship might tear the democratic system asunder. Berelson and others not only reflect the democratic revisionists' general concern for stability, but predicate that stability on low levels of involvement by large lots of people. This, too, has been incorporated in the democratic revisionist's general case.

On the basis of examining only two major democratic revisionists, the recurring themes of that literature are apparent: (1) attention is focused upon national institutions; (2) the democratic ideal is revealed in representative government; (3) representative government has been achieved; (4) voting is the only major political activity available to the mass public; (5) political stability is the prime objective; (6) stability generally requires low rates of mass participation.

If all of this has begun to sound remarkably familiar, it should; for democratic revisionism is the contemporary flagbearer of classical liberal democracy. All of the ingredients are there; the differences are a matter of tone arising from the fact that the basics of liberal democracy have been achieved in many Western nations of the world. Thus the "revision" was actually a "return"—a return to the principles of John Locke. It does not seem to matter whether one proceeds on the basis of survey research as Berclson does, or pure logical deduction, as formal theorists do, such as Anthony Downs in *The Economic Theory of Democracy*;[56] liberal premises lead to liberal conclusions. There just is no need for more participation. A liberal amount of participation is not a "liberal" amount.

The Challenge Rebutted

In opposition, many modern democratic theorists were quick to assert that the revisionists misconstrue major aspects of the democratic theory they challenge. This applies to the very unity that revisionists label "the classical theory of democracy." Carole Pateman calls the notion of a classical theory of democracy "a myth,"[57] while John Plamenatz, in even more rancorous style (when refering specifically to Schumpeter), condemns the revisionist attack as "ignorant and inept and . . . worth discussing only because it has been taken seriously."[58] What so irks these democratic theorists is that the diverse characteristics the revisionists conglutinate to form the classical theory of democracy do not exist as an expression of any theorist in specific, nor as an accurate account of democratic theory in general. Quite simply, the revisionists have lanced a bugaboo.

Even if one were to accept the revisionists' "cut and paste" version of "traditional" democratic theory, it is clear that they have misunderstood that "traditional" democratic theory was never intended to be descriptive, but prescriptive of political reality. Those who so carefully measured the distance between political reality and democratic ideals have only rediscovered a major characteristic of ideals—they are unachieved. To reject theories on the basis of such misapprehensions is unfortunate, but more regrettable yet, the revisionists lack the ideals that could enable them to share in goals and other valuables that germinate from those ideals. By myopically focusing upon voting, the revisionists ignore the other varieties of more meaningful participation; by tunneling their attention toward representative institutions at the national level, they avoid on the periphery of their vision the diverse levels and congeries of communities that await more meaningful forms of participation. Furthermore, the revisionists simply seem unaware of the many benefits that may accrue to society and the individual as a result of participation. If participation is restricted to voting, the individual especially will be hampered, as John Stuart Mill claimed a century ago: "a political act, to be done only once in a few years, and for which nothing in the daily habits of the citizen has prepared him, leaves his intellect and his moral dispositions very much as it found them."[59] No benefits will be conferred, however, if participation is discordant with political stability—and that is exactly what the revisionists claim. This contention is so essential to the revisionist case that it behooves us to return to it.

Though Berelson and his associates are not alone in averring that positive effects stem from citizen apathy, their case is atypical. It will be remembered they postulate that mass public apathy ameliorates the negative impact of the politicos. This is contrary to the more common contemporary case, which contends that it is not the active but the generally inactive segments of the population that pose a threat and demand buffering. (Those who wish to revise democracy on this basis hereafter shall be known as "elitist democratic revisionists" or simply "elitist revisionists.")[60] Seymour Lipset, for example, is most fearful that the common man might enter the political system, carrying with him deadly, antidemocratic virus. Seeing "profoundly antidemocratic tendencies in lower class groups," Lipset dedicates much of *Political Man* to analyzing Hitler, McCarthy, and other demagogic leaders who have led antidemocratic mass movements.[61] Others who join Lipset in the fear that the common political man is subject to demagogues include Durkheim, LeBon, Freud, Spengler, Ortega y Gasset, Mayo, Eliot, Niebuhr, Mumford, Talmon and Lippmann.

At first glance, there may not seem to be any significant difference between the two groups of revisionists; both view political stability as being contingent upon apathy and both happily consider America stable. It is only upon perusal that the logic which bifurcates the groups assumes practical importance. The elitist revisionists would extend participation throughout the political community *if* all possessed the attributes of the present participatory elites. Unfortunately, they do not. It is the elitist revisionist recommendation that the preponderance of the population remain outside the political arena, sadly stricken as the mass is with the antidemocratic virus. Berelson and his intellectual cohorts, on the other hand, would never prescribe a pervasive extension of participation, no matter how attitudinally democratic the new participants are. Apathetics in the system must remain apathetic to dissipate the dangers the politicos present by their proclivity toward rigid partisanship and fanaticism. To swell the ranks of the active is to augment the danger. Though both groups offer explanations as to why apathy and stability coexist, the explanations themselves cannot coexist. They are irreconcilable and mutually repugnant, thus necessitating a choice between them.

Berelson et al. create an equilibrium model that demands the exact attributes that exist in America. The construction of this model, however, is indeed unfortunate. The authors do not develop an equilibrium model with requisites for political stability and then discover that the American public satisfies them. Instead, they map the distribution of political attributes among the population while deeming the system to be stable and then fallaciously conclude that the latter followed from the former. It is unjustified to confer equilibrium requisite status on any factor on the basis of its concomitant existence with "equilibrium." But the problems with their "model" are not limited to the logic of its equilibrium requisites.

Since the appearance of *Voting* in 1954, many political survey research reports on America have been published, but none have received more praise than the award-winning work, *Participation in America*.[62] Published in 1972 by Sidney Verba and Norman Nie, the work reveals the continued interest in the extent of participation in America. Their preliminary report ostensibly appears consistent with Berelson and other democratic revisionists. When analyzing participation in twelve political acts,[63] Verba and Nie reveal that for six out of the twelve activities reported, "the participation rate is less than 20 percent, and four of the remaining six activities are performed by less than 33 percent of the citizens."[64] The authors confess that they are tempted to "interpret these data to mean that 70 to 80 percent of the citizenry engage in no activity beyond voting, while 20 to 30 percent perform all of the more active types of participation."[65] This indeed has been the standard interpretation running through democratic revisionist literature and finding its clearest expression in Lester Milbrath's *Political Participation*. Simply stated, the same citizens repeatedly engage in the "gladitorial" acts of participation. But could it not be different citizens who engage in the different gladitorial acts? When Verba and Nie address this question they are forced to conclude that the standard assumption of overlapping activities was woefully in need of revision. It is worth quoting from the authors at length. "No activity in this set is performed by as many as one-third of the citizens. The range of frequency of performance of these activities is between 8 and 32 percent. Whereas this might suggest that two-thirds of our respondents engage in none of these acts, we find that, in fact, less than a third of the sample reports engaging in no such act. Sixty-nine percent of our respondents report engaging in at least one of these acts, and almost half our sample (47 percent) report engaging in two or more. Acts of participation are not clustered in a limited set of citizens."[66]

The damage to Berelson's argument should be evident. Whereas he found equilibrium and stability associated with a certain distribution that included nearly 40 percent apathetics, the actual distribution is, in fact, much more heavily skewed toward involvement and participation. Berelson's bank of apathy has been depleted and yet stability remains. It is certainly possible to say that this new distribution is the one associated with stability, but that could be said about every new distribution ad nauseam. It is also possible (and more cogent) to contend that there are many points of equilibrium, but this is only to say that equilibrium may be achieved with ever-increasing levels of participation and involvement. No, this damage is irreparable; Berelson's case for apathy has become untenable. If Berelson's argumentation is to be rejected as implausible, how do the findings of Verba and Nie affect the elitist revisionist's case for apathy?

Since the elitist revisionists support apathy on different grounds, their argument will be challenged in a different manner. The elitist revisionists do not see danger emanating from the involved segment of the population, for the activists (the elites) generally share libertarian values, and possess "democratic" attitudes which include supporting the "democratic" rules of the game. The real danger exists among the uninvolved segment, for they are the ones that harbor antidemocratic values and attitudes. Given the previously cited research by McCloskey, Prothro, and Grigg, there may be reason for such fear. To the extent that Verba and Nie report rates of participation and involvement beyond that assumed by the elitist revisionists, however, their case is also attenuated. If the additional participants continue to possess antidemocratic qualities, then the system must be capable of tolerating a degree of antidemocratic qualities, for the sytem remains stable. Even more encouraging is the prospect that an attitudinal change has occurred among the new participants. Participation is a socializing agent as well as medium. By participating in democratic processes, people may develop values and attitudes consistent with those processes. As stated earlier in this chapter, a premium should be placed on bringing the uninvolved, antidemocratic into the system where attitudinal changes can occur. The great danger that the elitist revisionists anticipate is precipitated by the sudden emergence of the antidemocratic into the political arena; the danger will remain as long as the antidemocratic lie outside the system, susceptible to the persuasion of demagogues. The elitist revisionist defense of apathy serves only to perpetuate the danger. Only by a slow and methodical incorporation of citizens into communities can this potential danger be nullified.

In conclusion, it is one of the great ironies in the tradition of democratic thought that the revisionists' attack upon a spurious species of democracy serves to create a contemporary group of democratic theorists who embrace many of the very characteristics under assault. The more the revisionists lambaste "classical" democratic theory for its emphasis on participation (among other things), the more contemporary theorists come to view participation as a political good and a goal toward which to strive. Rising to lead the counterassault against the revisionists, although not always from a participatory perspective, are such men and women as Peter Bachrach, Lane Davis, Carole Pateman, and John Plamenatz.[67] Contemporaneous with the critique came a spate of books designed to elaborate upon the ideal of participatory democracy. Among them were Fluno's *the Democratic Community*, Cook and Morgan's *Participatory Democracy*, Benello and Roussopoulos's *The Case for Participatory Democracy*, and Kramer's *Participatory Democracy*.[68]

Contained within the reply to the revisionists is a much more significant challenge, one aimed at a tradition no less lofty than classical liberalism itself. The attempt to overturn the revisionist version of democracy is also an attempt to overturn liberal democracy, for interlaced as they are, both are antithetical to high levels of citizen involvement in the political. Lockean liberal democracy may very well emphasize government "of" the people, and government "for" the people, but it does not provide for government "by" the people. It is sufficient that citizens participate in the process by which governmental decision makers are chosen—and even on that limited basis, participation need not be widespread. The political, as embodied in the state, is an autonomous sphere divorced from the everyday life of citizens in a liberal democracy.

Participatory democrats certainly are justified in challenging the liberal-revisionist formulation of democracy that operates on such minimal amounts of participation. But in rejecting the liberal perspective, participatory democrats unnecessarily rejected the "process" version of democracy. The inadequacy of the liberal position does not lie in the process definition of democracy, but in the severe limitations to the process that liberalism's view of man and the political dictates. If democracy is seen not as a process of *selecting* governmental decision makers but as a process of *making* decisions in all communities, then democracy acquires its rightful participatory nature. Moreover, if democracy as a process is then tied to the preconditions, concomitant conditions, and consequences of participation, it achieves the intricacy associated with democratic theory, without the conceptual fuzziness associated with "content" versions of democracy too often embraced by participatory democrats.

The new democratic theorists are interested in doing more than confronting democratic revisionism and its liberal democratic ancestry with an alternative conception of democracy, a conception more etymologically faithful to the word's literal meaning and which more clearly expresses the ideal. They also are interested in effecting the change toward a more democratic system, that is, toward a more participatory system. This leads to a very interesting convergence of interests; democratic theorists who emphasized the norm of participation turned to the behavioral literature on political parication to inform them of the nature of the phenomenon. The effort has not produced a satisfactory understanding of political participation or a guide to achieving a participatory world. The next chapter will clarify the reasons for this failure.

Before this work considers the means by which participatory democracy may be achieved, it is important to stress again the theoretical schism which exists between liberal democracy and participatory democracy. In opposition to C. B. Macpherson and his book *The Life and Times of Liberal Democracy*,[69] this work takes a firm stance against the casual association of the two. In almost every important aspect, participatory democracy contrasts with the liberal democracy of Locke that was readily adopted in American thought and action. It conceives of the political differently: liberal democracy separates the social from the political, associating the political with what is public, and the public with what is governmental; participatory democracy extends the political beyond what is governmental and may reject entirely the notion of what is public. It has a different view of man's nature; liberal democracy depicts man largely as self-interested, acquiring, and manipulative; participatory democracy views man in a much more favorable light, stressing his ability to conceive of and maintain communities through his sincere empathy with other people. It conceives of the proper set of institutions differently; liberal democracy seeks to fashion governmental institutions into a representative form and allow other institutions to favor the free acquisition of property; participatory democracy departs from the simple utilitarian view of institutions and communities and seeks to open them fully to popular participation. Finally, it differs as to the proper view of the good life. Liberal democracy stresses acquiring almost exclusively individualistic values; participatory democracy in addition stresses the value of life shared in common with others.

It is true, as Macpherson asserts, that neither form is dictatorial or totalitarian, but that is not sufficient reason to categorize them together. According to Macpherson the telling quality is that they both emphasize the equal right of every man and woman to full development and exercise of capabilities.[70] This position is open to two broad attacks; the first of which comes from Macpherson himself. In *The Real World of Democracy* Macpherson claims that all three real-world varieties of democracy share the same goal: "to provide the conditions for the full and free development of the essential human capabilities of all the members of society." [71] If this is so, participatory democracy not only shares this characteristic with liberal democracy, but with two patently nonliberal varieties of democracy as well. On the other hand, I am willing to argue that participatory democracy does provide for the development and exercise of human capabilities whereas liberal democracy does not. The unmitigated competition of liberal society does not afford the conditions or even the existent rights of individuals to grow and develop. No, participatory democracy deserves to be viewed as a nonliberal, nontotalitarian system.

Though not precisely a participatory democrat, John Stuart Mill has written a most fitting closing for a chapter on participatory democracy as a political ideal.

"From these accumulated considerations it is evident that the only government which can fully satisfy all the exigencies of the social state is one in which the whole people participate; that any participation, even in the smallest public function, is useful; that the participation should everywhere be as great as the general degree of improvement of the community will allow; and that nothing less can be ultimately desirable than the admission of all to a share in the sovereign power of the state." [72]

3

Liberalism and Participation Research

The Presence of Liberalism

DEMOCRACY IS A PRIMARY POLITICAL GOOD. TO ACCEPT DEMOCRACY as a political ideal of necessity is to recommend the extension of participation as a goal worthy of pursuit. In the words of Arnold Kaufman, perhaps the first to address participatory democracy as such, "the persistent truth is that participation is an essential condition of the good society and the good life."[1] How to generate more participation becomes the dominant question; developing a theoretical framework which embodies a strategy for achieving higher levels of participation is the goal of this chapter.

In some ways, the burden of outlining a strategy for participation is made lighter by the fact that political participation has been the preeminent concern of political scientists over the past two decades or more. Vast amounts of empirical research findings are at our disposal. Yet despite all that is available, the literature does not lend itself well to cumulative recommendations for participation. Although it points consistently to the important relationship between social participation and political participation, alleging that a general social basis underlies political participation, problems in the research limit its utility. Part of the trouble concerns contradictory findings and needless variations in operation and measurement, but the major impediment relates specifically to the theoretical perspective upon which the research efforts are based. Much of our empirical research into political participation has been predicated on the liberal interpretation of the world. Most of the unambiguous traits of liberalism can be found in the empirical research into political participation: a basic division between social and political spheres, limitation of the political sphere to government, an emphasis upon restricted forms of participation (especially voting), and an antiparticipation bias. *Perhaps the most important conclusion to draw from this discovery is not simply that most of those engaged in participation research, in effect, have been practicing liberal theorists, but that the dominance of liberal perspectives has constituted a major obstacle to the development of compelling theories of participation.* Since liberal assumptions lead most naturally to liberal conclusions, it is very difficult to employ liberal-based research toward achieving the nonliberal goal of participatory democracy. To utilize fully the findings, it is necessary to incorporate a broader perspective of the political. This, however, threatens the entire social participation/political participation relationship with tautology. Fortunately, there is a way out, but it entails a complete restructuring of participation research based on nonliberal conceptualizations. The foundation of this necessary restructuring *will follow* the presentation of the general liberal model of participation and the research, which both constitutes it and is derived from it.

Liberalism is the tradition of thought into which Americans are born. As political socialization affects our everyday thoughts and actions, so does liberalism affect our theoretical political thinking—in ways that often are unrecognized. When we assume "no particular" perspective on the political world we observe and study, we all too often are assuming the perspective liberalism has proffered. This is certainly the case in our study of participation. To establish the presence of liberalism, it is necessary to analyze the participation research literature. Such an analysis shall reveal the unambiguous traits of liberalism: a basic division between social and political spheres, limitation of the political sphere to government, an emphasis on restricted forms of participation (especially voting), and an antiparticipation bias.

The research literature's dominant position on the origins of participation is that it is a learned response to the environment. Sidney Verba and Norman Nie made the significant discovery that by controlling on statistically the affects of social class, the relationship between age and voting became more linear than curvilinear, leading them to suggest that the "data seem compatible with a gradual learning model of political activity. The longer one is exposed to politics, the more likely one is to participate."[2] Since that time, the consensus of research opinion has been, as Milbrath and Goel's review indicates, that "political participation is a *learned* social role."[3]

If participation is a *learned* response, then participation must result in some change in the psychological disposition of the individual who participates. The research literature offers a number of important psychological dispositions which may be seen as the result of some participatory experiences and the causes of others. The research tendency has been to use them separately; but it would be more meaningful to combine them. The configuration of psychological dispositions that incline an individual to offer a participatory response may be termed a "participatory persuasion." It consists of such traits as social interests, concerns, gregariousness, sociability, efficacy, and internal locus of control. As these traits develop, so does the participatory persuasion and the likelihood that an individual will later seek a participatory response. Participation thus breeds participation.

Though the view that participation is gradually learned and operates through the development of a participatory persuasion may contribute to our understanding, it does not say very much about what kinds of experiences lead to political participation. Throughout the vast participation literature, nothing emerges as more clearly related to political participation than what has been termed "social participation." Social participation, alternatively called "organization involvement," "voluntary association participation," "associational participation," and the like, often has been found to form the closest association with political participation of any phenomena measured. Thus the elementary model that dominates the research literature is:

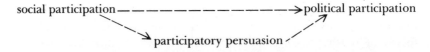

social participation — — — — — — — — — — — →political participation

participatory persuasion

From the large number of supportive studies it is possible to select three major efforts for illustrative purposes. In 1969, Norman Nie, G. Bingham Powell, Jr., and Kenneth Prewitt published a major two-part article entitled "Social Structure and Political Participation: Developmental Relationships." The authors employ three measures of social structure: urban residence, social status, and organizational involvement while they operationalize political participation by measures of the following activities: talking about politics, contacting local authorities, contacting national authorities, being involved in electoral campaigns, and joining political organizations and political parties. Based on a five-country study, Nie, Powell, and Prewitt conclude that although social status relates highly to political participation, "organizational involvement is the predictive variable with the most strength."[4] In the United States, for example, the correlation between organizational involvement and political participation is an impressive .523.[5] Since each of the five nations (the United States, United Kingdom, Germany, Italy, and Mexico) would rank high on a modernity scale, the authors were unsure that the findings would apply to developing nations as well. Hence they extended their investigation to include India, and discovered "striking confirmation" that in every nation they studied, "organizational involvement is the strongest predictor of participation."[6] Using the same data set, Paul Burstein comments that "perhaps the most surprising result is the consistency with which the best predictors of participation—media and organization involvement—work their effect.[7]

David Sallach, Nicholas Babchuk, and Alan Booth present a second significant study in their article "Social Involvement and Political Activity: Another View" (1972). Focusing on the United States, the authors test the effects of information access, voluntary association membership, and a sense of powerlessness on a multiple measure of political participation. Consistent with much of the contemporary thinking concerning political participation, such as that which Verba, Nie and Kim offer in their important monograph, "The Modes of Democratic Participation: A Cross-National Comparison,"[8] Sallach, Babchuk, and Booth do not simply combine the measure, but establish three distinct dimensions of political participation: voting, political group membership and active political participation. They measure active political participation by talking to public officials, working in elections, attending political meetings, and contributing money to political causes. They report "The data strongly supported the hypothesized relationship between membership in voluntary groups and voting behavior, political group membership and active participation. . . . The stable relationship which voluntary association membership established with each form of political activity suggests that similar social bases underlie differential forms of participation."[9]

Marvin Olsen in his important article, "Social Participation and Voting Turnout," continues the progression of thought by asking "if active participation in voluntary associations can mobilize individuals politically, why can't participation in other organizations such as churches or communities have the same effect?"[10] By separating church and community organizations from voluntary associations in general, Olsen establishes three measures of social participation. Though Olsen seems to broaden the independent variable from voluntary association to social organization participation, the actual construction is a bit more narrow than most. Though there may be good reasons to distinguish among participation in church organizations, community organizations, and voluntary organizations, most operationalizations would categorize all three under the same rubric, voluntary associations. Olsen's construction of the dependent variable could not be more narrow; he measures political participation only in terms of voting. With the relationship so specified, Olsen discovers that participation in "all three positively affects voting turnout and does so separately thus indicating none of the zero-order [relationships] are spurious."[11] When the three types of participation are combined into the "Social Participation Index," the strength of the relationship to voting increases and "hence does reflect the overall dimension of social participation."[12] This overall dimension of social participation withstands extensive controlling procedures and is found to be the "most important predictor of voting turnout,"[13] when political orientations (such as the factors in my "participatory persuasion") are considered intervening variables.

From several very different types of research design, the same general conclusion can be drawn: there is an exceptionally strong relationship between social participation and political participation. The general support for this relationship is substantial and almost unparalleled in social science research. Marvin Olsen asserts "every voting turnout study has found these two variables to be fairly highly correlated."[14] Sallach and his associates maintain that "when coupled with previous research, [their data] seem to establish the preeminence of voluntary group membership in predictions of political activity."[15]

Since the relationship between social participation and political participation is specified in so many different manners, there may be great confusion concerning the logic of the nexus. The greatest disparity arises between those who examine voluntary association membership and those who study a more active form of participation. On the basis of his research, Marvin Olsen states that the "social participation effects on voting are cumulative. The greater the number of one's organizations, the more likely he will vote."[16] Other scholars substantiate the existence of this cumulative effect, including Sidney

Verba and Norman Nie. In *Participation in America* (1972), they find the cumulative effect to operate on a combined political participation index, "the more organizations to which an individual belongs, the greater is his rate of activity.[17] But is it mere membership, or active involvement that accounts for this occurrence? Verba and Nie make clear that:

The individual who is a *passive* member in one or more organizations is no more *likely* to be active in politics than the individual who belongs to no such association. In contrast, the active organizational member is much more likely than the nonmember to be politically active, and this political activity rate increases as one moves from single membership to multiple membership. These data strongly suggest that affiliation with associations relates to increased political activity because it affords the individual an opportunity to be active within the organization.[18]

Testifying to the great impact of social participation, Verba and Nie confirm that activity, even in "manifestly" nonpolitical organizations, will increase political participation.[19] For example, activity in recreation groups, the least politically-oriented voluntary associations studied, results in a substantial increase in political participation. In fact, the size of that gain is the same as the average improvement in the more politically-oriented organizations. If there is a political content to the organizational-participation experience—the occurrence of political discussions or the group's involvement in community affairs—the leap in political participation is even more dramatic. This is true only for those active in the organization, thus indicating the primacy of activity: "The data . . . make clear that exposure to political discussion and community activity in an organization has an impact on those who are active in organizations."[20] There is no corresponding improvement upon the participation rates of passive members. They are unaffected by the presence of political stimuli.

The presence of the social/political distinction is also apparent in the only other variable that can rival social participation in its impact upon political participation, *social* class. The influence of social class seems to follow exactly the same channels as social participation. Social class converts into a measurable variable (SES or socio-economic status) by constructing an index of educational, income, and occupational achievement. It is not high education, a large income, or possession of a prestigious job that is important, but the sets of experiences that these measures represent. What do these sets of experiences have in common? Each provides the individual with knowledge of his social world. Each fosters in the individual the skills necessary to live effectively in that social world. Each improves the individual's confidence that he can act in that world. Thus social class itself is an indicator of effective and extensive social (and therefore political) participation.

It is clear that in their study of participation, political scientists have adopted the most important distinction that liberalism offers. As there is a basic division between social and political spheres in liberalism, so there is a basic distinction between social and political participation in political science. We may ask if the other dominant characteristics of liberalism also appear in political science research into participation. For example, is the political taken as synonymous with government, and is participation taken in a narrow sense, often restricted to no more than voting? One need only refer to the same social participation/political participation literature for an answer. Throughout the literature, the range of phenomena taken as indicators of political participation varies from narrow to very narrow. The broadest scope is provided by Sallach, Babchuk, and Booth, who operationalize political participation by measures of voting, belonging to explicitly political groups (e.g., political party), talking about politics, contacting elected officials, contributing money to campaigns, attending political meetings, and working in elections. Though this may seem to cover much ground, close attention reveals that each measure relates the political to what is governmental. Keep in mind, this is the most encompassing functional definition. At the other end lies Marvin Olsen who accepts only voting as a measurement of political participation. This observation applies not only to the full range of literature that examines the social participation/political participation relationship, but to the entire literature related to political participation. Consider the much more recent study of political participation by Verba, Nie, and Kim in *Participation and Political Equality*. "By political participation, we refer to those legal activities by private citizens that are more or less directly aimed at influencing the selection of governmental personnel and/or the actions they take. Though this is a rough definition, it is adequate for delimiting our sphere of interest. It indicates that we are basically interested in *political* participation, that is, in acts that aim at influencing *governmental* decisions. Ours is a broad conception."[21] (Italics by original authors.) The authors make no bones about the fact that the political is what is governmental. When they claim that their incredibly narrow conception is broad, they mean that their conception of political participation includes more than just voting; it includes a few other government-focused activities. The typical study, including the most important in the area, *The American Voter* and *The Changing American Voter*, limit participation to voting.[22]

It is difficult to deny that those who have engaged in behavioral research into political participation have been practicing liberal theorists. No distinction that they make is more important than the division of life into social and political spheres, with the political narrowly conceived. Throughout the social participation-political participation literature, and throughout the participation literature generally, the political is viewed as that which relates rather directly to formal government; in its operational form political participation often means nothing more than simply voting.

As far as the antiparticipation bias within the participation-research literature is concerned, that was indicated in the previous chapter's discussion of challenges to the participatory democratic ideal. Throughout the entire effort to revise the democratic ideal with results of participation research, the pervading view is that America is fortunate not to have rates of mass participation higher than what they are.

The Nonliberal Alternative

The liberal view of politics is based on a basic distinction between spheres of life, the social (what is sometimes called "private") and the political. In the world in which we now live, it is almost impossible to maintain liberal distinctions. If the bifurcation of life into political and social spheres was ever useful, it is not any longer—so great has been the interpenetration of the two. Assuming that there was once a logic to the division, can we continue to cling to the preconceptions of liberalism when General Motors has a gross sales in excess of the GNP of most nations of the world (and a standing in the world community to match), when multinational corporations have built an incredible spiderweb network of international relations, when "public" regulation of life has expanded into almost all areas of human activity? Who can now say that there is any meaningful boundary between the two, far less specify what that boundary is? Yet that is exactly what we have done in our participation literature, and it is upon that untenable distinction that liberal theories of participation rest. If we are to develop strong theories of participation, we must reconceptualize our notion of the political. This is particularly important since it can and will be argued that the liberal bias against participation interferes with the creation of theories to aid us in understanding participation.

It has been difficult for the participation research literature to maintain the distinction between social and political participation. Verba and Nie were acutely aware of the trouble when they wrote that "The possible overlap between our political measures and our measures of organizational activity illustrate the great difficulty that exists in determining the exact boundary between political participation and participation in the nonpolitical sphere [social participation]. There is no clear conceptual answer."[23]

I do not believe that the precautions Verba and Nie took succeeded in distinguishing between the political and the nonpolitical (i.e. the social), but at least they made the attempt. The confusion can be considerable when no such careful effort is extended. Lester Milbrath, in his encyclopedic summary of political-participation literature, offers us the following relationship in bold type: "persons who are active in community affairs are much more likely than those not active to participate in politics."[24] What is nonpolitical about activity in community affairs? The author never lets us know.

The deficiency is corrected in the second edition of *Political Participation* now coauthored by M. L. Goel. In fact the very first word of the introduction begins the discussion of what will be considered political. The actual definition appears in the second paragraph.

Political behavior, then, is behavior which affects or is intended to affect the decisional outcomes of government. The politics of nongovernmental organizations are excluded from this definition. Behavior which affects the decisional outcomes of a church or a corporation, for example, even if it were typically political in form and content, would not be considered political behavior by this definition. Politics now can be defined as the process by which decisions about governmental outcomes are made.[25]

By reviewing all of the major research efforts into political participation, Milbrath and Goel's book has come to reflect rather accurately the preconceptions of that literature. Thus captured within the quotation cited is the schizophrenia concerning the political, which not only hinders the development of research and theories of participation, but probably also impedes the development of our discipline, since our definition of the political is fundamental to what is developed. The authors clearly recognize that the political extends well beyond the boundaries of government, but they will nevertheless dismiss behavior which is "typically political in form and content" if it is not directed toward government. In the preceding paragraph, Milbrath and Goel misconstrue a conception of the political (Robert Dahl's use of the political system), which is unmistakably intended to move the boundaries of the political beyond what is governmental in order to justify their restrictive use. In the name of precision the authors ignore a good deal of what is considered to be political—even by them. In the name of precision, the authors revert to the preconceptions of liberalism.

It is time that we move beyond liberalism and the depoliticalization which is associated with its basic distinctions. We must get beyond such definitions of the political as that which is offered by A. Gordon Dewey: "No matter how the question may be obfuscated, whenever it tends to involve a utilization of the machinery of government then it becomes a 'political issue'; those concerned with it are involved in 'political activity'; and the phenomenon becomes one of these which it is the function of the political scientist to observe." [26]

Yet in going beyond such definitions, we run the risk Milbrath and Goel rightly indicate; we do risk making the political so ubiquitous that necessary distinctions cannot be made. The task is evident; we must seek a broad view of the political, a view that allows necessary and precise distinctions to be made. Our ability to compile, organize, and aggregate participation research findings, in short, our ability to create compelling theories of participation rests on this broad view.

If the political is not a sphere of life, then what defines it? Ironically, Milbrath and Goel lead us in the right direction when they reject behavior that is typically political in form and content because it is part of the wrong sphere. We must seek a view that relates the political to behavior and activity that is somehow "typically" political, that is, "essentially" political. Fortunately, the quest for a nonliberal view of the political was completed in the first chapter when the political was depicted as activity *related* to group decision making (not to be confused with acts simply of decision making), and the three main dimensions of the political were delineated: the nature of the activity, the group,

and the issue involved. Isn't this view of the political exactly the conclusion that Milbrath and Goel were trying to avoid when they rejected the "politics of nongovernmental organizations . . . behavior
which affects the decisional outcomes of a church or a corporation?"

From the perspective of the new view of the political, the problems
in the social participation/political participation literature become
clear. The distinction between the two is unwarranted because all participation relates to the decision making of groups, and all group decision making, by definition, is political. Of course, there are important distinctions to be made among acts of participation, but they are
not neatly divisable into "social" and "political" categories. Assuming
this view, much of what Nie, Prewitt, and Powell measure as "organizational involvement," Sallach, Babchuk, and Booth call "voluntary
association involvement," Alford and Scoble conceptualize as "voluntary association participation," Erbe considers "organizational participation," Marvin Olsen terms "social participations," and Verba and
Nie examine as "organizational activity," is activity related to the decision making of groups. It is political activity.

It is because the political is an important part of social participation
that we find social participation revealing many of the same characteristics as political participation. Social participation of one kind increases other forms of social participation in the same way that it does
political participation; in both cases the effects of social participation
are cumulative.[27] Social participation and socio-economic status are
correlated in the same fashion as political participation and socio-
economic status. Social participation distributes across the life cycle in
precisely the same manner as political participation: in a curvilinear
pattern until social class is controlled, and then in an almost linear
pattern.[28] Social participation has even been found to generate democratic norms in precisely the same manner as political participation.[29]
Is there any wonder why social participation consistently is found to
relate highly to political participation? The answer is clear. Social participation and political participation are not generically discrete phenomena: they are both forms of the very same *political* phenomenon,
participation. The social participation/political participation relationship is misleading, for it associates the effects of one expression of political activity with another.

It may seem possible to avoid this conceptual confusion by conve-
niently defining the political narrowly as that which is governmental,

but this comes at the cost of missing much of what is phenomenologically political. The much preferable alternative is to restructure the participation literature, incorporating the new view of the political. Politics must not be seen as a *sphere*, but a *type* of individual activity. It must be linked to the everyday life of individuals. Only with emphasis on the actual experiences of participation of individuals in their everyday life can we hope to surmount the barriers of liberal conceptualizations and construct a truly compelling theory of participation.

Rejecting the liberal perspective does not necessarily mean that we must also reject all research conducted under its influence. If a research effort is able to penetrate to the empirical world in which we live, then it is likely to say something about it, no matter which perspective informs and guides it. Thus one need not be a Marxist to recognize the validity of many interrelationships between the economic order and government. In the same manner the correlations between participation variables remain valid; it is the way that the research findings are incorporated into a theoretical framework that must change.

To restructure the participation literature, we must begin with what has been identified. Although very little could be done with the observation within the liberal perspective, it does appear as if participation is a learned response, one that develops over almost the entire lifetime of the individual. It also would appear from the research literature that experiences of participation that contribute to future participatory responses probably act through the development of an activist orientation to the world, what has been called a participatory persuasion. Although participatory experiences generally make a positive contribution to one's orientation toward participating in the future, it is quite possible in some cases that participation will be such a negative experience that it will diminish the likelihood that an individual will participate in the future. In any event, both the view of participation as gradually learned and the view that participatory experiences contribute to future participatory experiences through the development of a participatory persuasion are worth keeping.

With that in mind, it is necessary to look again at what has been found in participation research. In operational form, what has actually been correlated is simple acts of participation. Adding the individual's psychological disposition toward participation as a mediating factor, an alternative theoretical formulation can be offered. We are no longer concerned with the elementary model from the liberal perspective:

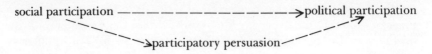

Instead, we are interested in particular acts of participation within particular communal settings. It may be the activity that varies. For example we may seek the relationship between frequency in attendance within a social club and the likelihood that an individual will run for elective office within that social club.

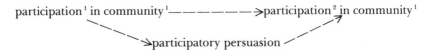

Or, a researcher may be interested in the correlation between voting in a social club and voting in a school board election:

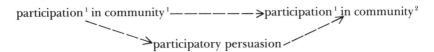

In constructing a theoretical framework for understanding participation, we ask what type of participatory experiences lead to a positive participatory persuasion; we also ask what type of participatory experiences, in what type of communities, lead to what type of future participatory experiences, in what other types of communities. The guiding light for answering these questions is the Proximity Hypothesis. Stated simply, the closer two experiences approximate each other, the more likely that there will be a transference from one experience to the other. The two diagrams can be used as illustrations. In the first case, the type of participation varies, not the setting. Therefore, the closer attending social club meeting (participation[1]) approximates the experience of running for office in that social club (participation[2]), the more likely there will be transference between the two. In the second figure, the community varies and not the type of participation. Therefore, the closer voting in the social club (community[1]), approximates voting in a school board election (community[2]), the more likely there will be transference between the two. And a third dimension along which the Proximity Hypothesis can exist is the issue involved.

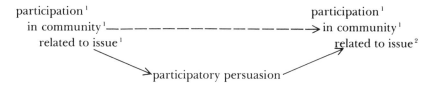

In this case, the closer voting in the social club on where the next meeting will be (issue[1]) approximates voting in the social club on whether to expell a member (issue[2]), the more likely there will be transference between the two.

The reader may have already identified the possible dimensions along which a participatory experience can approximate another (type of activity, setting, and issue), as the dimensions of the political previously discussed. Now that the political is not tied to government as it is in liberal thought, the dimensions of the new view of the political assume significance in opening new research perspectives and strategies. Governmental participation can remain a research subject, but it will not be the only research subject. Relationships among nongovernmental forms of participation will be as important to the political scientists in developing theories of participation as will forms of governmental participation. Redefining the political as activity related to any group decision making provides the necessary theoretical basis for identifying proximity dimensions and developing a sophisticated theory of participation based on the Proximity Hypothesis. Within the three-dimensional space of the political (activity, setting, and issue), each participatory (political) experience can be identified, and its proximity with other participatory experiences can be mapped.

It is possible to provide greater indication of the ways participatory experiences can approximate each other. It is best to begin with the three dimensions of activity, setting and issue.

Activities may approximate each other in at least the following ways:

  A. The nature of the interaction
    1. Formal
    2. Informal
  B. Its relationship to decision making
    1. Direct: acts of decision making

2. Less direct: voting for others who will make decisions
3. Indirect: having less defined input into decision making

Settings may approximate each other in at least the following ways:
  A. The nature of the setting
    1. Unorganized setting
    2. Organized setting
    3. Community
  B. The nature of the community
    1. Governmental
    2. Nongovernmental, geographically based
    3. Nongovernmental, not geographically based
  C. The size of the community
    1. Small: a family
    2. Intermediate: a corporation
    3. Large: a nation

Issues may approximate each other in at least the following ways:
  A. How many people are affected
    1. Large numbers: the whole nation
    2. Intermediate numbers: the Jewish population
    3. Small numbers: residents of a particular neighborhood
  B. The impact of the issues
    1. Negligible: the decision to grant an honorary award
    2. Medium: the closing of a small college
    3. Strong: the decision of the United States to go to war

Although this discussion does not, and indeed cannot, anticipate the best distinctions within a proximity dimension, it does illustrate the kinds of distinctions that may be useful. Utilizing such an approach, it should be possible to specify the likely effects that specific events of participation have on each other. Although the idea of proximity has not received attention within the research literature, it is very possible that proximity links participatory events within the four modes of participation identified by Verba and Nie in *Participation in America*: communal activity, campaign activity, voting, and particularized contacts.

With continued analysis of participation research, it is likely that other dimensions of proximity soon will emerge. One that seems apparent now is proximity in terms of time. The closer participatory events occur in time, the more likely they will have an impact upon one another. Since this operative view of the political places much stress on seeing participation as experience within an individual's life, we must not forget that it is within individuals that the participatory persuasion is developed and proximity occurs. It also may be fruitful to establish a psychological dimension of proximity, one relating to the motivation for individual participation. An individual may participate in a particular issue because of the utility he expects from it (instrumental participation), or because of his desire to share with others in a common enterprise (expressive participation).

It would be interesting to test the degree to which individuals in a liberal society, in relation to the analysts of that society, have incorporated into their thinking such basic liberal distinctions as the social/political dichotomy. Further, it would be interesting to know the degree to which the liberal perspective interferes with the impact of proximity. For the general population the interference could not be great; if it were, the empirical relationship between "social" participation and "political" participation would not be so strong. The apparent consistency of the Proximity Hypothesis with the findings of participation research, and the dead end which liberal approaches to participation theory find themselves are compelling reasons why analysts should not uniformly continue to adopt liberal categorizations—even if political actors do. When liberal categories are adopted, they should be consciously chosen for the purpose of revealing the life-worlds of participants; they should be consciously rejected if they are found not to be helpful.

The Effects of Liberalism

It is difficult to deny that liberal tenets have been incorporated into participation research, and this being so, participation research misses much of what should be defined as phenomenologically political. Despite commonplace perceptions to the contrary, the political continues to be associated with government. Accordingly, broad definitions of the political consider actions, other than voting, that are intended to influence what government does. To the degree that research is conducted on nongovernmental forms of participation, they are lumped together, viewed as social participation, and seen as independent variables influencing participation in government. When attention is placed upon "theoretical" considerations, they reflect liberal considerations as well. The major theoretical concerns tend to be such liberal obsessions as voting rights, opportunities to participate (rather than actual participation), representation, and democracy (constructed from the preceding liberal considerations).

Some progress has been made in the study of participation. Recognition that participation is a learned response to the environment, and that it is mediated through psychological dispositions are important contributions. These findings have not been incorporated into a more encompassing theory of participation, however, and the reason lies with the acceptance of liberal perspectives. Of these, none is more significant than the division of the world into social and political components. Since research findings related to nongovernmental participation are placed under an entirely different rubric (social participation) than those related to governmental participation (political participation), we cannot adequately trace the complex network of individual experiences that develop gradually into a participatory response. The breach between the social and political spheres is too great to transcend. Within the liberal perspective, it makes no sense to attempt to transcend the distance. After all, what road map shows us how to get to Washington, D.C., starting from somewhere in France?

We will never be able to develop fruitful theories of participation based on the severely curtailed analysis presented within the liberal perspective if we do not conceive of participation as generically the same, regardless of the community in which it occurs. The chains which link participatory experiences are broken in critical spots by liberal formulations. The only hope for a strong theory of participation is to transcend such notions as the split between social and political spheres, the restriction of what is political to what is governmental, and the undue emphasis upon participation in the limited form of voting. In transcending these limitations, we break from liberalism and begin to move toward a nonliberal perspective on participation. As we know, this nonliberal perspective produces its own views of participation, representation, and most importantly, democracy, which will rival the liberal versions.

It is just as important to the development of participation theories that we break from liberalism in another way. The lack of development of theories of participation is all too understandable, given the normative response of liberalism to participation. Within liberal thought there is certainly no urgency to develop a theory of participation, for participation is not something to be sought. There is little benefit, and perhaps considerable harm, expected from participation—to the participating individual and the community in which participation occurs. A nonliberal emphasis on the potential value of participation is as essential to the development of a compelling theory of participation as is leaving behind liberal formulations.

The emphasis placed on developing a compelling theory of participation is well warranted in terms of the major concerns expressed in this work. Such a theory would enhance understanding of the essential element of democracy—participation. A strong theory of participation, based on a nonliberal view of the political, will identify the chains that link participatory experience. These linkages, discussed in terms of the Proximity Hypothesis, provide not only the necessary basis for understanding participation, but also for developing a strategy to achieve higher levels of participation in all communities. The complete mapping of proximity dimensions could provide the direction necessary to prescribe a specific sequential strategy for enhancing participation in any particular community. The importance of this possibility will become evident in the next chapter as a strategy for increasing participation in government is explored.

4

The Workplace Connection

Exploration of the Proximity Hypothesis

THERE IS AN IMPORTANT CONNECTION BETWEEN THE WORLD OF work and the world of government. Despite a long-standing tradition positing that the two are tied in some manner, the conjunction has never been well specified. Many idiosyncratic facets related to particular theorists help account for this failure, but the most significant systematic reason derives from the tenets of liberalism. It is the view of liberalism that the workplace and government exist in different spheres of life—spheres that ought to be kept separate. That notion does not prevent inquiry into the general effects of the social sphere on the political sphere and vice-versa, but it does hamper the ability to discern the interaction between certain communities, such as the workplace and government, and to build theoretically on the interactions examined. To establish more fully the theoretical nexus between the workplace and government, it is necessary to transcend liberal tenets and the conception of the political on which they are based. Having reconceptualized the political so that it is rooted in the everyday existence of man, the relationship between the workplace community and government becomes clear and open to elaboration. Although the Proximity Hypothesis is appropriate to the analysis of any participatory events, the predominance of research on governmental participation makes the utility of proximity more apparent in its elaboration. The task of elaboration is before us. Specifically, this chapter will explore the logic of the workplace-government relationship through the Proximity Hypothesis, establish the theoretical traditions that form its foundation and provide the evidence that supports its existence.

The Proximity Hypothesis provides a conceptual, as well as an empirical, guide for establishing commonalities among political (i.e. par-

76

ticipatory) experiences. The greater the proximity between two participatory experiences, the more likely the two will be associated. Or,
to state the principle negatively, the greater the gap, the less the impact. As presented in the opening chapter, there are at least three dimensions to the political: the activity in which the individual engages,
the issue towards which it relates, and the setting in which it occurs.
Each of these dimensions, in turn, can become dimensions of proximity. They may be illustrated by utilizing participation in government as the "dependent" variable. The first manner in which factors
related to the "independent" variable may approximate participation
in government is in the nature of the activity. As also indicated in the
first chapter, human interaction in any community consists of social
activity, political activity, and political action. Since acts of participation fall along the spectrum incorporating parts of political activity
and political action, we would expect acts of participation rather than
social activity more closely to approximate participation in government. Furthermore, we would expect acts of participation more
closely to approximate participation in government to the degree that
dimensions of participation, such as mode, intensity, and quality, are
similar in experiential structure. Factors related to the independent
variable also may approximate participation in government through
the nature of the issues involved. When issues in some particular community affect people in the same manner and intensity as do issues
related to government, then a second kind of approximation exists. A
third manner in which approximation can occur is by virtue of the
characteristics of the setting in which participation occurs. Government exists in a highly organized setting characterized by a high degree of formal interaction. Activity related to decision making often
assumes routinized characteristics within such well-delineated authority structures. Participation in communities that are organized and
characterized by a high degree of formal interaction will have more
impact on participation in government than would participation in
unorganized settings, or organized settings with a low degree of formal interaction.

To the three basic dimensions of the political must be added several
other possible dimensions of proximity. Since we are comparing different participatory events, the time at which they occur may be important. The temporary dimension of proximity would indicate that
events that occur closest in time are likely to have the most impact on
each other. Participation in government is almost entirely restricted to

adults; the set of experiences likely to have the greatest impact on participation in government are other adult participatory experiences. There is also the possible proximity of individual motivation to consider. Participation in government within the dominant view of liberalism is seen largely as an instrumental activity; one enters into it to increase one's own interest. It is likely that other experiences viewed in terms of utility are likely to approximate participation in government the most. Among those individuals who see governmental participation as being more expressive than instrumental, however, it will be other expressive experiences that will approximate most their participation in government.

On the basis of this discussion of the Proximity Hypothesis, the type of phenomena that should have the most impact on participation in government would be participation (similar in mode, intensity, and quality) of adults motivated to participate for the same basic reasons, within organized social settings characterized by a high degree of formal interaction, concerning similar types of issues. For these reasons it can be hypothesized that participation in government is approximated most by participation in the workplace. This is the workplace connection. To increase participation in government, it is most efficient to increase participation in the workplace.

The following section will elaborate on the logic of the workplace connection in terms of the Proximity Hypothesis and examine some of the more important ramifications that may be derived from it. Imagine, if you will, two friends discussing the minutia of their daily existence as they stroll down a city street. The billboard in front of a theater attracts the attention of one of them. When he moves closer to examine the stills from the movie (which look very enticing), he notices that the starting time for the next feature is only minutes away. This prompts an immediate exchange concerning the merits of seeing the movie. Though they are both agreed that the motion picture is worth seeing, one insists that the movie should be seen at some other time because they already have committed themselves to another social activity for the evening. The other agrees. These two people properly constitute a group (though not a community) and their discussion concerning the movie qualifies as participation (activity relating to the decision making of a group). But by the standards derived from the Proximity Hypothesis, this participation is not likely to make much of an impression on either participant's decision to run for county sheriff or any other involvement in governmental activity. The actions, issue, and setting are just too far removed from participation in government.

This is the very conclusion derived from Marvin Olsen's research. When Olsen examined the effects of "social participation" on "political participation," he included measures of interaction among friends and neighbors in his "social participation." While involvement in voluntary associations, church organizations, and community organizations was strongly related to the most popular form of participation in government (voting), interaction among friends and neighbors was not related. It is likely that friend and neighbor interaction did not produce participation because of the nature of the activity, the related issues, and most especially, the setting involved. As Olsen himself commented: "We must look beyond the political system for many of the crucial causes of political participation. In addition to the commonly examined factors of age and education, we must give special attention to the individual's involvement in *organized* social activities which may have little or no formal connections with politics."[1] In this manner our attention is directed toward the proximity dimensions related to the nature of the group and the nature of the activity. An elaboration of these and all of the proximity dimensions will proceed through a discussion of what is conventionally accepted as the origin of governmental participation, childhood socialization.

Individuals are born into an organized social setting, the family, but it is unclear how important the family is in fostering participation in government. It is certainly true that the family plays a nearly indispensable role training the individual for communication within the social world. The family is a prime agent in transmitting social values and other aspects of the culture. It is within the family that the individual is likely to first experience forms of cooperation and conflict. None of this general social participation, however, comes close to approximating participation in government. Although there is participation within the family, it is unlikely that this participation provides good training specifically for participation in government. Though the family is an organized social setting, interactions within that setting are not often formal. Decision making is seldom routinized with clearly delineated lines of communication and authority. It is a rather remarkable family in which the mother, acting as chairperson, convenes the weekly meeting of the family to receive petitions and discuss matters of the budget. No, decision making is much more likely to be conducted in simple, informal exchange. This means that much of the range in the mode of participation within government will not be represented in familiar experience. It is also true that the family is not likely to entertain issues that approximate those considered by government. Another lack of approximation exists along the temporal dimension. Many of the experiences of a child within the family are as temporarily removed from participation in government as experiences can be. The events in the life of an eight year old are a decade removed from his ability to vote. In most ways government is an adult enterprise, and most children must grow up (at least chronologically) to assume an active role in that enterprise. A final lack of proximity is likely to occur along the proximity dimension of motivation. It is much more likely that participation in the family is the result of expressive motivations than is participation in government. Once again, governmental participation is most often viewed as instrumental behavior.

An individual's exposure to organized social settings is quite limited during childhood and adolescence (the period through the age of at least sixteen). Aside from the family, the only similar setting to which almost all children are systematically exposed is the school. In comparison with the family, social interactions within the school are more formal; and yet like the family, the school is unlikely to provide a direct experiential vehicle for participation in government. Participation in school (here conceived as elementary, junior and senior high schools) is characterized by a similar lack of proximity. Though there probably is greater proximity between school and governmental participatory experiences in terms of the mode of participation, there is a clear breach in terms of the quality of participation. This is evident in that students do not possess a full slate of civil liberties, and, as a result, most student participation is little more than pseudo-participation. On that basis, it would be difficult for student participation to be instrumental in motivation. There is little parallel between the actual issues that confront students and those that confront adults making governmental decisions. Issue areas in which students may be effective are not at all similar to those concerning governmental participation. This very fact has led researchers to examine the effects of community participation on student attitudes.[2] Last, but not least, school participation is often temporally removed from most governmental participation.

If children do experience participation in the family and the school, the lack of proximity of such preadult experiences attenuates their significance as training for participation in government. It is quite possible, however, that children do not experience participation in the family and school. For example, Robert Weissberg finds that neither the family nor the school provides the necessary basis for participatory democracy in the United States.[3] Readers need only consult their own memory as to how great their participatory training was in the family and the school.

The Proximity Hypothesis challenges some of the basic tenets of the political science discipline. Since concentrated research on political socialization began in the 1950s, it has been assumed that childhood experiences hold the key to understanding adult political behavior. This is most clearly captured in the "persistence theory" of political socialization. In the words of Fred Greenstein, "the more important a political orientation is in the behavior of adults, the earlier it will be found in the learning of a child."[4] Herbert Hyman even attempts to link politics as a learned behavior with the persistence theory of political socialization. "The importance of such a formulation [of politics as learned behavior] to the understanding of political systems is self-evident, humans must learn their political behavior early and well and persist in it. Otherwise there would be no regularity, perhaps even chaos."[5]

The logic of the persistence theory is dubious to say the least. The theory comes close to portraying a political condition in which very little changes (a view that may have appeared accurate in the late 1950s and early 1960s). A child acquires his basic orientations early in life (and thus presumably from the family); the orientations persist through adolescence to adulthood, at which time they are transferred by the subject—now an adult—to his children. The cycle repeats itself ad infinitum. We know that this is not the case, however, for major changes do take place. Certainly changes occur in the early years, but fundamental modifications in the outlook and behavior of citizens occurs in later years, too. One need only consider the incredible decrease in governmental trust and belief in governmental responsiveness during the decade between 1964 and 1974, or the equally precipitous decline in party identification to realize that dramatic changes can occur among the adult population. These changes often occur as a result of historical events. The results of historical events (known as "Zeitgeist effects") such as the war in Vietnam and the Watergate affair[6] can have devastating effects, especially on those close to them. Yet the persistence model practically ignores these changes.

We know on an individual basis that the persistence model is not a generally accurate model of the socialization process. Is the reader the same person politically that he or she was as a child? If the answer is no, then the occurrences accounting for the change are likely to move us right out of childhood into adolescence and adulthood. At the very least we must concur with Niemi and Jennings that while "maleability is higher among the young, there is graphic evidence that change occurs in the middle years also."[7]

An early, albeit weak, challenge to the dominant view of political socialization came from Orville Brim and Stanton Wheeler in their two essays entitled, *Socialization After Childhood* (1966).[8] The authors concede that the most durable learning occurs in childhood, but claim that childhood does not prepare us for everything; thus significant socialization must occur after that period. On this base has come a growing body of literature assigning significant weight to adult experiences as sources of socialization to politics. Lewis Edinger's 1967 study of elites in France and Germany find that "adult socialization experiences . . . were consistently highest in relationship to (elite) attitude."[9] Donald Searing replicated this study in Venezuela, Israel, and the United States and reported "one potentially important characteristic held in common by the best predictors for all five groups (France and Germany plus the three additional countries) was that they generally isolated adult[10] . . . rather than pre-adult socialization experiences."[11] Allan Kornberg's study of American and Canadian elite comes to the same conclusion;[12] while Kenneth Prewitt's state legislator research leads him to surmise that "early political socialization is apparently unrelated to major aspects of incumbent orientation."[13] Perhaps the most critical appraisal of all comes from R. W. Connell, who reviewed fifty studies in which comparative data from parents and children within the same family were present. He states that "it appears from a substantial body of evidence that processes within the family have been largely irrelevant to the formation of specific opinions."[14] It is understandable that Donald Searing comments that "in explaining political outcomes, one naturally looks to adult attitudes, not to the attitudes of children. But if adult attitudes are the phenomena of interest, why have socialization investigators interviewed children?"[15]

It is not necessary to dismiss the impact of childhood experiences to establish the importance of adult experiences. The gradual learning model stipulates that any participatory interaction will contribute to future participation, including participation in government. But it is unreasonable to expect childhood experiences to lead very directly to participation in government. The experiences of a child, even when they are participatory, do not approximate governmental participation. At a minimum, childhood experiences can contribute to the development of an individual's participatory persuasion, which is then mediated through adult participatory experiences and orientations. This is precisely what Donald Searing contents in "The Structuring Principle."[16] The Proximity Hypothesis can provide guidance to the linkages that extend from childhood to adult participatory experiences. A very good example of establishing such linkages can be found in "Adult Voluntary Association and Adolescent Socialization."[17] In that article, Michael Hanks and Bruce Ecland link participation in extracurricular activities in high school with membership in adult voluntary associations, and then link membership with governmental voting.

The significance of adult experience contributes to the understanding of the powerful relationship that formed a dominant part of the preceding chapter: the relationship between participation in social organizations and participation in government. *Effective* participation in social organizations is largely an adult experience and thus approximates participation in government along the very important temporal dimension. Approximation exists along other dimensions as well. Though the issues entertained by social organizations may not often parallel government issues, the structure of the group and the formal nature of many of the interactions do form an analogue to government and interactions within government. The combination of these factors makes social organization participation a potent influence on governmental participation. It is, however, not the most potent influence.

Though adults encounter more organized social settings than children, not all of these settings are equally pervasive in adult life. Certainly the family is most intimately tied to adult life, but another institution rivals it. As W. E. Moore states: "In modernized societies, occupation represents a central place in life organization for a vast majority of adult males and a substantial minority of adult females. In temporal terms, occupation is challenged only by the family as the major determinant and locus of behavior. . . . In view of this overarching significance of occupation in the life of modern man and woman, it is surprising that occupational socialization appears not to

*Table 1   The Work Force in America, Number and Percentage of
the Working Age Population* [19]

Year	Working Age Population*	Labor Force	Percentage of Population
1890	41,799	21,833	52.2
1900	51,438	27,640	53.7
1920	74,144	40,282	54.3
1930	89,550	50,080	55.9
1935	95,460	53,140	55.7
1940	101,560	56,180	55.3
1945	106,700	65,290	61.2
1950	112,210	64,749	57.7
1955	118,832	68,896	58.0
1960	119,759	72,142	60.2
1965	129,236	77,178	59.7
1970	140,182	85,903	61.3
1975	153,449	94,793	61.8
1977 (Jan.–Apr.)	157,683	97,546	61.9

*For the figures years 1890 to 1955, working age population was considered
fourteen years and older. For the figures years 1960 to 1977, working age
population was considered sixteen years and older.

have excited scholarly interest proportional to its importance." [18] The
family's impact upon governmental participation is minimized by its
lack of proximity. If we exclude the family, it would be difficult for any
other community to rival the workplace in terms of its ubiquity. Table
1 indicates precisely that the number of Americans who are part of
the workplace has increased in both absolute and relative terms since
the turn of the century.

The workplace has more than its presence in adult life (or the fact
that interest groups are often derived from occupations), recommending it as the *key* community linked to government. Participation
in the workplace approximates participation in government because
the workplace provides an organized social setting that approximates
government in terms of its interaction patterns. Since the decision-
making process of both communities is formal, participation in the
workplace is likely to approximate participation in government in

terms of the mode, quality, and even intensity of participation. Proximity in the intensity of participation is tied closely to the parallel that
exists in the importance of the issues considered in the workplace and
in government. Like government, decisions in the workplace deal
with primary values. Workplace decisions determine things as basic as
how well an individual will be able to provide food, clothing, and shel-
ter for his or her family. They also determine the way the rest of
society will look upon that individual, for a person's social status is
tied to that person's occupational status. For these reasons, participation in the workplace is characteristically instrumental. With so many
Americans experiencing the workplace at one time or another, and
with the very close approximation of the workplace and government,
there is good reason to believe that participation in the workplace will
have a powerful effect on participation in government.

The Theoretical Tradition

Based on a reconceptualization of participation relationships and an
elaboration of the Proximity Hypothesis, the previous section posited
a close relationship between participation in the workplace and participation in government. Though the process leading to this postula-
tion may be considered original, the identification of a connection between the workplace and government is in no way novel. Not only
does a growing body of contemporary writings address the existence
of the connection, but a long tradition of thought links the workplace
to government in one form or another.

Before the tradition is examined, two specifications should be offered. The literature does not organize or develop its thoughts concerning the workplace connection as they are organized and developed in this work; thus the reader must keep the reconceptualization
in mind throughout this section. The second point is that the survey
will not attempt to be exhaustive. It will seek only to relate a few of the
typical connections. Though there is some sense of development, the
reader should not demand that it be clear or progressive. The logical
thread is often transparent when it is not, in fact, broken.

The first tradition of thought to deal systematically with the workplace connection was utopian socialism. The tradition begins with
Robert Owen. For Robert Owen, society was to have become a federation of cooperative communities governed by producers, and the

total capitalist system was to have been replaced by a system of management incorporating workers, employers and government.[20] Thus the worlds of work and government were to enter into partnership. For Louis Blanc, government was to act as a reforming agent of the world of work.[21] First by nationalizing key industries, and then by supplying capital for the construction of national workshops, government could re-create society. For Pierre-Joseph Proudhon, the relationship between the worlds of work and government was not to be so congenial.[22] Through a horizontal system of mutualism among communes established to organize economic life on a cooperative basis and through a vertical system of federalism among associated communes, Proudhon developed plans to do away entirely with formal government, as embodied in the "state." Though the creative impulse of utopian socialism was to remain with us, the visions of a new society based on a revision of the worlds of work and government, were not to be realized.

Emile Durkheim broke from the tradition of utopian socialism, but continued the thought that gave empirical substance to the flow from the "economic" to the "political" by making economic units formally part of government. Durkheim correctly perceived a relationship between the State and secondary organizations, but interpreted that relationship to be one of mediation. As quoted earlier in this work, a "nation can be maintained only if, between the state and the individual, there is intercalated a whole series of secondary groups near enough to the individuals to attract them strongly in their sphere of action and drag them, in this way, into the general torrent of social life."[23] The very next sentence in that passage adds, "we have shown how occupational groups are suited to fill this role, and that it is their destiny."[24] Occupational groups play more than a simple role of mediation in Durkheim's scheme for "there is even reason to suppose that the corporation will become the foundation or one of the essential bases of our political organization."[25] It is apparent to Durkheim that occupational divisions are becoming more salient to politics than other societal divisions; he actually foresees a time when corporations would become "the elemental division of the State, the fundamental political unity."[26] Durkheim continues his prognostication:

Society, instead of remaining what it is today, an aggregate of juxtaposed territorial districts, would become a vast system of national corporations. From various quarters it is asked that the elective assemblies be formed by occupations, and not by territorial divisions; and certainly, in this way, political assemblies would more exactly express the diversity of social interests and their relations. They would be a more faithful picture of social life in its entirety. But to say that the nation, in becoming more aware of itself, must be grouped into occupations—does not this mean that the organized occupation or corporation should be the essential organ of public life?[27]

Making "the organized occupation or corporation" the "essential organ of public life" is Durkheim's version of French syndicalist thought. The syndicalist movement, which reached its peak during Durkheim's life, is a child of anarchistic thought such as that produced by Proudhon. As a result of its heritage, syndicalist thought is imbued with a deep suspicion of government; in fact, the doctrine of syndicalism may be seen as a blueprint for replacing the existing form of government. The elementary unit of the replacement part is to be the *syndicats* (local groups of workers in the same trade or industry). These *syndicats* actually control the larger trade unions of which they are a part. It is believed that the trade unions could provide the basis of representation to the national assemblies, when they do not replace governmental structures by assuming their functions. In this manner "governmental" control could be exercised by individuals within their small work groups.

Certainly Durkheim's expectations of the future have not materialized any more than the hopes of the French syndicalists, but that is not our major concern. As misled as they might have been about the shape of the future, the syndicalists nevertheless make a general connection between the world of work and the world of government. This element bonds all of the previous examples; each expresses a belief that the two worlds are, are to be, or should be joined. Specifying the nature of the connection, of course, is a recurring problem, but not every effort to articulate the relationship has proven as futile as Durkheim's. Beginning with John Stuart Mill, a train of thought develops that has gained credence with the passage of time.

The second chapter of this work clearly indicates that J. S. Mill is aware of the benefits that derive from participation. He contends that as a result of participation, the individual becomes "consciously a member of a great community," in effect enters "a school of public interest," and receives an "education of the intelligence and of the sentiment." To him "any participation, even in the smallest public function, is useful."[28] What is particularly relevant to this discussion is that

Mill sees these benefits deriving from participation in spheres other than "public" affairs. As Carole Pateman states, "perhaps the most interesting aspect of Mill's theory is an expansion of the hypothesis about the educative effect of participation to cover a whole new area of social life—industry."[29]

In language unmistakably similar to that which he uses in regard to public participation, Mill claims that a cooperative industrial organization leads to "the conversion of each human being's daily occupation into a school of the social sympathies and practical intelligence."[30] This training is of undeniable relevance to the public realm, for Mill thinks that no situation could better bring the individual to recognize "the public interest as his own," than a "[communal] association"[31]—a cooperative work arrangement. A cooperative work arrangement is "not that which can exist between a capitalist as chief, and the work-people without a voice in the management, but the association of the labourers themselves on terms of equality, collectively owning the capital with which they carry on their operations, and working under managers elected and removable by themselves."[32]

Thus the major contribution of Mill is to begin to specify the nature of the bridge between the world of work and the world of government in terms of the experiences of individuals. Things that occur in the world of work affect the way a person behaves in the world of government. What has been presented, however, is more an extrapolation than an explication of Mill's thinking. At no time did the "workplace connection" occupy a central spot in his work. Such a privileged position would have to await the writings of others.

The workplace connection appears in the writings of the political left—within the works of anarchists, communists, and orthodox socialists alike. The workplace connection also manifests in the works of the "distributists,"[33] who lie on the political right. But nowhere is the workplace connection drawn more clearly than in the writings of the guild socialists. Most scholars mark the birth of guild socialism with the writings of G. S. Hobson published in the A. R. Orage weekly, *The New Age*, in 1912. Though I concur with this view, the discussion of guild socialism should begin before 1912 with some of its antecedents.

Guild socialism historically is premised on a favorable view of the guild system that was prevalent during the medieval period of history. The lasting attraction to the guilds is not to be captured in a mere description of guilds. They are something more than associations of men designed to uphold standards of product quality and protect the interests of the guild members. Part of the guild's appeal is evident in the notion of community—a community of workers who regulate themselves. Another part is expressed in the nature of work associated with guilds. The enticing vision of the happy craftsman, hard at work producing things of utility and beauty, remains with us today. Whatever the reason, numerous social theorists after the Industrial Revolution call for a restoration of the guild system. Among the first to issue such a call is John Ruskin, who goes so far as to recommend in *Fors Clavigera*[34] that existing trade unions should convert themselves into self-governing guilds. Ruskin's call for restoration makes him a precursor of guild socialism, but only distantly so, for he tends to concentrate only on different forms of art guilds and does not elaborate upon the possible connections that guilds could have to government. This void soon is filled by one of Ruskin's disciples, William Morris. Morris takes Ruskin's views of art guilds and incorporates them into his "socialist" vision of the world, but never does he create a complete theory with guilds occupying the central position.[35] This is achieved by one of Morris' disciples, A. J. Penty.

In 1906, Penty presented a modern version of guilds in *The Restoration of the Gild System*.[36] Given his extensive theoretical treatment of the subject, some think that Penty justly deserves the credit for originating guild socialism. A convincing case could be made if it were not for the fact that Penty's "modern" version of the guilds is not modern at all. Rather than adjust a preindustrial phenomenon such as guilds to the modern world, Penty would have us return to the golden age we left behind. Penty's conception of restoring the guild system is based on returning production to its preindustrial form. Goods are to be produced by hand in the tradition of the craftsmen. It is to be a new age of handicrafts. In and of itself, *The Restoration of the Gild System* is nothing more than sterile nostalgia. The modern, industrial world could never voluntarily return to any previous epoch.

Thus the stage is set for a thinker who revives the idea of guilds and makes the connection between the world of work and the world of government all within the reality of an industrial setting. That man is S. G. Hobson, whose thoughts should be viewed both from a societal and individual perspective. At the macro-level, Hobson calls for the organization of workers into guilds according to their occupation. These guilds would then enter into "comanagement" of public affairs with government (this distinguishes guild socialism from syndicalism, for syndicalism would have workers' organizations replace government). More accurately, Hobson stipulates that guilds would be autonomous in regard to industrial issues, with government playing a more dominant role in other functional areas of public concern. On the micro-level, Hobson is interested in the effects that this arrangement would have upon individuals. He seeks to have an active citizenry and thinks that his system of guild socialism would produce the desired effect. "Politics is largely a question of psychology. Economic subjugation brings in its train certain definite psychological results which, in their turn, colour and dominate politics. . . . Is it not abundantly clear that a community, four-fifths of which is rendered servile by the wage system, cannot possibly slough off the psychology of servility and claim to be a community of free men politically whilst remaining servile economically?"[37]

The synthesis of a modern industrial age with the guild system continues in the thoughts of G. D. H. Cole. Whereas guild socialism is an appealing idea in the hands of Hobson, it becomes a more fully developed theory and gains mass appeal in the hands of Cole. At the basis of Cole's work is the same motive as that found in Hobson. As S. T. Glass observes, "Cole made it clear that his chief motive in advocating workers' control was the same as Hobson's—to create an active citizenry out of the working class."[38] Cole, as clearly as Hobson, makes the workplace connection: "The industrial system . . . is in great measure the key to the paradox of political democracy. Why are the many nominally supreme but actually powerless? Largely because the circumstances of their lives do not accustom or fit them for power and responsibility. A servile system in industry inevitably reflects itself in political servility."[39]

The "circumstances" of most people's lives are such that they do not participate. Participation is a learned response. If in one setting individuals are not afforded the opportunity to participate or do not participate when there is an opportunity, then their response is very unlikely to be participatory when presented with a new setting. Cole laments that "over the vast mechanism of modern politics the individual has no control . . . because he is given no chance of learning the rudiments of self-government within a smaller unit."[40] This is especially true with the workplace and government. People must be encouraged to participate in the decisions that affect their lives "not only or mainly to some special sphere of social action known as 'politics,' but to any and every form of social action, in especial, to industrial and economic fully as much as to political affairs."[41]

In the early 1920s guild socialism suffered a precipitous decline. But the demise of guild socialism did not bury an awareness of the workplace connection that serves as one of its basic premises. Recognition that the worlds of work and government are inexorably linked continues unabated among political theorists of diverse persuasions. For example, it appears in the writings of a new strain of Marxist thought.

The earliest and probably still the most eloquent statement of the workplace connection in this literature belongs to the Italian Marxist, Antonio Gramsci. Gramsci is deeply impressed by the early writings of Marx and the concern that they displayed for man. It is within these early writings that Gramsci discovers a Marx who is disturbed by the processes of human interaction within the workplace, for it is there that man experiences the most severe forms of alienation. In his personal search for an answer to the dehumanizing effects of the work processes, Gramsci sees hope (presumably from the window of his Mussolini prison cell) in the workers' councils that spread in Italy during the early 1920s. The workers' councils could provide the sorely needed opportunity for control within the workplace. But more than this, the councils could serve as institutions of higher learning for the working class. Through participation in the councils, workers could acquire the skills, capacities, responsibilities, and confidence that would allow them to assume a more active role in other areas of their lives. In particular, participation in the councils would allow the workers to break out of the servile roles for which they are trained and prepare for their future positions as governors of the State. Thus the workplace could create a more politically active proletariat; it could create the revolutionary working class of which Marxists have always dreamed.[42] The train of thought that Gramsci begins is continued by such theorists as the Italian group, the "IL Manefesto," and the French Marxist Andre Gorz. Gorz believes that the only route to revolution available in advanced capitalist countries is through worker participation and control of the workers' councils.[43] In this way the concerns expressed in the early writings of Marx are reborn in contemporary considerations of the workplace.

Interest in the workplace connection is not restricted to Marxist theorists; concern for the topic has entered the contemporary scene with a burgeoning group of thinkers establishing the workplace connection in their own writing. From among them at least the following should be mentioned: Chris Arygyris, Peter Bachrach, Ernest Barker,

C. George Benello (and Dimitrios Roussopoulos), T. B. Bottomore, Terrance Cook (and Patrick Morgan), Erich Fromm, G. David Garson, Edward Greenberg, Tom Hayden (and John Case), David Jenkins, Henry Kariel, C. B. Macpherson, C. Wright Mills, Carole Pateman, David Thompson, Tony Tompham (and Ken Coates), and Graham Wooten.[44] I will allow T. B. Bottomore to speak for this group:

Can we accept that democratic government which requires of the individual independent judgement and active participation in deciding important social issues, will flourish when in one of the most important spheres of life—that of work and economic production—the great majority of individuals are denied the opportunity to take an effective part in reaching the decisions which vitally affect their lives? It does not seem to me that a man can live in a condition of complete and unalterable subordination during much of his life, and yet acquire the habits of responsible choice and self-government which political democracy calls for.[45]

From these various theorists emerges the idea that there is a connection between the world of work and the world of government, a connection mediated through individual experiences. Individuals tend to develop psychological characteristics congruent with the social settings to which they are exposed. This is especially true of the workplace. An unparticipatory workplace will produce the "servile" character that Cole and Gramsci lament, while a participatory workplace will produce the active citizen that Mill and Wooten praise.

The Evidence

Each of the two preceding sections make an important contribution to the discussion of this chapter's topic. There is a long intellectual history to the workplace connection, and the logical case for its existence is compelling. The combination of these two factors could lead reasonable people to assume that such a vital empirical question has attracted sufficient quantitative research to allow some determination concerning the nexus between workplace and government participation. Yet this is not the case. The amount of research confronting the question is incredibly sparse. The only encouraging aspect to the situation is that although the amount of research is miniscule, that which does confront the subject tends to support the existence of an empirical connection between participation in the workplace and participation in government. It will be the purpose of this portion of the argument to review the empirical evidence for the workplace connection. The first part of the review will focus on studies that examine the complete workplace connection; the second part will review studies, which, when placed together, address the workplace connection.

After two decades, Almond and Verba's *The Civic Culture* remains relevant to an examination of the workplace connection. In the eleventh chapter Almond and Verba turn their attention to the effects of nongovernmental participation on governmental participation. Utilizing terminology that indicates that their research constructions are not reconceptualized, the authors state: "The question is whether there is a close relationship between the roles that a person plays in nonpolitical [nongovernmental] situations and his role in politics [government]. Is there some strain toward homogeneity in these roles?"[46]

Almond and Verba are concerned particularly with the relationship between the participatory stance taken in the crucial settings of the family, school, and workplace, and the participatory stance assumed in reference to government. The authors would have preferred to examine actual participation rates, but unable to secure that information, they must employ responses based on memory. The manner in which Almond and Verba approach their subject is particularly relevant. Though they do speak of a direct link between participation in nongovernmental spheres and government, they more often speak of that relationship incorporating an intervening psychological state. The major component of that psychological state is efficacy, which the authors consistently find to relate strongly to participation in all of the five nations that they study.

Consistent with the elementary model advanced in this work, Almond and Verba report that participation in family, school and job relates to patterns of political participation in each nation and that the associations are mediated largely through the intervening psychological state of efficacy. In a statement consistent with the discussion of the Proximity Hypothesis, the authors conclude that there "appears to be a rank order in the strength of connection between nonpolitical types of participation and political competence: the connection becomes stronger as one moves from family to school to job participation."[47] When considering orientations toward participation in government, the authors stress that "of crucial importance here are the opportunities to participate in decisions at one's place of work."[48]

Almond and Verba do more than distinguish the workplace as the most important setting for predisposition toward governmental participation. Before discussing the importance of the workplace, the authors examine the effects of organizational participation on governmental participation.[49] Almond and Verba come to the same conclusion as the social scientists cited in the preceding chapter: there is an impressive correlation between the two phenomena. What is significant about the Almond and Verba study is that it includes organizational participation with workplace participation when elaborating the reasons for the workplace connection. Hence they recognize that the same logic that links workplace participation to governmental participation also binds organizational participation to participation in government. The parallel is so compelling that Sallach, Babchuk, and Booth actually employ measures of organizational involvement to test the relationship between occupational variables and governmental participation.[50]

Almond and Verba trace the workplace connection from participation in the workplace (as remembered), to psychological dispositions derived from participation in the workplace, to participation in government. In doing so, The Civic Culture becomes one of the very few research projects to examine empirically the complete logical chain of the workplace connection. Several other studies come close to providing the desired breadth. Lewis Lipsitz in his 1964 article "Work Life and Political Attitudes: A Study of Manual Workers,"[51] examines the skill level of workers vis-à-vis their political attitudes. To the extent that skill level can be associated with participation, then workers who can participate in issues related to their jobs are less fatalistic, have a greater sense of internal locus of control, and are more efficacious. Though there is no difference in low-level acts of participation in government such as voting, highly skilled workers do participate more frequently in more-demanding acts of governmental participation such as active campaigning. The work of William H. Form also comes close to tracing the workplace connection from beginning to end. In his article, "The Internal Stratification of the Working Class: System Involvements of Auto Workers in Four Countries,"[52] Form indicates that skilled workers participate significantly more *both* inside the workplace and outside the workplace in numerous social settings.

Most other relevant research considers just one or the other link of the argument. Since they require other studies to complete the chain, they can provide only partial support for the workplace connection. Composite support for the workplace connection may assume several different forms, but the most common employs a variety of the general model adopted in this work:

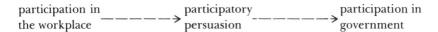

participation in the workplace ——————> participatory persuasion —————> participation in government

In this variety of support, it is possible to assemble one set of research findings to establish the first linkage and a different set to establish the second. More specifically, if one can document that participation in the workplace will foster the psychological traits associated with the participatory persuasion, and if it can be indicated on the basis of another set of research findings that there is a close relationship between the traits associated with the participatory persuasion and participation in government, then the workplace connection is inferentially made.

The first linkage of the workplace connection model, the nexus between participation in the workplace and the development of psychological traits associated with the participatory persuasion, has not received the attention it deserves in the research literature. Despite that fact, it is possible to marshall support for its existence. The most relevant work is Robert Blauner's *Alienation and Freedom* (1964).[53] Blauner contends that the "nature of a man's work affects his social character and personality."[54] In order to subject this contention to critical examination, Blauner compares four forms of work organization, each of which is represented by factories in four different industries: automotive, textile, printing and chemical. Within each factory, Blauner concentrates on four key dimensions: workers' control, integration of the work group, the existence of an occupational community, and the status of the occupation. For our purposes, the first dimension is most important, for it relates directly to workplace participation.

The four work organizations differentially allow workers to participate in the decisions that govern their lives in the workplace. At the lowest end of the participation scale lie the textile workers and the automotive workers. According to Blauner, the composite personality portrayal of the textile worker is that he is "resigned to his lot . . . more dependent than independent . . . lacks confidence . . . is humble . . . the most prevalent feeling states . . . seem to be fear and anxiety."[55] The "social personality of the auto worker . . . is expressed in a characteristic attitude of cynicism toward authority and the institutional system."[56] In contrast, the chemical workers and the printers are allowed considerably more participation in their workplace decisions. The personality of the average printer differs remarkably from the previous descriptions. The printer's personality is typically "characterized by . . . a strong sense of individualism and autonomy," and has a well-developed sense of "self-esteem and a sense of self-worth." Consistent with the postulations in this work, Blauner observes that the printer possesses a "solid acceptance of citizenship in the larger society" and is very well prepared "to participate in the society and political institutions of the community."[57] This obviously lends support to the linkages of the workplace connection. Even though the chemical workers do not have the complete freedom of control and participation that characterizes the printers, many of the same observations apply to them. The participation that they share in group decision making contributes to their well-developed sense of confidence and self-esteem. It is possible that some of the differences in psychological disposition may be attributable to the original recruitment patterns of the various workplaces. Nevertheless, there does appear to be a strong positive relationship between participation in the workplace and the development of psychological traits associated with the participatory persuasion.

The second link of the model, that which exists between the participatory persuasion and participation in government, is not difficult to discover, for the psychological attributes that constitute the participatory persuasion consistently are found to relate to various forms of governmental participation. Efficacy is one of the prime components of the participatory persuasion and is one of the psychological measures most often correlated with participation. Though the impact of political efficacy is challenged by a few scholars such as Robert Weissberg,[58] the weight of opinion still rests on the opposite side.[59] For example, McPhersen, Welsh and Clarke establish the reliability and stability of political efficacy over a series of presidential election voting.[60] With only a few exceptions, the significant relationship between political efficacy and participation withstands controlling procedures.

Furthermore, the relationship remains constant with a more general form of efficacy. As Lester Milbrath indicates, "persons who feel more effective in their everyday tasks and challenges are more likely to participate in politics."[61]

The participatory persuasion is composed of more than efficacy. Though such characteristics as sociability and sense of civic duty have been found to be associated similarly with forms of governmental participation, the supportive research is not as extensive as that concerning efficacy.[62] In reference to sociability, Milbrath has stated that "sociable personalities are more likely to enter politics than nonsociable personalities: this is especially true of political activities that require social interaction."[63] Milbrath supported this proposition twice in his own research, once in 1960 and again in 1962.[64] Another psychological measure that is part of the participatory persuasion is "locus of control." Though it has emerged only recently in participation research, it appears to have significant consequence for participation.[65]

There is, then, a set of psychological traits that predispose an individual toward participation; this set of traits is shown to be positively related to forms of government participation. In a sense, these diverse research findings may be considered "positive" support for the second link in the workplace connection. Another group of research findings supports the workplace connection, but in a "negative" sense. These findings are tied to the concept of alienation. If the reader will recall the assemblage of psychological traits that constitute the participatory persuasion, and then imagine the opposite, he will have some impression of a syndrome negatively related to participation. It is contended that the converse of a participatory persuasion is somewhat captured by the concept, alienation. The converse is even expressed in the meanings of the words. Whereas participation denotes a "taking part in" something, alienation signifies "being apart from" something. There is an equally strong research literature that negatively associates cynicism and alienation with governmental participation.[66]

It is somewhat simplistic to view alienation and the participatory persuasion as counter-opposites and to expect an invariant inverse relationship between participation and alienation. For example, it is quite possible for alienation and efficacy to combine under some circumstances. When they do, the resulting participation is likely to assume unconventional forms, ranging from mere protest to more

extremist activity.[67] Other refinements in our theory concerning alienation are bound to follow from the growth of research that exists on
the subject.[68]

Employing the elementary model, there are thus two routes by
which the second link of the workplace connection—the relationship
between the participatory persuasion and conventional governmental
participation—can be established. The first, or "positive" route directly relates the individual traits that are constituent members of the
participatory persuasion to participation in government. This is accomplished through the attributes of political efficacy, general effec-
tiveness, sociability, civic duty, and locus of control. The second, or
"negative" route traces the opposite of the participatory persuasion,
"alienation," to an unparticipatory or unconventional response to
government. As with the direct route, this path also indicates a clear
relationship between the participatory persuasion and participation
in government. In summary, it should always be the scholar's desire to
achieve greater levels of reliability in his empirical research. But given
the underdeveloped nature of our discipline, the empirical link between the participatory persuasion and governmental participation
must be considered fairly well supported.

With this, the argument concerning composite support for the
workplace connection is complete. There is yet another form of argumentation, however, that relates generally to the workplace connection. It concerns the fourth factor listed by Blauner, occupational
status.

It was stated in the previous chapter that social class is among the
factors most strongly related to participation in government. To
gauge the effects of social class on governmental participation, social
class first must be transformed into a variable. This is accomplished by
constructing the composite index, SES, which derives from measures
of income, occupation, and education. Though each of these interre-
late, they are sufficiently discrete to warrant separate entry. The indicator of greatest concern to us is occupational status. As part of the
measures of social class, occupational status highly relates to participation. An individual's occupation, apart from the amount of
money he makes, is an important consideration of the degree to
which a person is likely to participate in government.

There are several alternative ways of measuring occupational status, but a choice among them is alleviated by the fact that they produce very similar results. Occupations which are considered profes-

sional—doctors, lawyers and others—always receive higher status scores than manual labor occupations. It is important to realize that the rankings of occupations according to status also ranks factors related to status. The most crucial among these is control over one's work experience. The higher the status of an occupation, the more likely that occupation permits the individual to control major facets of his worklife. Though professors and automotive assembly-line workers may earn approximately the same amount of money, the professor's status is higher and his ability to control his worklife considerably greater. Reiterating and applying the case stated earlier in this chapter, to control one's worklife is to participate in the decisions that govern that worklife. Thus a high-status job relates to participation in the workplace; and since a high-status job also relates strongly to participation in government, participation in the workplace is indirectly related in this argument to participation in government. The workplace connection is once again advanced.

The salient parts of this argument have received attention from other theorists and social scientists. Carole Pateman proclaims that it is "almost part of the definition of a low status occupation that the individual has little scope for the exercise of initiative or control over his job and working conditions, plays no part in decision making in the enterprise and is told what to do by his organizational superiors."[69] When examining high-status occupations, Seymour Lipset comes to a consistent conclusion. These occupations do provide the opportunity to learn and develop that is essential to acquiring a disposition toward participation. As Lipset avers, the "upper occupational groups have job activities which continue their intellectual development."[70] Continuing the argument, he asserts that the "relationship of occupational activities to political skills has long been evident in the backgrounds of the organizers and leaders of political movements."[71] This fact is illustrated by many of the professions. Lipset maintained that law, journalism, teaching, and the ministry provide job activities that encourage the individual to develop participation-related characteristics. Theorists and social scientists also recognize that there is a relationship between occupational status and participation in government. Lester Milbrath summarizes the relevant research by stating that "persons of higher occupational status are more likely to participate in politics."[72]

Robert Lane, however, discovers behavior that appears prima facie to contradict this proposition. His investigation of the "common man" of an eastern city reveals him to be more active in the world of government than his occupational status would have indicated.[73] Rather than contradicting the major thrust of the argument, however, Lane's research actually supports it. It is not the status of an occupation, but the life experiences associated with the status that is significant. High status jobs are associated with more participatory work experiences. Though the occupations of the men whom Lane studied were of low status, they are not characteristic of low status jobs. The workers in Lane's research do have the opportunity to interact with their fellow-workers, can express themselves in a number of different ways, could develop a variety of skills, and do participate in decisions related to their work. Their work lives are more characteristic of upper-status rather than lower-status position. Thus Lane's study produces the same conclusion as did Blauner; in regard to governmental participation, the most salient workplace feature is participation.

The workplace connection and several forms of argumentation for its existence have been offered. Though the research conducted on the workplace connection clearly tends to support it, the research is not proportionate in either quantity or quality to the significance of the subject. Until strong research designs, including those which approach the workplace connection from a dynamic perspective, are brought to bear on the topic, we must piece together what evidence is available.

To entice the interested reader, there are reports that provide strong indications of the workplace connection in dynamic form. There are several major American examples of dramatic increases in participation in the workplace, and in each of these cases there has been a corresponding change in the affected workers' governmental participation. Richard E. Walton, who observed the changes in work institutionalized at the General Foods plant in Topeka, Kansas, reports that after the innovation, there was an appreciable increase in the workers' community involvement.[74] As the HEW report, *Work in America* states in reference to the General Foods plant, "many workers have been unusually active in civic affairs—apparently, significantly more so than is typical of the workers in other plants in the same corporation or in the same community."[75] From experience at the Procter and Gamble plant in Lima, Ohio comes the same conclusion. Neil Mc-Whinney, a UCLA psychologist working for Procter and Gamble as a consultant, relates:

One of the striking features in our "pure" open systems plant is that workers take on more activities outside the work place. The most visible involvements had to do with community racial troubles. Following major disturbances in the small city where they live, a number of workers organized the black community to deal directly with the leaders of the city and industry. . . . Blue collar workers won elections to the city school board majority office and other local positions. Nearly ten percent of the workforce holds elective offices currently. . . . We have noted that open systems workers join more social clubs and political organizations.[76]

Two examples of the participatory effects of restructuring work cannot confirm that there is always a workplace connection; neither can the existence of other empirical evidence. But in conjunction with the long intellectual history, and the logic of the Proximity Hypothesis, the empirical evidence does make the workplace connection seem quite likely. Although there is no space within the present volume, it would be interesting to use the Proximity Hypothesis to explore the antecedents of workplace participation, in the same way that the antecedents of government participation were explored in this chapter.

5

The Importance of Work

Introduction

NO EXAMINATION OF PARTICIPATORY AND WORKPLACE DEMOCRACY could be complete without consideration of the subject of work. The workplace may have become our focus of attention because of its connection with government, but the case in favor of extensive and effective participation in the workplace extends well beyond its effect on generating participation in other communities (most notably, government) to the importance of work itself. Participation in the workplace is demanded in the name of unalienated and meaningful work, as well as participatory democracy. This chapter will discuss the various dimensions of the claim that meaningful work is a goal in itself worth pursuing. The discussion will offer a preferred formulation of work, describe work as being central to our lives, present a synoptic history of work in terms of work being viewed as an intrinsic versus extrinsic value, witness the conflict between these values in the American context, investigate the price paid when the intrinsic value of work is denied, and give some impression of work in the future—if intrinsic values dominate. Throughout the discussion, the connection between the participation of workers and the intrinsic value of work will be stressed.

Work occupies a central position in the lives of men and women. One recurring theme of our analysis has been an emphasis on the everyday life of individuals, and such an emphasis places work most immediate in our vision. The normal events of an individual's life—birth, illness, marriage, and death—all relate to the occupational endeavors of others. The very names that we choose to call ourselves reflect the importance of work in our lives: Smith, Baker, Miller, Cook, and Mason. Though the absolute number of hours the average American works may have declined considerably over the last century, the

102

average work week is still very close to forty hours. With a minimal amount of mathematical computation it becomes clear that forty hours is nearly one quarter of the 168 hours available in a week. Alotting the individual two weeks of vacation, the average working individual still spends more than a third of his or her nonsleeping life working. If we believe that human experience has any effect upon the lives of individuals, we cannot disregard an activity that occupies as much as one third of an individual's conscious life. Of course, working is generally an adult activity and so this assessment can relate unambiguously only to adults pursuing conventional working lives. Yet previous chapters have emphasized the importance of adult experiences in relationship to adult behavior, and so from that perspective, the impact of working should not be taken lightly. The arm of work is exceptionally long. While much of preadult life is spent preparing to work, work is not something that can be left behind at the time of retirement any more than work can be left behind at the end of the day. Work has a serious effect upon people across their entire life span.

Before a more complete discussion of work can insue, greater clarity must be brought to the concept of work. Work has been defined and utilized in so many ways, however, that a brief yet meaningful exposition is very difficult. The *Oxford English Dictionary*, for example, has compiled ten pages, three columns per page, of major variations in usage.[1] It is clear from that listing that work is generally considered as a form of activity that entails an actor and usually something acted upon. Attempting to synthesize the most constructive aspects of the various conceptions, a useful definition of work would be "activity that is designed to create things of value for other people."

This definition would seem to apply to work and labor, yet there is a crucial distinction between the two, a distinction that has some basis in the thought of Hannah Arendt, as expressed in *The Human Condition*.

Whatever we do, we are supposed to do for the sake of 'making a living'; such is the verdict of society, and the number of people, especially in the professions, who might challenge it has decreased rapidly. The only exception society is willing to grant is the artist who, strictly speaking, is the only 'worker' left in labouring society. The same trend to level down all serious activities to the status of making a living is manifest in present-day labour theories, which almost unanimously defined labour as the opposite of play. As a result, all serious activities, irrespective of their fruits, are called labour, and every activity which is not necessary either for the life of the individual or for the life process of society is subsumed under playfulness.[2]

According to Hannah Arendt, there is an important distinction between activity a person must do to live, and activity that supplies things of value which extend beyond the satisfaction of survival needs. This kind of activity can be chosen more freely, can be more creative, meaningful, and satisfying. Activity that sustains biological life is labor; activity that is the purely human providing of nonsurvival values is work. Though this bifurcation may differ from some usages, there are very good reasons for its acceptance. From the beginning of classical economic theory, the term *labor* was used as the expression of a man's work as a commodity. It is therefore not surprising that in everyday language *labor* has more harsh connotations than *work*. We speak of a criminal being sentenced to twenty years at "hard labor," and refer to a woman in the pain of childbirth as being "in labor." Viewing labor as the alienated state of work, which appears occasionally in the writings of Marx and often in the writings of such contemporary theorists as Erich Fromm,[3] is based on strong arguments concerning the usage of the word. This conceptualization will be adopted for use in this work.

The distinction between work and labor expresses a difference in who values the activity and the way in which the activity is valued. Moving away from the distinctions of Hannah Arendt, the fundamental characteristic of labor is that it produces things of value for other people. It is because the locus of value is with other people that factors related to labor are largely established by other people. Thus in initial stages, the conditions of labor, the methods of labor, and the pay for labor are determined by processes that largely exclude the laborer, who merely offers his effort for what the market will exchange for it.

Labor has instrumental value for the laborer; since other people value the outcome of his effort, the laborer can exchange his time and energy for the means to support his biological existence. It is very unlikely that the laborer will find the product or outcome of his labor valuable, and even less likely that he will value the activity that creates the product. Work is different. Though the worker does produce things of value for other people (that is, things with exchange value), he also finds value in what he is doing, and therefore is likely to find the outcome of what has been accomplished valuable. This alters the previously accepted definition. Labor alone is "an activity designed to create things of value for other people." Work, on the other hand, is "an activity that is valuable in itself for the worker, as well as an activity that produces things of value for other people." Herein also lies the essential difference between leisure activities such as hobbies and work activities. Whereas work is an activity that is valuable in itself *and* creates outcomes valued by other people, thereby creating exchange value, leisure activities are valuable to the actor but not generally to other people. If labor is seen as the activity of producing things of value for other people, and leisure activities as essentially producing things of value for the actor, then work may be viewed as a meaningful synthesis of the qualities related to labor and leisure.

The essential distinctions among labor, leisure activity, and work, as ideal types, rests on their relationship to two factors: whether the activity is meaningful in itself to the actor, and whether the activity generally has exchange value. The categorization appears as follows.

	Labor	Leisure Activity (hobbies)	Work
Activity which is valued in itself	−	+	+
Activity which has exchange value	+	−	+

The primary distinction between labor and work, that of whether activity of exchange value also is valued in itself, relates very closely to the notion of intrinsic versus extrinsic value. The division is at least as old as Aristotle, who claimed that health, being internal to man is an autonomous good, something desirable for itself, while wealth, being external to man, is a mere utility, forever a means to something else.[4] Though these qualities will often be discussed as if they were dichotomous, it is more accurate to conceive of them as if they were opposite ends of a continuum. As Aristotle has indicated, health represents a good example of an intrinsic value; wealth a good example of an extrinsic value. In terms of our present discussion, labor can be seen as valuable only in an extrinsic sense to the laborer for he does not find meaning in the activity of producing. Work is valuable intrinsically to the worker for he does find meaning in the activity of creating things.

The basic distinction between labor and work from the point of view of intrinsic versus extrinsic values is illustrated by the example of the artist. The artist does not write, paint, play an instrument, or whatever he does simply because of the money or other external rewards that may accompany that activity. The very fact that it is so difficult to support oneself through the arts is a clear indication of this proposition. The artist engages in the activity because of its value not only to other people, but to himself—and probably most importantly to himself. Since the activity is freely chosen and has worth to the individual, it becomes a creative expression of the individual and contributes to his health and growth. In this way work relates to the higher needs of man—autonomy, self-expression, self-actualization. The artist is a worker in a world full of laborers.

The intrinsic versus extrinsic value dimension is the most significant aspect to the meaning of work. It divides the history of work and helps explain some of the tensions in our modern world. In fact, many contemporary theories of work are restatements of the basic distinction between intrinsic and extrinsic values. The discussion of the significance of work will center upon this value dimension.

Having secured the conceptual distinctions between work and labor on one hand, and intrinsic and extrinsic values on the other, it is necessary to make a few statements to clarify terminology. The word, work, will be employed as the generic expression for the phenomenon that includes both work and labor. Whenever the discussion highlights the intrinsic-extrinsic distinction between the two activities, the words *work* and *labor* will appear in italics. In this manner, the presentation can proceed with minimal interruption for explanation.

Work as an Extrinsic Value

As Adriano Tilgher indicates in his famous survey of work through the ages, *Homo Faber*,[5] over the vast length of human history, work generally has been viewed as a curse, or certainly no better than a necessary evil—valuable only in terms of the external things that it could provide. Work was not a separate category of action among primitive tribal gatherings, but as soon as work was differentiated from the rest of life's activities, it acquired undesirable significance. The ancient Greek philosophers were undeniably disdainful of work; given the basic Greek division of life into private and public spheres, it could not be otherwise. There was little or no value assigned to activity within the private sphere, and that is exactly where work was trans-fixed. The Greeks could not even express the notion of a gentleman's work without resorting to the negative construction, *ascholia*, mean-ing that he was "not at leisure."[6] Why would anyone wish to work when the Greek word for the curse that was work, *ponos*, has the same root as the Latin, *poena*, "sorrow." The view of work as little more than an unfortunate requirement of life became part of the ancient Chris-tian tradition as indicated by the story of the Garden of Eden, that place from which Adam and Eve fell to a world of toil and sorrow. Genesis graphically describes life after the fall: "In the sweat of thy face shalt thou eat bread, till thou return unto the ground."[7] It is worth noting that the same idea of a golden age from which man fell is repeated in other cultures. The accounts of a prehistoric paradise contained in the ancient Sanskrit epic of India, *Mahabharata*,[8] and that which is described by the Chinese philosopher, Chuang-tzu, are vir-tually the same.[9] They were times in which no work was done and there was no need for knowledge.

Though there were some changes of attitude in the Middle Ages, the negative image of work persisted. Work remained to the Christian of the Middle Ages a curse and the punishment of God, but there were several interesting twists to the interpretation of that punish-ment. At the foundation of the partial revision may well be the twelfth-century figure, Joachim of Flora.[10] It became part of the Joachite millenarism that through work one could somehow become part of the plan by which a new world order, a thousand years long, could come into being. Perhaps there was a greater purpose to the punishment. Upon this base, other variations of interpretation could be spawned. If work were indeed punishment for original sin, then what better way to express righteousness than to work hard and well? Thus there emerged in the Middle Ages the idea that work could have great import, although in itself, it created a terrible plight. This theme was echoed in the Reformation. Work was important because success in work and in accumulating and dispersing wealth indicated that a person might be one of the few who would gain access to heaven. As Max Weber explained the belief, "the gods bless with riches the man who pleases them, through sacrifice or through his kind of conduct."[11] The stress on sacrifice created the great irony in the belief system: to be really pleasing to the deity, neither the riches nor the work that produced them could be pleasing.

Both in its emphasis on work as a money-making enterprise and its deemphasis on all human activity (including, if not especially, working) as pleasurable, Calvinism provided a very suitable environment for the growth of industrial capitalism.

For one of the great creations of industrial capitalism was the idea of work as a purely monetary activity completely separate from sentimental considerations of its suitability or desirability, in human terms, for the people involved in it. The religious content in all this has, needless to say faded almost entirely by now. But capitalism has not, and neither have the Calvinistic-capitalistic ideas of work. The Calvinistic ideas fitted in marvelously well with the type of work that was created by industrial capitalism . . . the Calvinistic disagreeableness of work undoubtedly facilitated the acceptance of the new manufacturing methods. Was it not in the order of things that work should be performed for money alone, regardless of its unpleasantness (and, indeed, that it ought to be unpleasant)?[12]

It is most important to understand, however, that this image of work, which is so closely associated with industrial capitalism, did not spring full-grown from Calvinism. Something provided the conduit through which certain facets of Calvinistic thought, stripped of religious significance, became material for industrial capitalism. That something was liberalism.

Our earlier discussion of liberalism stressed that the emergence of the social sphere between the previous divisions of private and public diminished the importance of the political by a process that included the reification of politics. The preeminence of the social did not mean the emphasis was placed on all forms of social endeavor. Man, the true man washed of metaphysical hobgobblins, was economic man. Therefore, economic analysis was the proper subject of thought; economic gain the proper subject of action. Liberalism, as the paramount secular philosophy, had little room for the unnecessary categories of religious thought and action. The dismal science was its embodiment.

Following the interpretation of theorists such as Sheldon Wolin, liberalism has been described as "a philosophy of sobriety, born in fear, nourished by disenchantment, and prone to believe that the human condition was and is likely to remain one of pain and anxiety."[13] The inheritance of such Calvinistic notions as sobriety, fear, and anxiety is clear, but what happened when liberalism became heir to the idea that work had value only in terms of being a means to mitigate scarcity? Once liberalism "liberated" man of his common religious bond with other men, and stripped work of its religious import, all that was left was grim necessity. Locke stated it unambiguously: the "law man was under was rather for appropriating, God commanded, and his wants forced, him to labor."[14] Man had to work hard to eliminate necessity from his life, but since it was not simply necessity, but fear and anxiety that provided the real motivating forces, there could be no actual limit to his labor.

The combination of man characterized by biological existence and dominated by material needs, and work as the means of satisfying those needs, which provided the potent and obnoxious mixture that would find its most complete expression in the early phases of industrial capitalism. As we soon shall see, the classical "liberal" economists such as Adam Smith, William Petty, David Hume, James Mill, John Stuart Mill, Alfred Marshall, and those who followed in that tradition could not have structured work the way they recommended without this limited definition of man. As Sheldon Wolin properly states, "Having reduced man to mere externality and stripped him of conscience, it was easy for the liberal economist to treat him as a material object."[15] Work is nothing more than the means to sustain the existence of this material object.

Capitalism is in some senses the younger brother of liberalism, although they did grow up together. The very basis of capitalistic thought rests on the foundation of liberalism. An emphasis on the individual, on relentless activity, on competition, on unmitigated pursuit of self-interest, on the attempt to rationally maximize values, and on the use of some noninterfering mechanism to determine distribution of things valued (market rather than government) is something both liberalism and capitalism share. Yet the most important bond lies with the liberal notions that the values to be stressed are material (property). In fact, there are no real intrinsic values related to man. Within the liberal system of thought, the whole notion of individual self-development, apart from creature comforts, is almost absurd. That is why Bentham scoffed at the idea of self-knowledge and awareness being goals worthy of pursuit. He said, "by interest he [man] is at the same time diverted from any close examination into the springs by which his own conduct is determined. From such knowledge he has not, in any ordinary shape, anything to gain,—he finds not in it any source of enjoyment."[16]

Thus contrary to popular belief, the view of work as only extrinsically valuable was not a product of industrial capitalism; industrial capitalism inherited the perspective from the past. Industrial capitalism, however, viewed and continues to view work as only extrinsically valuable in its most powerful, consistent, and extreme institutional expression. Industrial capitalism most significantly altered in an undesirable fashion the nature of work. Elemental to industrial capitalism was a concern for techniques of operation. It was assumed that a single best way to produce goods existed, and that this was discernible. The best overall manner to organize production would be identified by subdividing each act into its smallest component part. Surely industrial capitalism was not the first to be concerned with techniques or even the first to employ analytical processes in search of the best organization. Long before the birth of Christ there were accounts of division of labor. Xenophon related this account in his biography of Cyrus the Persian: "In the large cities . . . one trade alone, and very often even less than a whole trade is enough to support a man; one man for instance makes shoes for men and another for women; and there are places even where one man earns a living by only stitching shoes, another by cutting them out, another by sewing the uppers together, while there is another who performs none of these operations but only assembles the parts." [17]

With industrial capitalism, however, there was a qualitative leap in the concern for techniques, a concern fostered by a major change in the degree of mechanization. The greater the extent of machinery utilized, the more attention had to be paid to techniques, and the more complicated those techniques became. At least in the beginning, techniques do not produce their own ends or goals. Techniques require a recognized end toward which to strive. The logic of the system was provided by capitalism. Industrialization was to be organized in such a manner as to maximize efficiency and production; profit was to be the measure of success. These concerns were well-illustrated in Adam Smith's *The Wealth of Nations*. In the following passage, which is the most well-known of that famous work, Smith describes the way that an estimated 240 times the amount of goods could be produced, if they were not manufactured individually.

In the way in which this business is now carried on, not only the whole work is a peculiar trade, but it is divided into a number of branches, of which the greater parts are likewise peculiar trades. One man draws out the wire, another straightens it, a third cuts it, a fourth points it, a fifth grinds it at the top for receiving the head; to make the head requires two or three distinct operations; to put it on is a peculiar business, to whiten the pin is another; it is even a trade by itself to put them into the paper; and the important business of making the pin is, in this manner, divided into about eighteen distinct operations.[18]

The particular techniques that Smith describes may be the most efficient, they may be the most productive, and they may be the most profitable at a high level of demand, but they are not the most meaningful or satisfying organization of work for the workers. Imagine what work would mean in the pin factory, and imagine the effects of such work on workers. On second thought, there is no reason to imagine the effects of highly fragmentized work on those who perform the tasks, for Smith himself provides the description.

The man whose life is spent performing a few simple operations . . . has no occasion to exert his understanding or to exercise his invention in finding out expedients for removing difficulties which never occur . . . and generally becomes as stupid and ignorant as it is possible for a human creature to become.
  [And if such work be widespread] all the nobler parts of the human character may be, in a great measure, obliterated and extinquished in the great body of people.[19]

To many minds the extrinsic value of work found its ultimate expression and manifestation in Adam Smith's pin factory; unfortunately, this is not the case. The stress on the extrinsic value of work led to the wanton subdivision of labor within the pin factory, yet even Smith did not carry this process to its end. There are smaller subdivisions of work to isolate than the eighteen tasks. What Smith failed to accomplish in 1776, Frederick W. Taylor completed a century and a third later. Since Taylor provides such an excellent example of man as merely economic man (having only material needs but also having insatiable material desires, thus man the consumer), and work as only extrinsically valuable, it would benefit us to concentrate on his work. In doing so, no attempt will be made to offer a full and balanced account of Taylor's entire system.
  For all its pretention, Taylor's "scientific management" based on "time and motion" studies, was nothing more than an extension of the same subdivision principles that had influenced Adam Smith. Taylor was not satisfied to limit subdivisions to the "peculiar trade" level of Smith, however; he wished to further divide each "peculiar trade"

into its component actions. If greater efficiency, productivity, and thus profit could result from the identification of the overall enterprise's component parts, would not the same gains result from viewing each component part as if it were a whole and identifying its component parts? Is there not a most efficient way to draw the wire, straighten and then cut it? Is there not a particular stance, position of the hands and motion of the arms which will most effectively put the pins into the paper? This was the intention of Frederick Taylor: to observe and then specify the most efficient manner to complete each component of a production process. Having discovered the best manner to perform each task, it was only necessary to provide the correct equipment, locate the right person for the job, and offer him the necessary incentives for him to perform the operation as specified. Within such a system, all parts would benefit in the only manner that made any difference—monetarily.

One of Taylor's most famous experiments concerned the handling of pig iron at a Bethlehem Steel plant. After months of careful observation and analysis, Taylor and his colleagues were convinced that the individual production rate of twelve and one-half tons per day could be raised beyond forty-five tons per day. To test the redesign based on their observations, the scientific management team chose a strong but mentally dull immigrant. These were the instructions that he was issued: "You will do exactly as this man tells you tomorrow, from morning till night. When he tells you to pick up a pig and walk, you pick it up and walk, and when he tells you to sit down and rest, you sit down. You do that straight through the day. And what's more, no back talk. . . . Do you understand that? When this man tells you to walk, you walk; when he tells you to sit down, you sit down, and you don't talk back at him."[20] The team could not have been more pleased with the results. The immigrant did as he was told (while not talking back) and loaded an impressive forty-seven and one-half tons during that day.[21]

To be effective, the Taylor system required a large degree of cooperation on the part of the workers. Only if they were willing to subject themselves to the treatment that the pig-loading immigrant received could the alterations founded on scientific management be instituted. To entice the workers to abandon all control over their work and work-life, Taylor proposed to offer rewards. The incentive system was based entirely on the external value, money. If the worker cooperated and produced at the level expected, he would receive his wages plus a handsome bonus, which varied from 30 percent to 100 percent of his base pay. The range of incentive had to vary because workers themselves varied. The most important single characteristic is intelligence. By Taylor's general calculations, it would require an additional 30 percent to move the dullest of workers to accept the new procedures; with the more intelligent workers, double the pay may be necessary.

Given the economic value system that scientific management embraced, a high premium was placed on locating the worker with just enough intelligence to perform the required task. Any more than the minimum would produce either a dissatisfied worker (which is economically disadvantageous), or require a larger bonus (which also is economically disadvantageous). Intelligence—or the lack of intelligence—is thus an important part of Taylor's system of work. Using pig-iron loading as an example, it was difficult to locate the right person for that job. A pig-iron loader, Taylor stressed, must be "so stupid and phlegmatic that he more resembles the ox than any other type." Certainly the "man who is mentally alert is entirely unsuited to what would, for him, be the grinding monotony of work of this character."[22] "Seven men out of eight" simply would not do, and the eighth is so difficult to find that he should be prized indeed; "a man so stupid that he (is) unfitted to do most kinds of laboring work, even."[23] In this case, Taylor failed to arrive at Smith's further conclusion concerning the human consequences of his own system. Though there may be resistance in the beginning, scientific management could produce the kind of worker it required—one as stupid and ignorant as it is possible for a creature to become, to cite Smith. Scientific management need not rely on recruitment, for it provides its own "on-the-job debilitation."

Though the description of scientific management, which is so reminiscent of Charlie Chaplin's famous movie, *Modern Times*, is disturbing (indeed, dystopian novels, such as Zamiatin's *We* have been based upon it),[24] the reader may have taken refuge in thinking that it only applied to the extremes of manual labor operations, such as pig-iron handling. This belief is not only erroneous, it misses the real appeal of the system. Scientific management procedures may be applied to almost any productive enterprise. As Frederick Taylor stated: "While there are millions and millions of different operations that take place, yet these millions of complicated or composite operations can be analyzed intelligently and readily resolved into a comparatively small number of simple elementary operations. . . . Under scientific management there is nothing too small to become a subject of scientific investigation."[25] This is also true of any economic-political system. The Marxist emphasis on "scientific" approaches, became very vulnerable to such things as scientific management. Lenin, for example, had a very strong interest in Taylor's scientific management. He urged that "We must organize in Russia the study and teaching of the Taylor system and systematically try it out and adapt it to our own ends."[26]

Scientific management possesses the potential to take complex procedures and formulate them into simple sets of operations. The construction of a sophisticated computer, for example, need not require workers who understand electronics. If scientific management is correctly applied, a worker need only know that the "blue wire connects to the blue terminal." Of course, someone must understand the entire system and perform creative thinking to reduce complicated operations into their component parts. In Taylor's schema, this is management. "All possible brain work should be removed from the shop and centered in the planning or laying-out department."[27] This is important to Taylor because the "time during which the man stops to think is part of the time that he is not productive."[28] And so it has come to pass, as Conrad Arensberg indicates, that things such as inventiveness "once a part of every artisan's work, has now become instead the career job of the technician and the research man. The loss for democracy, and even work interest, is clear; no one denies it."[29]

It should be noted that scientific management principles apply to management as well as line-workers. Virtually everyone (including the corporate heads if they have scientific management experts to advise them) has another person instructing him what to do. But in such a situation, an incredible irony is created: in this hierarchial management schema, few workers have the breadth of knowledge to really understand the jobs they are performing. Each must rely on another to determine what to do and how to do it. "This inability of the man who is fit to do the work to understand the science of doing his work becomes more and more evident as the work becomes more complicated, all the way up the scale. . . . The law is almost universal . . . that the man who is fit to work at any particular trade is unable to understand the science of that trade without the kindly help and cooperation of men of a totally different type of education."[30]

Within the scientific management system, an overbearing concern for efficiency, productivity, and profit led not only to the rampant division of labor and specialization, but to a strict construction of

command into an unambiguously hierarchical form. The tightly bureaucratic form, so characteristic of scientific management, was but a
refinement of what already existed. The ideal pyramidal command
structure was viewed as a requisite of effective management and therefore efficient production.[31] Industrial capitalism's general dependence
on bureaucratic forms of organization was recognized by Max Weber,
bureaucracy's first and foremost theoretician. Maximization of profit
required structure and control (or so it was thought), so Weber was
led to claim that "Indeed, without it [bureaucracy] capitalistic production could not continue."[32]

Thus man's relations with the machines and management associated with industrial capitalism were premised on the acceptance of
work as only extrinsically valuable. If work has only extrinsic worth,
then it should be organized according to the imperatives of efficiency,
productivity, and profitability, regardless of its brutal effects upon
workers. These effects are immaterial, and of no concern to man, who
is nothing but an externality himself.

As our discussion of work in contemporary America will reveal, our
present situation is inherited from such sources as protestant ethics
and liberalism—traditions that view work as valuable only in extrinsic
modes. This value perspective allowed, nay encouraged, work to be
fragmented and routinized, and workers to be isolated and regi-
mented. Many social thinkers still believe that this is the way things
should be. For example, Nels Anderson, writing under the aegis of
the UNESCO Institute for Social Science, consistently suggests that
this organization of work is the proper one. His value position is
clearly expressed in his description of the modern worker:

The worker naturally may form a love for his place of employment, and this
may grow with the years; but in general he is quite ready to move without
emotion from one work place to another, just as he gets rid of one automobile
for another. His attachment to the workplace is usually in proportion to his
dependence on it and the money he earns there. That the workplace does not
utilize his whole personality is of little concern; he would probably resist that
because the major part of his personality finds expression in the nonwork
sphere. It is in the nonwork sphere that he looks for the satisfaction which
counts for him. What he wants mainly from the work place is money, and in
this respect the manager is no different. He too would leave the enterprise for
a better job with higher pay.[33]

Fortunately there is another tradition, one that recognizes work as intrinsically valuable. It is captured in this statement by Karl Mannheim.

Once work habits and skills have been acquired and implemented a way of life in which workmanlike contributions are socially esteemed, pursuit of workmanship becomes an urge. . . . Once a person is trained for significant and self-expressive work, working means joy and the withdrawal or denial of work is not only painful but disorganizing to the personality. Hence utilitarian psychology based on the concept of homo economicus is only partially correct in asserting that the unpleasantness of work can be overcome by pecuniary compensation alone.[34]

Work as an Intrinsic Value

It was not until the Renaissance and its emphasis upon "man as creator" that work received more than isolated recognition as being intrinsically valuable. The attitudinal shift during this period may be detected even in writings not intended to eulogize work. A good example is Thomas More's *Utopia*.[35] After the Renaissance the growth of this view of work increased dramatically. By the nineteenth century, work as an intrinsic value was one of the central concerns of European social thought and gave birth to a number of social experiments designed to achieve this new vision. Realization of the idea continued to spread until the intrinsic value of work was heralded as one of the great social truths in our contemporary world. Unfortunately this "great social truth" did not supplant the previously entrenched notion that work was only of extrinsic value. It could do no better than coexist with it.

The name of Karl Marx must be among the first included in a discussion of those who stressed the intrinsic worth of work. For Marx, *work* was the key factor in the self-actualization of man in the world, and, as such, the Marxist revolution is largely a revolution of work. As Erich Fromm summarized Marx's position, *work* "is the self-expression of man, an expression of his individual physical and mental powers. In this process of genuine activity, man develops himself; work is not only a means to an end—the product—but an end in itself, the meaningful expression of human energy; hence work is enjoyable."[36] Unfortunately, not all of work is a genuine expression of man. This is especially true under a capitalistic system, which defines work purely in terms of its extrinsic value, money. Marx recognized the danger that exists when work is extrinsically valued. "The need for money . . . is therefore the real need created by the modern economy, and the only need which it creates. . . . This is shown subjectively, partly in the fact that the expansion of production and of need becomes an *ingenious* and always *calculating* subservience to inhuman, depraved, unnatural, and imaginary appetites."[37]

Capitalism, a system premised on the extrinsic value of work, is bound to have devastating effects. As Marx described in *Das Kapital*:

Within the capitalist system all methods for raising the social productiveness of labor are brought about at the cost of the individual laborer; all means for the development of production transform themselves into means of domination over, and exploitation of, the producers; they mutilate the laborer into a fragment of a man, degrade him to the level of an appendage of a machine, destroy every remnant of charm in his work and turn it into a hated toil; they estrange him from the intellectual potentialities of the labor process in the same proportion as science is incorporated in it as an independent power.[38]

It is Marx's contention that as "individuals express their life, so they are. What they are, therefore, coincides with their production, both with what they produce and with how they produce."[39] Thus in the capitalist system, which has perverted work into forced, meaningless *labor*, man becomes the "crippled monstrosity" that Marx described.

The condition of man in the capitalist system is characterized by Marx as one of alienation. Nowhere does he give fuller expression of this than in his early work, the *Economic and Philosophical Manuscripts*. "The object produced by labor, its product, now stands opposed to it as an *alien being*, as a *power independent* of the producer. The product of labor is labor which has been embodied in an object and turned into a physical thing; this product is an *objectification* of labor."[40] He continues his argument by asserting that since work no longer clearly expresses the worker's essence, he "does not fulfill himself in his work but denies himself, has a feeling of misery rather than well-being, does not develop freely his mental and physical energies but is physically and mentally debased. The worker therefore feels himself at home only during his leisure time, whereas at work he feels homeless."[41]

The importance of work may be gauged by the effects of worker alienation. When man becomes estranged from his work, the impact is not limited to that one area of his life. He not only becomes alienated from work life and the things he produced, but becomes alienated from other people, his potential, and even himself. "A direct consequence of the alienation of man from the product of his labor, from his life activity and from his species life is that *Man* is *alienated* from other men. What is true of man's relationship to his work, to the product of his work and to himself, is also true of his relationship to other men, to their labor and the objects of their labor.

"In general, the statement that man is alienated from his species life means that each man is alienated from others, and that each of the others is likewise alienated from human life."[42]

Though Marx may have been the foremost theorist of the intrinsic value of work, he was neither the first nor the last to make the case. As early as Rousseau, work was accorded significant meaning. Rousseau believed that the work of a craftsman conferred dignity upon life and therefore prescribed craftwork for his Emile. In fact, Rousseau was so strongly linked to a positive view of work that upon his death the representatives of various trades marched in his funeral procession carrying signs which read: "To the man who restored the honor of useful industry."[43]

The intrinsic value of work is evident in the intellectual traditions from which Marx most heavily borrowed. Hegel, for example, conceived of *work* at the macro level as the driving force in human history and at the micro level as the "act of man's self-creation."[44] The utopian socialists who preceded Marx reinforced this notion of the intrinsic value of work. Though the thought of Saint-Simon is more accurately seen as precursive to socialism, the importance of work is evident in his writings. It was Saint-Simon who claimed that *work* is the fountainhead of all virtues, and in words that sounded like a Biblical curse, but conveyed an entirely different message, proclaimed that "all men shall work."[45] His glorification of *work* was not a denial that the actual practice of work was an abomination, so the attacks upon him by his archrival in the field of social theory, Charles Fourier, were largely unfair. (As a matter of fact, Saint-Simon was much more aware of the untoward effects of industrialization than Fourier.) How could work be the prize virtue, Fourier wondered, when it most often was "an agreed upon, indirect form of slavery?"[46] After all, were not workers forced by necessity to "spend twelve, often fifteen consecutive hours . . . crouched in an unhealthy workshop . . . [within this] veritable industrial hell?"[47] To Fourier, this was not the product of a just God who would provide enjoyable work even for animals; it was the product of man and civilization. Hence, Fourier rejected the *labor* (and almost everything else) of his contemporary society, but retained the belief that *work* was the key to human happiness. It became his objective to reconcile work with the great motivating and justifying principle of pleasure, which was accomplished by stripping from work all of the *labor-like* characteristics that society had added. When people freely chose what they did, work became the type of self-expression that fostered individual development. This same theme is continued by Robert Owen, who many consider to be the actual founder of socialism. It was Owen who first coined the phrase, "working class," and the Factory Acts of 1833 and 1847 were largely a result of Owen's forceful preachings. Thus the cases of Saint-Simon, Fourier, and Owen illustrate Jonathan Beecher and Richard Bienvenu's contention that work became one of the predominating interests of European social thought by the beginning of the nineteenth century, and that the "most striking aspect of this relatively new concern was the almost universal attempt to establish productive work as the prime activity of a healthy society and the mark of a virtuous man and citizen."[48]

The praise that Marx showered upon Saint-Simon, Fourier, Owen, and the other utopian socialists who preceded him was equalled by the contempt he displayed toward those who carried on the same tradition within his own lifetime. Marx had little patience for those who could not offer "scientific solutions" to the problems inherent in industrial capitalism. His animosity, often more vehement than that shown the capitalist enemy, should not be allowed to obfuscate the fact that Marx and his contemporary utopian socialists shared many of the same views, especially as they concerned work. As with Marx, Pierre Proudhon, Peter Kropotkin, and others believed that work was an intrinsically valuable enterprise closely tied to the well-being and development of man. They recognized that the industrial capitalist order had given work its most extreme expression as an extrinsically-valued activity. They theorized that work could best assume its rightful dignity and worth in some form of voluntary and mutual association, a notion that Marx, of course, dismissed as misguided and dangerously naive.[49]

The intrinsic importance of work appeared in other strains of socialist thought. Prime examples are the nineteenth-century theorists who have been cited as the forebearers of guild socialism. To them, work was an expression of man in the world; it was the way that man made his existence concrete. It is not surprising, then, to find such men as John Ruskin and William Morris equating *work* with "fellowship, with love, with the liberating vitality of the artist."[50] In fact, Ruskin's emphasis on the value of art and his belief that work could be an art-like expression of man's creative powers led to his stinging critique of work within the industrial capitalist order. An appreciation of the intrinsic significance of work is not limited to the mainstream varieties of socialist thought. For example Berdyaev, who sought to fuse socialism with religion, spoke of *work* as "the great reality of human life."[51] He saw that in *work*, "there is a truth of redemption and truth of the constructive power of man."[52]

Thus along many tangents of socialist thought, the intrinsic importance of work can be discerned, but this should not lead the reader to associate this view of work with socialist thought alone. Many modern variations of thought have attributed great significance to *work* as a formative factor in human development. For example, one need not delve deeply into the musing of Henry David Thoreau at Walden Pond to discover that his view of work places its intrinsic value paramount.[53] A more influential expression of this theme of *work* as a formative factor in human development is found in the psychoanalytic school of thought. Among the writings of Freud, the founder of the school, one can find the foundation for such expression. As Freud contended, "Laying stress upon the importance of work has a greater effect than any other technique of reality living in the direction of binding the individual to reality. The daily work of earning a livelihood affords particular satisfaction when it has been selected by free choice."[54] The same theme is articulated more clearly by the second most influential personage in the school, Carl Jung, who claimed that the "best liberation [from the grip of primitive and infantile fantasy] is through regular work. Work, however, is salvation only when it is a free act and has nothing in it of infantile compulsion."[55] Wilhelm Reich maintains the Freudian theme concerning work by insisting that there is no contradiction between *work* and a sexually fulfilling life, although there may be some contradiction between *labor* and sexual satisfaction.[56] Contemporary psychoanalysts continue the stress placed upon *work*. Erich Fromm, for example, averred that in "the process of work, that is, the molding and changing of nature outside of himself, man molds and changes himself."[57] Given the central role

, that *work* plays, if expression through *work* is thwarted, the negative impact upon man will be great.

On the contemporary scene the central nature of *work* finds expression among a seemingly endless number of schools of thought. Even among those who reject many standard bases of values—existentialists for example—*work* emerges as an important phenomenon. To the existentialist, there may be no ultimate justifications for man's life, but this does not preclude the possibility of meaningful human activity. The extension of man into the world not only remains significant, it acquires a new and more complete meaning for the existentialist. Only when man is highly committed to an important project can life assume even the semblance of significance. Camus makes clear how central work is: "without work all life goes rotten; but when work is soulless, life stifles and dies."[58]

Thus rather than forget the message that was first formed in the Renaissance, modern man has elaborated upon it. The acknowledgement of *work's* significance, however, still stands in opposition to the actual conduct of work in the contemporary world. America is no exception. We accept the importance of work as an intrinsic value, but continue to act as if work were nothing more than employment. The next section will give substance to Alasdair Clayre's claim that "Work and a concern for the quality of work, far from being the essential element and center of all life, as in Carlyle, Marx, Ruskin or Morris, frequently seemed subordinate to the simple earning of money."[59]

Work in Contemporary American Thought and Practice

The historic battle between the view of work as intrinsically valuable, and the view of work as only extrinsically valuable is present in the thought and practice of work in contemporary America. Though both views have been inherited, they have not been well integrated. The resulting clash is one of the great sources of tension today; given the amount of time spent working, it is a tension that cannot be ignored easily. Let us take a closer look at the thought and practice of work in America. Before we do, it might be helpful to clarify further the distinction between intrinsic and extrinsic values.

Earlier in this chapter health and wealth were offered as polar opposites of a continuum that runs from the intrinsic to the extrinsic ex-

treme. To give more substance to this distinction, it is possible to specify characteristics that occupy specific points along the continuum. As
the example of wealth has indicated, pay for work lies at the extrinsic
polar extreme (although it should be noted that if pay is taken as a
sign of individual worth, it moves away from the extrinsic pole). Lying
close to that point would be most other financial rewards, such as the
usual array of fringe benefits. Many of the working conditions related
to a job would fall toward the extrinsic end, but not too distant from
the center. These would include having good working hours, a sufficient number of well-scheduled breaks, and pleasant physical sur-
roundings. The center of the continuum is occupied by factors related to fulfilling the assigned task and supervision related to that
task. Thus such factors as whether the worker is provided all the information and material necessary to complete the task, and whether
he is fairly supervised combine extrinsic and intrinsic features. Closely
aligned with supervision are matters related to evaluation; does the
worker know what is expected of him and how he will be judged? Toward the intrinsic end lie job characteristics such as whether the job
presents a variety of things to do, requires a high-skill level, and encourages the worker to be creative. Further along the continuum in
the direction of intrinsic values are features that concern the autonomy of the worker. Does the worker make many of the decisions related to what to do on the job and how to do it? These types of qualities are crucial in terms of intrinsic values, for without the exercised
ability to make decisions related to the job, the worker can never
really develop. Thus at the most extreme intrinsic position are those
job qualities that result in the development of the entire person and
not just "the worker." The discussion of work characteristics along the
intrinsic-extrinsic value continuum is represented as follows:

Extrinsic-Intrinsic Work Value Continuum

```
          fringe    working     task                      task
---pay---         ---         --- ---supervision---       ---
        benefits  conditions support                   evaluation


          job variety,                        personal
       ---             ---autonomy---                  ---
        skill, creativity                    development
```

The subject of work has attracted a number of theoretical approaches in America. Though the details of these approaches vary,

they do seem to have a common basis in the distinction between intrinsic and extrinsic values. To illustrate this point, let me choose three leading theorists whose work has been utilized to study work in some systematic manner: Herzberg, McGregor, and Maslow. The approach of Frederick Herzberg has always been one of a dual dedication.[60] As a managerial expert, it has been his objective to be efficient, but at the same time he wished his efficient management to be humane. Perhaps his most recognized accomplishment is his two-factor approach to worker satisfaction, known as the "motivation-hygiene theory." It is Herzberg's contention that those factors that lead a worker to be satisfied with his job are not the same as those that cause dissatisfaction. Dissatisfaction is usually associated with such factors as company policy and administration, supervision, interpersonal relations, working conditions, pay, and the like; while satisfaction is usually associated with such factors as achievement, recognition for achievement, the work itself, responsibility, autonomy, and growth. The reader will notice immediately that the distinction between those factors that can breed dissatisfaction (called hygiene factors) and those that breed satisfaction (referred to as motivators) is essentially the difference between extrinsic and intrinsic values. If a particular job does not provide the extrinsic rewards a worker thinks it should, then the worker will be dissatisfied. But to be satisfying, the job must be intrinsically rewarding.

Douglas McGregor emphasizes a different point, but the same underlying reliance on the extrinsic-intrinsic value continuum can be detected.[61] It is McGregor's objective to specify two major opposing points of view concerning the human worker. Theory X reads as if it could have been written by Thomas Hobbes as a liberal expression of man. The average worker is irresponsible, self-centered, and not very creative or energetic when it comes to serving any other interest but his own. These workers force management to take all of the initiatives related to work and force management to utilize traditional carrot and stick approaches to motivate workers to do their job. Only extrinsic rewards are necessary, for workers only respond to extrinsic rewards. The opposite position could have been written by Rousseau. Theory Y reverses cause and effect. If workers qua workers are indolent, passive, resistant to change, lack responsibility, and so on, it is because they have been made that way. Management can motivate workers in a different way, for workers are responsive to intrinsic values related to their job. If workers are allowed the opportunity to express themselves, make decisions, be creative, all will benefit from the results. McGregor's utilization of the extrinsic-intrinsic value dimension relates to the human nature of the average worker and the style of management that should accompany the rejection of Theory X as an accurate description of the worker.

Though Abraham Maslow did not begin his quest into what motivates humans with work organizations in mind, it did not take long for him and other people to make the application.[62] At the basis of what motivates humans is a hierarchical set of needs, and at the base of those needs lies the extrinsic-intrinsic value distinction.

Maslow's Hierarchy of Needs

Self-Actualization Needs (to realize more of one's potential)

Self-Esteem Needs (Self-approval, approval by others, prestige)

Social Needs (acceptance and affection)

Safety Needs (protection of the physical self, and one's life situation)

Physiological Needs (hunger, thirst, sex, sleep)

According to Maslow, almost everyone has these five basic types of needs. They are arranged so that the lower level needs predominate until they are satisfied. After satiation, the average person then directs his attention on the next highest need. The truly healthy and happy person is in a position to deal, and deal successfully, with his needs of self-actualization. As Maslow makes clear in *Eupsychian Management*, "The only happy people I know are the ones who are working well at something they consider important. . . . This [is] universal truth for all my self-actualizing subjects." From Maslow's perspective workplaces prevent the full development of individuals unless they address in the normal course of working the individual's higher-level needs. These needs center upon intrinsic values.[63]

The extrinsic-intrinsic value dimension can be found in the work of each theorist of work organization who has been examined. It is important to realize that this is not merely characteristic of these particular men, but of a large portion of those who dedicate their intellectual activity to thinking about work. I just as easily could have discussed Chris Argyris and his view that the general human personality development from immaturity to maturity is hampered in conventional workplaces because authority structures force workers into adopting immature roles and behavior.[64] The same could be said for the work of Rensis Likert[65] or Arnold Tannenbaum[66] without any substantial change in conclusion. At the base of modern thinking concerning work lies the same extrinsic-intrinsic value conflict, which historically has accompanied the examination of work.

If the theoretical considerations concerning work have shifted toward an emphasis on the intrinsic since the writings of Frederick Taylor, what has happened to the actual practice of work? Even a quick glance into contemporary workplaces reveals that there has been movement toward a recognition of the importance of work, although that shift has not been as pronounced as in the writings concerning work. Certainly the conditions of industrial shops are nowhere near as dismal as those of the early twentieth century when management attempted to conform to the principles of scientific management developed by Taylor. It is no exaggeration at all to claim that most workplaces, to an appreciable extent, achieved that nefarious goal. The advent of the "human relations" school of management[67] was to ameliorate many of the most appalling features. Within this school there existed the fundamental realization that the major problem with Taylorism was that its view of human nature was seriously misconceived. Scientific management simply did not admit to even the possibility that intrinsic values could be pervasive. Since it structured work as if the only thing of value to be derived from working was money, work in a Taylor-inspired system could not be satisfying, for so many of the basic human needs and desires were left unfulfilled. Though no one has established the empirical existence of Maslow's exact hierarchical ranking of needs, research has indicated that once the basic needs for existence and security have been satiated, other needs, such as those related to esteem, autonomy, and self-actualization, do come into play.[68] How many of the needs beyond existence and security could be satisfied by the robot-like performance of work scientifically managed? Yet the fact that it addressed even the material needs proved to be the undoing of the system. It is only when workers are at subsistence wages or lower that physical sustenance and security are likely to be of overwhelming concern, and it is only when these two most basic needs are in jeopardy that workers would allow themselves to be victimized under scientific management. Thus only under conditions of dire necessity would the Taylor system, based exclusively on extrinsic rewards, prove successful. Under other conditions, it is likely to produce malcontent people and they, it must be assumed, do not make the best workers.[69] Scientific management contained the seeds of its own destruction; by lessening the severity of material needs, it undermined its own viability. Taylor often insisted that his sympathies were primarily with the workers. In terms of the self-destruction of scientific management, perhaps he was correct.

From management's point of view, the charge against scientific management ironically must be that it does not remain efficient, productive, and profitable. Unless conditions are similar to those when swarms of hungry immigrants were forced to take any available employment to avoid starvation, the system could not motivate men and women to labor. When it came to actual organization of work, rather than writing about the organization of work, the emphasis upon human relations within the "human relations" school of management was at least as much a concern for economic expedience as it was a concern for humanitarian values. In practice, the human relations school was to improve conditions within workplaces, but only to the extent that economic values dictated. Whenever humanitarian causes did not carry economic advantages, they were likely to be lost amid a myriad of other concerns. Whenever economic concerns could be pursued without consideration for humanitarian aspects, they often were. Since most basic objectives were economic and not humanitarian, if it were profitable to institute apparent rather than real humanitarian changes, then that was done. It is most important to understand that the "human relations" school did not reject the dominance of the extrinsic values of work; it was in fact premised upon that view of the worth of work. The basic operational difference between it and Taylorism is that the human-relations school recognized that worldly conditions had changed, and given its more complete and accurate view of human nature, realized that work had to be organized in a manner that was more congruent with the lessening of necessity.

Though the human relations school, which began with Elton Mayo's Hawthorne studies in the 1920s,[70] did ameliorate conditions surrounding work, it all too often left the actual content of work untreated. In both our thoughts and actions, that tradition is strongly with us today. Take for example the recent Biddle and Hutton article, "Toward a Tolerance Theory of Worker Adaptation." The authors stated objective is to examine "the ways in which people can achieve toleration of what is to them, and may appear to others as, an unsatisfying or impoverished work situation."[71] The authors solution is to manipulate the physical environment; they do not address the actual unsatisfying or impoverished work situation. It is an inheritance of the human-relations school that a search for a change in the conditions surrounding work rather than a change in the actual work content would be sought. It is the result of the human-relations school that work that remains dull and meaningless has been made pleasant. It is the sad conclusion of Lawler and Rhode, after their careful review of the literature, that "Evidence abounds that people are motivated by intrinsic rewards, yet this often isn't taken into account when organizations, jobs and information and control are designed."[72] This situation creates a particular strain on workers; although so much has obviously changed, little has been done to enhance the intrinsic value of work.

Work as an Intrinsic Value Denied

What happens when we deny in the structuring of work that work has intrinsic value? The previous theoretical argumentation makes clear its answer. The contradiction between the centrality of work and work designed as if it had only extrinsic value is a source of great tension. Since work is a primary means of expression and linked closely with human development, it cannot be made an artless drudgery without having profound effects. Certainly much more is at stake than a disappointing worklife. The central nature of work assures that the negative effects of work designed as if it had only extrinsic value cannot be confined to the hours spent at the place of work. Ramifications of bad work (work that is only extrinsically valuable) will be experienced in other areas of the worker's life. One conclusion to be drawn from this contention is that exogenous solutions to bad work are not likely to be effective. Those who seek solution in the form of leisure activities, for example, neglect to consider the import of the work experience. Hence even Marx was misled when he claimed that as a result of the work experience, the "worker therefore feels himself at home only during his leisure time, whereas at work he feels homeless."[73] That which is bred at work will be carried home. To those who have advanced the "leisure" solution, Robert Blauner replied bluntly that they underestimate "the fact that work remains the single most important life activity for most people, in terms of time and energy, and ignores the subtle ways in which the quality of one's worklife affects the quality of one's leisure, family relations, and basic self-feelings."[74] Man is not, in Ferdynand Zweig's words, "one person at home and a different person at his work, he is one and the same man. He projects his personal worries, frustrations, and fears on to his workplace, and vice versa from workplace to home."[75] Continuing the argument in a somewhat hyperbolic fashion, Georges Friedman stridently claims that "fragmentation of labor does not always cause the worker to seek leisure activities of greater scope in order to compensate for his frustrations. It may tend instead to disorganize the rest of his life and to arouse aggressive tendencies and outbursts of savage self-assertion through indulgence in all kinds of stimulants, in alcohol, in games of chance or luck, or in habits or bouts of 'conspicuous consumption,' brutal amusement . . . mass-spectacles disguised as 'sport' or 'artistic' events . . . and crime and horror films."[76] The contention that is being forcefully proposed is that bad work, work designed to maximize the extrinsic value of work (labor), has a powerfully negative effect on the lives of individuals.

But is this actually the case? On the contemporary research scene, Harold Wilensky was the first to formulate conceptually alternative responses to work as an intrinsic value denied. In his article, "Work, Careers, and Social Integration." Wilensky stipulates two rival hypotheses.[77] The "spillover" hypothesis predicts that the characteristics of the workplace experience will spill into an individual's nonworking life. The "compensatory" hypothesis predicts that if a person's worklife is not intrinsically valuable or rewarding, he or she will compensate for it in nonworking life. The hypotheses were not adequately examined until Martin Meissner did so in 1971.[78] In testing the rival hypotheses (as well as the possibility that worklife would have no impact), the first factor Meissner examined was the ability of workers to make decisions and control various parts of their working life. When a worker's choice of action (discretion) was limited by the spatial, temporal, and functional constraints of the work process, his capacity for meeting the demands of nonwork activity requiring discretion was clearly reduced. In testimony to the potency of work experiences, fifteen of the sixteen possible relationships between indicators of work *constraint* and indicators of nonwork activity that require discretion (organizational involvement) were negative. The relationship tended to be the strongest when measures were the most demanding, as when constraint was correlated with the average number of organizational offices held. The "spillover" hypothesis also was supported by measures of social isolation. Rather than compensating for their work experience when work is socially isolating, workers reduce their exposure to situations in which they have to talk in nonwork settings. As Meissner adds, "Lack of opportunity to talk on the job is associated with dramatically reduced rates of participation in associations, that is, in activity commonly believed to help integrate individuals into the community."[79] Meissner aptly entitled his article "The Long Arm of the Job," for the reach of workplace experiences would seem to be long indeed.

Perhaps it is possible that the reach of workplace experiences is sufficiently long and strong that the claims of Georges Friedman are not overstated. Selecting the area of health to illustrate, there is ample evidence to relate work to physical and mental well-being. In this regard the investigators of the HEW study, *Work in America*, have compiled an impressive number of studies that make this very connection. Concentrating first upon physical well-being, there is the obvious relationship between dangerous work—say deep-shaft mining—and physical health, but the effects of work extend well beyond the obtrusive examples. A recent fifteen-year study of life expectancy found that satisfaction with work is the single *best* predictor of longevity.[80] The relationship remained strong under control procedures. Working women live longer than women who do not work; housewives on the average do not live as long as blue-collar workers.[81] In Italy, a study linked the effects of adverse working conditions to the process of aging.[82] Work-related characteristics have been found to correlate with one of the nation's top killers, heart disease. More specifically, heart disease was discovered to be associated most strongly with job dissatisfaction,[83] low self-esteem,[84] occupational stress,[85] excessively rapid and continuous changing of jobs,[86] and an incongruity between job status and other aspects of the person's life.[87] When to this is added a spate of research findings that relate work characteristics to numerous other less serious ailments such as peptic ulcers[88] and arthritis,[89] the belief grows that work is intimately related to physical health.[90]

Work appears to have a similar impact upon the mental health of individuals. Though the concept of mental health is difficult to define, it normally denotes the demonstrated capacity of an individual to live productively in society. To C. M. Solley and K. Munden, who have analyzed the phenomenon, this means that the mentally healthy individual derives satisfaction from a variety of sources, has a realistic image of himself, sets reasonable standards, and involves himself in the world around him.[91] Hypothetically, work can be related to each of these criteria; empirically, work-related characteristics have been related to a variety of measures of mental health. According to national surveys reported by Angus Campbell, Philip Converse, and Willard Rodgers in *The Quality of American Life*,[92] the unemployed as well as those dissatisfied with work report being less satisfied with their lives in general, less satisfied with where they live, less trusting of other people, fear most that they will have a nervous breakdown, and confess to being the most out of control of their lives. Many of the same conclusions seem to hold when specifically addressing working women. Working women report being more satisfied with their lives and less hampered by emotional distress than their nonworking counterparts. The social scientists at the Institute for Social Research have found job dissatisfaction to be related significantly to the development of psychosomatic illnesses, low self-esteem, anxiety, tension, and disrupted social relations with others.[93] Bertil Gardell in his Swedish sample found an array of mental health problems related to work structured as only extrinsically valuable.[94] These results remained valid after control for age, sex, education, income, quality of supervision, and pay satisfaction in mass production industries. In other research efforts, low socio-economic status (which is related definitionally to occupation and logically to work participation as previously discussed)[95] was linked to high rates of psychiatric hospitalization and symptomatology, while long periods of unemployment were discovered to relate to psychiatric hospitalization and suicide.[96] One of the most disturbing facets of the mental-health research[97] is the mounting evidence that ties job dissatisfaction with drug abuse.[98] Not being mentally present is one way to cope with meaningless and monotonous work. In direct contrast to all of this, a strong positive correlation has been found repeatedly between job satisfaction and good mental health.[99]

It is not accidental that the subjects of physical and mental health were chosen to illustrate the powerful impact that work has on the lives of individuals. If work could be demonstrated to affect people in ways as fundamental as their health, then it is likely that work affects all that we do. One very interesting example appears in the research of Theodore Kemper and Melvin Reichler. They found that *both* the husband and wife's satisfaction with their marriage correlates significantly with the husband's *intrinsic, but not extrinsic* satisfaction with work and that the effects were indifferent to social class.[100] Though

work experiences may indeed affect all that we do, we ought not leave
the topic without addressing the explicit focus of this entire exposition—the political world. According to Harold L. Sheppard and Neal
Q. Herrick in their study *Where Have All the Robots Gone?*, younger
workers are less likely to be authoritarian, and when forced into occupational positions characterized by little variety and autonomy, they
are more likely to become alienated.[101] In testimony to the workplace
connection, alienated workers are less likely to vote. Indeed, in a Kal-
amazoo study, 47 percent of the alienated workers did not vote in the ·
1968 presidential election in comparison to a 25 percent nonvoting
rate among those not alienated.[102] The alienated workers were found
to feel politically inefficacious and have negative attitudes toward the
political system. But even more disturbing is the discovery that when
alienated workers did vote, their support was twice as strong for Wallace than was that of the nonalienated worker.[103] This is significant.
Although George Wallace was to amend his positions significantly in
years to come, in 1968 his positions were still chauvinistic and demagogic. Alienation most often strikes the young; consistently, young
workers voted for Wallace by a ratio of six-to-one compared to the
oldest workers surveyed.[104] May the reader be reminded that those
supporting Wallace, especially the young, were not workers originally
characterized by authoritarian traits. This means that George Wallace
found his greatest support among the youngest, least authoritarian
and best-educated of workers. Thus Sheppard and Herrick concluded that jobs with little variety, autonomy, and responsibility—jobs
constructed according to the extrinsic value of work—can lead to politically undesirable attitudes and behavior. This conclusion is supported by A. K. Korman who demonstrates by citation that "there is a
substantial body of literature that points to the conclusion that work
experience marked by hierarchical approaches to leadership, specialization of duties and routinization of tasks tends to be associated with
attitudes and behaviors that can be described as noncivil libertarian in
nature."[105] Bad work can affect all we do.

Though Arthur Kornhauser's study, *Mental Health of the Industrial
Worker*, is already a classic in the field of industrial health, its importance extends far beyond that limited field. So many of the crucial
contentions of this thesis find expression in Kornhauser's work that it
provides an excellent basis for summary and conclusion.[106] In Kornhauser's study, 40 percent of the workers surveyed revealed symp-
toms of mental illness. Work was undeniably the dominant institution

in the workers' lives; it ranked above family, leisure, and social activities in its ability to command the attention of workers. This did
not, however, make work a dominant life *interest*, for only 25 percent
considered what they did sufficiently rewarding to choose it again as
their occupation. (This is clear indication that the respondents considered their activity to be *labor*, not *work*.) Given the central role that
work plays, it is imperative that it be worthwhile. Workers, of course,
are interested in extrinsic values such as wages and vacations, but they
also are concerned that their jobs be challenging and intrinsically rewarding. As the reader would expect, those workers who were forced
to operate in the monotony of a boring job (work designed according
to its extrinsic value) were more likely to become dissatisfied with their
jobs. More is at stake than dissatisfying work, for the centrality of
work insures that other areas of a person's life will be affected deeply.
Thus those who were trapped in an unrewarding work life (laborers)
were not only more likely to be dissatisfied, but were also more likely
to suffer from low self-esteem, a feeling of helplessness, alienation,
and to be plagued by a variety of mental disorders. The impact of
worklife on the individual's psyche is important in influencing the degree to which individuals engage themselves in the world around
them. The workers who were the most dissatisfied and whose mental
health was the most impaired were the least likely to vote or participate in community organizations. Bad work is debilitating.

A number of studies indicate that a satisfying life at work requires a
combination of both extrinsic and intrinsic values. Patricia Voydanoff
reports that both extrinsic and intrinsic values were related to job satisfaction,[107] while A. L. Kalleberg reports that measures of both types
of values were found to have an independent effect on job satisfaction.[108] Yet it could be argued that the intrinsic values have greater impact. In Kornhauser's study, for example, the intrinsic values were
most intimately related to mental health; pay could not assuage the
alienating effects of meaningless work. Jobs cannot be interesting,
challenging, meaningful, and expression of the self, a learning experience and the like (i.e., embrace intrinsic values), as long as they are
designed only to maximize efficiency, productivity, and profit (i.e.,
embrace extrinsic values). If we persist in our present course of acknowledging the intrinsic worth of work, but designing work as if it
has only extrinsic value, then as the HEW research team has contended, we will continue to confront the problems that bad work
creates: "a consequent decline in physical and mental health, family

stability, community participation and cohesiveness, and 'balanced' sociopolitical attitudes, while there is an increase in drug and alcohol addiction, aggression and delinquency."[109] In conclusion, consider the words of Simone Weil, "No society can be stable in which a whole stratum of the population labors daily with a heart-felt loathing. This loathing for their work colors their whole view of life, all of their life."[110] Bad work is debilitating. ·

The Intrinsic Value of Work Affirmed?

Work in America must be restructured so that it is more intrinsically satisfying. But how is this to be done? Throughout the entire argument of this work, it has been a major contention that intrinsic values are achieved through an active, not a passive process. It would follow that for work to embrace the values of individual self-development, work must involve workers.

This is no idle claim; the contention that workplace participation is linked to satisfaction (and therefore to intrinsic values) is strongly supported in research literature. The Shepard research in 1969 revealed a positive relationship between level of work autonomy and general job satisfaction.[111] This conclusion is consistent with previous research conducted on workplace participation. Jacobson in 1951 found that workers were more satisfied when foremen and shop stewards allowed them to participate.[112] Morse and Reimer in 1956 compared satisfaction scores for authoritarian and democratic groups and found that the democratic groups were more satisfied.[113] In 1967 Marrow, Bowers, and Seashore reported on a company that introduced a participatory style of leadership. At that time they concluded that the participatory style seemed to increase satisfaction. A follow-up study several years later showed that levels of satisfaction remained high.[114]

The survey of work in contemporary America reveals that much progress has been made, but that much more need be accomplished before the intrinsic value of work is realized. Projecting our concerns into the future, there is a good possibility that this will be the case. As large portions of the population find their basic material needs satisfied, they are likely to increase their demands that work become a better source of self-respect, and that it provide more fully nonmaterial (intrinsic) rewards. At the same time workers are likely to continue their demands that rights and liberties, once only applicable to participation in government, be applied to the workplace as well.[115] Since civil rights and liberties form the foundation for participation, this reform will act to augment participation in the workplace. This is critical, for without workplace participation, it will be difficult, if not impossible, to satisfy the nonmaterial desires of workers.

It is possible to envision restructured work in terms of art. The art that was taken from the artisan can be returned to workers in the future. The more work becomes expressive and a means of developing individual potentials, the more work comes to resemble art. Work can involve the creative use of abilities, inspiring pride in the product and pleasure in the production. Although work will differ from the contemporary view of art in that it will be more of a collective than individual enterprise, each worker will have the opportunity to be an artist. Each worker will be one artist within a group of artists, working together in a common purpose. The workers of the future will have no need to separate working life from the rest of their lives. With work acquiring a new art-like quality, all of life can acquire the holistic quality necessary to achieve intrinsic values.

This description of work in the future intentionally has a utopian air. It is a description of work as it could possibly be. There are, however, powerful forces pushing work in the opposite direction. One threat lies in the body of thought that would have work not change, or if it did change, to return work to a form more purely an expression of extrinsic values. Consider the statement of Milton Friedman, which pertains to whether work should be organized by corporate officials to achieve values other than the extrinsic value of profit: "Few trends could so thoroughly undermine the very foundations of our free society as the acceptance by corporate officials of a social responsibility other than to make as much money for their stockholders as possible. This is a fundamentally subversive doctrine."[116]

When corporate leaders believe that their only social responsibility is to make a profit, the form of work that will emerge is not very likely to be intrinsically rewarding to the workers. We might be able to dismiss the views of Milton Friedman, if it were not for the fact that he publishes his views in one of the country's most popular periodicals, *Newsweek*. Let us not forget that in the fall of 1976 Milton Friedman was announced as the winner of the Nobel prize in economics for the elaboration of his beliefs. There is no small amount of meaning in the fact that Friedman's intellectual heritage lies mainly with the British classicists such as Adam Smith, William Petty, David Hume, James Mill, John Stuart Mill and, of course, Alfred Marshall. There is much meaning in the fact that Friedman corrects those who call him conservative by stating that he is actually a "neo-liberal." The devastating views of work provided by liberalism are still very much with us.

Another threat comes from those who would break from the liberal tradition as represented by Friedman, but who would not seek to establish work as intrinsically valuable. Herbert Marcuse offers an excellent example. Whereas Friedman would have us work with a Calvinistic spirit, Marcuse would do away with work entirely so that we might be free to express ourselves in play and leisure activities all of the time. The Marcusian view of the good life is one in which automation has advanced so far that man is not required to engage in the scourge that is all work to meet his necessities of life. There is no such thing as a quality working life, for quality life and working are contradictory: "The more complete the alienation of labor, the greater the potential freedom: total automation would be the optimum. It is the sphere outside labor which defines freedom and fulfillment. . . ." Marcuse's view is no less a threat to establishing meaningful work than Friedman's view.[117]

Though many of the signs are hopeful, the chances that the view of work as intrinsically valuable will grow and be realized is difficult to assess. It is hard to say whether the views of Alasdair Clayre and Simone Weil concerning work will predominate. As Alasdair Clayre states the notion: "Though Rousseau expressed his ideas through a language of nature and virtue, Marx in terms of unalienated productive activity, and Ruskin and Morris through the evocation of forms of work that involve art, they have a strikingly similar idea of the human future. It will centre on work—but work set free from monotony and compulsion."[118] And Simone Weil completes the idea: "Our age has its own particular mission, or vocation—the creation of a civilization founded upon the spiritual nature of work. The thoughts relating to a presentiment of this vocation, and which are scattered about in Rousseau, George Sand, Tolstoy, Proudhon and Marx, in papal encyclicals and elsewhere, are the only original thoughts of our time, the only ones we haven't borrowed from the Greeks."[119]

6

Workplace Democracy

Introduction

A NUMBER OF DIFFERENT ROUTES LEAD TO A CONSIDERATION OF participation within the workplace. Participation in the workplace is an efficient means to generate greater participation within government. Participation in the workplace is also a crucial element in creating more meaningful work. Since participation is the essential ingredient of democracy, a discussion of participation within the workplace is potentially a discussion of workplace democracy, if participation within that community is widespread and effective.

This conclusion and the implications that follow are often missed for the dominant liberal view does segment the world in such a fashion that terms such as *democracy*, and communities such as the workplace, are divided and placed in different categories. *Democracy* is a political term and belongs in the public category with other expressions which relate to government, while the workplace belongs in the social sphere. Since the political, according to liberalism, does not apply to the everyday social and private components of our lives, we can only apply political terminology to them in some figurative manner. That is why we speak metaphorically of family "politics," or economic "democracy." In changing our conception of the political, it becomes clear that the political is present in our daily lives whenever our activity relates to group decision making. It is equally clear that democracy may relate to any community, but it especially should apply to the workplace, given the importance of that community.

On this base, a number of topics related to workplace democracy will be explored in the following pages. There is a substantial European tradition of thought associated with workplace democracy, although, it is not always called that. The origins most relevant to this discussion lie in the genre of socialist writings which emphasize decentralized decision making, and in the anarchist tradition. Many of the thinkers who were surveyed in the chapters related to the workplace connection and the intrinsic value of work also are important to workplace democracy. It is not accidental that the recognition of the impact of workplace participation on participation in government and the intrinsic value of work is linked to the advocacy of workplace democracy. Closely tied to the advocacy of workplace democracy has been action in its behalf. Significant attempts to increase workplace democracy have been made in Europe and the United States. Underlying this entire investigation is the important question of what legitimately constitutes workplace democracy. With this standard, it is possible to examine critically both the contemporary forms and the advocates of workplace democracy.

In European Thought and Action

Though Phillippe Buchez in 1831 was the first to use a phrase with the equivalent meaning of workplace democracy, "republic in the industry,"[1] it is clear that the tradition of thought linked to workplace democracy precedes him. What is not clear is the proper time with which, or theorist with whom, to begin the review of thought related to workplace democracy. When exhibited in the form of cooperative work efforts, the general heritage of workplace democracy is probably as old as man himself. The roots of workplace democracy are exposed in medieval communes and cooperative guilds, but it is probably best not to investigate the origins prior to the industrial revolution, for the industrial revolution initiated the process by which workplaces were transformed into their modern variant.

Two genres of literature contribute seminally to the theoretical heritage of workplace democracy: utopian socialism and anarchism. The utopian socialist tradition is identified in Frederick Engels' work, "Socialism: Utopian and Scientific": "Then came the three great Utopians: St. Simon, to whom the middle-class movement, side by side with the proletarian, still have a certain significance; Fourier; and Owen, who in the country where capitalist production was most developed, and under the influence of the antagonisms begotten of this, worked out his proposals for the removal of class distinction systematically and in direct relation to French materialism."[2] Given the coincidence of their writings, it almost appears as if these contempo-

raries were responding to the very same stimulus. Each of the found-
ers of utopian socialism produced their most celebrated work associated with workplace democracy during the years 1821–22: Saint
Simon, *Le Système Industriel*; Fourier, *Traité d' Association Domestique
Agricole*; and Owen, *Report to the County of Lanark*. Each of the theorists
had formulated their basic ideas in this regard during the years
1813–14; Saint Simon, *De la Réorganization de la Société Européenne*;
Fourier, *La Théorie des Quatre Mouvements et des Destinées Générales*; and
Owen, *A New View of Society*. Though a distinct part of utopian socialist thought, Saint Simon ought not be identified with workplace democracy. Saint Simon does identify the potential significance of small
social units based on industrial relationships to the restructuring of
society, but there is nothing necessarily democratic about those units.
In fact, it was Saint Simon's contention that capitalists were the natural leaders of the units, and on that basis, Saint Simon formulates a
rather elitist system of rule.

A more clear ancestor to workplace democracy is Charles Fourier.
He prescribes the good life in terms of self-governing units known as
phalanstéres. These phalanstéres are collectivities that cooperate in
the efforts related to joint production and consumption. There is a
democratic quality to the notion that individuals within the phalanstéres may choose what work they wish to do, and change the work
they are doing almost as often as they like. There is at the same time,
however, a very undemocratic quality to the cooperative units, which
stems from Fourier's view of human nature and extends to the structure of the phalanstéres. Fourier believed that individual human
nature did not change and that there were a limited number of personality types. The assumption that human nature is fixed allowed
Fourier to fix immutably the structure of the phalanstéres. Since any
population of 610 men were likely to possess all of the possible personality types, Fourier specified the size of his collectivities to be 1220,
adding a woman for each man. Not only is the number of members
fixed, but every other structural aspect is also unchanging. Fourier
believed that he had established the perfect order for human choice
and expression, but in removing the ability to decide on the very
structure of the phalanstéres, he created a system limited in democratic expression.

It is Robert Owen, the third person identified by Engels, who establishes the clearest precedent for workplace democracy. Owen believed
that all should work and that work placed individuals in a common

bond with each other. This bond was strengthened by uniting common distribution with social property and equal privileges. Politically this means that all members of the community have equal participatory rights and opportunities based on their mutual interests. Achieving this will be a matter of education; among other things men are not well trained in principles that would allow them to act in concert, except to defend themselves or destroy others. The participatory plan will be accomplished in each single village community before it is achieved in the overarching community. In this way the new society will grow out of the old one in an evolutionary manner.

The train of thought begun by Saint Simon, Fourier, and Owen became the socialist tradition and within that tradition there continued to be expressions related to workplace democracy. One good example is expressed through the thought of Louis Blanc, who believed that it was possible for the government to sponsor workplace democracy by financing social workshops. For the first year, government organizations would be responsible for the operation of the workshop, but after that year, the workers would elect those who were to administrate the workshop. The distribution of income would vary according to the development of the workshops. At first the workshops would distribute income inequitably, but as the workshop system matured, the formula for distributive justice would become, to each according to his needs, from each according to his abilities. Blanc foresaw a time when workshops would not only transform national politics, but lead to international harmony, based on the commonality of worklife experiences.[3]

The possibility of workplace democracy did not escape the thought of socialism's master theorist, Karl Marx, although it must be stated that his views concerning workplace democracy were not always in high relief. The major reason for this was that Marx insisted that his variety of socialism was scientific, not utopian. It was the mark of utopianism to talk about what did not exist; it was the mark of scientific inquiry to address what does exist, and what predictably would exist. Thus he spends very little time describing the very desirable communist society that will follow the successful proletariat revolution. Nevertheless it is possible to indicate the compatibility of Marx's thought with workplace democracy. It can be seen in Marx's description of events contained in "The Civil War in France." Marx was obviously taken with the emergence of the Paris Commune. He begins the last paragraph of the work with the statement that "Workingmen's Paris,

with its Commune, will be forever celebrated as the glorious har-
binger of a new society."[4] What was the Paris Commune of 1871 to
Marx? Earlier in the work he makes it clear that the "Paris Commune
was, of course, to serve as a model to all the great industrial centers of
France. The communal regime once established in Paris and the secondary centers, the old centralized government would in the provinces, too, have to give way to the *self-government of the producers*."[5] It
can be seen in the famous passage in the third volume of *Das Kapital*
where Marx describes freedom in material production: "Freedom in
the field of material production cannot consist of anything else but
the fact that socialized men, associated producers, regulate their in-
terchange with nature rationally, bring it under their common control, instead of being ruled by it as by some blind power; that they
accomplish their task with the least expenditure of energy and under
conditions most adequate to their human nature and most worthy of
it."[6]

It, of course, can be seen in the brief glimpse that we get of the communist utopia in "German Ideology" where Marx describes the situation in which it is possible "to do one thing today and another tomorrow, to hunt in the morning, fish in the afternoon, rear cattle in the
evening, criticize after dinner."[7] Within all of this may be seen a decentralized system in which workers participate in the decisions which
govern their working life. It is thus possible to see within Marx's socializing of the capitalist means of production decentralization and
workplace democracy.

The second major body of thought to contribute to the idea of
workplace democracy is anarchism. The tradition of anarchism is so
varied that it is difficult to make summary statements about it. Perhaps the most that can be said is that central to most anarchist thinking is a radical and adamant insistence on autonomy. No agent of society, least of all national government, has the moral right to intervene
in the lives of individuals and dictate what they should or should not
do. Inherent in this insistence is the basic right to participate in, if not
outright decide, all those issues that affect one's life. This is especially
true regarding the workplace, for most anarchist thought pays particular attention to the ordering of production and the individual's relationship to that ordering. Since it is so difficult to offer a synoptic account of anarchist thought, it may be best to examine that tradition by
examining a few of the major thinkers who are in some sense repre-

sentative of that species of thought. The review will include mention of William Godwin, Pierre Joseph Proudhon, and Peter Kropotkin.

It is important to begin with William Godwin, not because he made a major contribution to the thinking related to workplace democracy, but because his *Enquiry Concerning Political Justice* is the first major treatise on anarchism.[8] Godwin's immediate reaction is to the brute engine that is the state. In rejecting the state, Godwin offers us a vision of small parishes of people who interact with each other on the basis of sincerity and trust. There is no need for laws or government, for virtuous and enlightened men and women can be persuaded as to the proper course of action through rational argument and accurate portrayal of the truth. This applies to all matters, including the structure of one's working life. Godwin contributes to the foundation of workplace democracy by stressing the decision making of all people related to the matters of their lives, but his work is not a direct ancestor to workplace democracy thought because he carries individual independence and self-determination too far. In Godwin's system there is no system of "community" decision making; there is only individuals making decisions. Without the existence of community, there can be no expression of democracy in the community of work.

The work of Pierre Joseph Proudhon is much more complete in terms of its development of workplace democracy.[9] Proudhon, persuaded by the ideals of the French Revolution, nevertheless indicates that it fell short by not applying the principles of liberty, equality, and fraternity to the "economic" sphere (workplaces), as it had to the "political" sphere (government). The critical element in achieving these goals is cooperation. Workers mutually form enterprises by contracting with each other in such a manner that all rights and obligations are specified and accepted. Mutualism in the form of cooperation through contracts extends vertically by having individual producers form associations, which in turn, federate into industries. A parallel structure is created on the basis of geographical units. The state must be abolished and all power of the state transferred to local units known as communes. These communes are created through contracts among various families; the communes, in turn, federate into provinces and states. Though there are central institutions in the society Proudhon envisions, they have authority only when their actions are accepted by the communes. All effective decision making is made at a level at which individuals may participate directly.

As the title of Peter Kropotkin's most famous work, *Mutual Aid*,[10] would indicate, Kropotkin is indebted to Proudhon for much of his thought—not the least of which is his obvious emphasis upon mutualism and its complement, federalism. Throughout his writings, Kropotkin succeeds in placing many of Proudhon's ideas in informative historical perspectives and correcting some of the contradictions that riddle the work of Proudhon. Yet it is not simply in the revision and updating of Proudhon that Kropotkin belongs in a survey of thought related to workplace democracy, but in his own, more original contributions. Though there are certainly a few such contributions to be found in *Mutual Aid*, it is in another work that Kropotkin offers some of his most interesting extensions of the tradition. Unlike many of his fellow anarchists, Kropotkin is willing to begin to build structures of reform within the existing order, which do not necessitate the overthrow of that existing order. In *Fields, Factories and Workshops Tomorrow*, Kropotkin specifies reforms which can counter excesses of specialization based on rampant division of labor.[11] He describes a system in which workers may move from factory to farm, rotating positions, and thus integrating society at a decentralized level. Kropotkin's overall emphasis is on decentralization and limiting representation so that individuals may participate effectively in the decisions which affect their lives.

The confluence of utopian socialism and anarchist thought is present in the writings of those associated with guild socialism. It is unnecessary to discuss in great detail the development of guild socialism, for that was done as part of the discussion related to the workplace connection. Instead, attention can be focused upon the structuring of workplace democracy within guild socialism, and certainly no better source can be consulted than G. D. H. Cole's *Guild Socialism Re-stated*. Within that work Cole states the basic goal: "the essence of the Guild Socialist attitude lies in the belief that Society ought to be so organized as to afford the greatest opportunity for individual and collective self-expression to all its members, and that this involves and implies the extension of positive self-government through all its parts."[12] Where does one begin to realize such a democratic vision? Cole makes clear that the proper point of departure is the workplace. "The factory, or place of work, will be the natural unit of Guild life. It will be, to a great extent, internally self-governing, and it will be the unit and basis of the wider local and national government of the Guild. The freedom of the particular factory as a unit is of fundamental importance, because the object of the whole Guild system is to call out the spirit of free service by establishing really democratic conditions in industry."[13]

The democratic principle of participation is thus applied horizontally to the internal operations of workplaces and then extended vertically to producer guilds. At a higher level of vertical ascent, the producer guilds will be federated into a congress of industrial guilds. Within that national guild there will be as many producer guilds represented as types of producing units identified and organized. Every individual has more than one role to play in life, however, and has more than one interest. For that reason Cole applies the same principle to every other functional activity. In addition to participation and representation in producer guilds, there also would be consumer guilds, collective utility councils, civic guilds, health councils, and the like. Since Cole distinguishes between the economic and political spheres (although he recognized the extension of the political, he does not reconceptualize it), there is a "political" counterpart to this structure. As the workplace was the basic unit in the production guilds, so the ward becomes the most basic unit in the "political" sphere. Direct participation is horizontally extended to the basic geographical unit of the ward, and functional representation is vertically extended to create communes, regional communes and eventually, the national commune. The different networks of functional representation are interlocked by providing guild representation in the commune assembly. Through such a system based primarily upon workplace democracy, Cole hoped to achieve his goal of active individuals in a participatory society.

European attention to workplace democracy was not limited to thought alone. There were numerous attempts to establish some work structure related to workplace democracy, and more often than not, that form had clear ties to particular social thinkers. Many of the early attempts to put workplace democracy ideas into practice were related to the thoughts of Robert Owen. Robert Owen established the first cooperative community of the industrial age in New Harmony, Indiana, in the year 1824. In 1833 he formed the Grand National Consolidated Trade Union, which was to spearhead the movement to put his ideas into practice. Though it was doomed to fade away in a short period of time, the ideas of Robert Owen were to give birth to the cooperative movement in England and other countries. The famous Rochdale Pioneers' Co-operative Society was based on the ideas of Owen.

Robert Owen was only one of several social theorists who contributed significantly to the cooperative movement. The thought of Charles Fourier inspired numerous attempts at cooperative living and also had a major impact upon the cooperative consumer movement. In France, a large number of self-governing workshops were created using the thought of Louis Blanc as the foundation. They, in turn, influenced the socialist fringe of the Christian movement in England, and as a result, cooperative workshops were created there. The same translation of thought into action can be seen in the case of Phillippe Buchez. The association of cabinet makers he created in accordance with his own beliefs eventually came to be used as a model for later producer cooperatives. In this manner the cooperative movement was one expression of the attempt to realize ideas related to workplace democracy.

Expressions of workplace democracy were not always as evolutionary and relatively peaceful as the cooperative movement. The unrest that affected various parts of Europe in 1848 included strident demands by German workers that they be included in the decisions governing their workplaces. Though these demands were not realized until the early 1920s, an important precedent related to action was set. One of the earliest examples of such an attempt at workplace democracy was the Paris Commune of 1871. The circumstances preceding the Paris Commune were no less complicated than the French politics of that period. The entire century, beginning with events related to the French Revolution, was wrought with the most severe unrest. Just prior to the Paris Commune, France had suffered a humiliating defeat in the Franco-Prussian War. After France surrendered, Paris refused to disarm itself, and when Louis Adolphe Thiers attempted to disarm the city by force and failed, the Commune became a reality. The reality was destined to be short-lived, for only during the month of April, 1871, were the elected representatives of the Paris Commune allowed to consider matters other than the defense of the Commune.

The most famous of all writings on the subject is Karl Marx's "The Civil War in France," which was made public a mere two days after the fall of the Commune. Engels observed that since "almost only workers, or recognized representatives of the workers, sat in the Commune, its decisions bore a decidedly proletariat character."[14] This led Marx to describe the essential character of the Commune as follows: "Its true secret is this. It is essentially a working-class government, the product of the struggle of the producing against the appropriating class, the political form at last discovered under which to work out the economic emancipation of labor." [15]

Though Marx clearly oversteps the facts to declare that the Paris Commune of 1871 was an authentic example of the dictatorship of the proletariat, it was indeed important in the history of practice related to workplace democracy. A majority of representatives were not of the working class, nor was the predominant ideological persuasion socialist, or even anarchist in the tradition of Proudhon, but the Commune did act to decree workplace democracy. The representatives announced that abandoned workshops were to be reopened under worker supervision and operation. As a result of military action against it, the Paris Commune came to an end too early to see anything come of the decree, but the verbal action itself was to establish an important precedent.

The next great historical event related to workplace democracy arising from violent means was the Russian Revolution of 1917. Though many theorists including Trotsky, Zinoviev, and Molvo wrote extensively on the Commune, it was Lenin who most completely developed the Commune as a precursor and parallel event to the Russian Revolution. In *Lessons of the Commune, The Problem of a Democratic Dictatorship, Memories of the Commune*, and perhaps most importantly, *The State and Revolution*, Lenin attaches international significance to the Commune: "The soviet power is the second universal-historical step or stage in the development of the Dictatorship of the Proletariat. The first step was the Paris Commune." [16] Lenin, of course, was a theorist whose political-philosophical thoughts were subject to his real world strategy. When the soviets no longer seemed to him to be a viable vehicle to carry Russia to communism, Lenin dropped reference to them as they quickly subsided in importance.

For a while, however, the soviets did function and were associated with the practice of workplace democracy. On February 27, four days after the strike of female textile workers in Petrograd, a soviet was created which combined the interests of Petrograd workers with soldiers. From this beginning, the idea of soviets spread until the provisional government legalized the existence of factory committees on May 23. Though these factory committees were intended to be limited to consultation, they assumed the operation of factories in cases where the factories threatened to close. In the same month the First Petrograd Conference on Factory Committees took place; within that body Lenin pleaded for some form of workers control. Finally in October, the uprising in Petrograd brought the Bolsheviks into power. A mere two weeks later the new government announced that workers' councils would be created to supervise the entire operation of the enterprises. The factory councils were to be responsible to local units of workers. Though the Central Council of Factory Committees insisted that the decisions of factory committees were to be binding on those who administered the enterprises, a new organization was created that challenged this position. The All-Russian Council successfully fought to limit the participation and influence of rank-and-file workers on the operation of their workplaces. Those who supported worker democracy were destined to lose; the first mortal blow came in January 1918 when the First All-Russian Congress of Trade Unions transformed factory committees into local units within the trade union structure. Despite its lack of longevity, the Russian experience in workplace democracy would contribute to the designs and experiences of other nations.

Aside from the Russian Revolution, the circumstances related to World War I provide the other great contribution of the period. It is possible to use Great Britain as an example. Several different movements pushed workplace democracy to the fore in Britain. First were the radical demands that accompanied the syndicalists. Though many provisions made the programme of the syndicalists unpalatable, there is little doubt that their stress on greater worker involvement contributed to the issue of workplace democracy. As early as 1912, syndicalist unions were demanding workers control in the enterprises of coal mining and railways. Of greater relevance was the shop steward movement. The shop steward movement represented a grassroots expression of protest against the leadership of organized unions that entered into no-strike agreements with government against the expressed wishes of the rank-and-file workers. It aimed to replace elite dominance with a system of shop steward representation that would allow the wishes of the workers to be articulated in union policy. This push for decentralized decision making was most clearly a part of the practice of guild socialism. In the years before the war guild socialism began to attract workers' support. During the period a number of small guilds were started. The most dramatic move was the attempt to revive Robert Owen's building guild of 1834. The building guild was most successful for a short number of years, but died in the post war depression.

Given the pressure from these movements and the urgency indicated by the fact that Britain was staggered by as many as one hundred strikes in progress at the onset of World War I, the British government had to respond to the workers discontent. The Whitney committee produced a plan by which employers and employees would be encouraged to cooperate through a system of joint consultation. The process would begin within workplaces by having employers meet with union officials. Cooperation was to be achieved at the district and even the national levels through an extension of the same principles of joint consultation. After the end of World War I, the pressure for cooperation subsided and the system of cooperation gradually faded as well.

Though there were several important attempts to institute worker participation in Europe between the world wars, the next extended period of activity came with the advent of World War II. This is perfectly obvious in the case of Great Britain, where the entire cycle of interest which manifested in relationship to World War I repeated itself with World War II. There does appear to be a cycle of interest in worker participation, but it is not simply a matter of revolving around the same circle, as some critics have claimed.[17] The forthcoming examination of contemporary forms of worker participation will indicate that real progress has been made in securing more complete forms of worker participation; the worker participation cycle is in fact a progressive spiral. Before examining the contemporary forms, however, it is necessary to discuss workplace democracy in American thought and action and set clear standards for the claim of workplace democracy.

In American Thought and Action

In some ways the American experience related to workplace democracy is little more than a reflection of European expressions, especially that of the British. This is quite evident in the American secular utopian settlements. The first attempt at a self-governing cooperative community was the New Harmony, Indiana, settlement of Robert Owen. Owen's vision of the proper way to live can be found in the statement of principles, which were set forth in the New Harmony constitution. "Our objective is that of all sentient beings, Happiness. Our Principles are:

1. Equality of rights, uninfluenced by sex or condition in all adults.

2. Community of property.
3. Freedom of speech and action.
4. Courtesy in all our intercourse.
5. Preservation of health.
6. Acquisition of knowledge.
7. "Obedience to the laws of the country in which we live." [18]

From these principles emerge a vision of community life that is energetic, participatory, and integrative. It is unfortunate that the reality of New Harmony was to be different. Despite these principles, there was very little to bind individuals to the community. This problem was aggravated by Owen, who, expecting that his ideas would spread to all, refused to turn away people because they were unfit. The centrifugal effects of individualistic squabblings could not be prevented. At one point the elected officials of the community decided to bring back Owen as an authoritarian leader, but it was too late to save the community. New Harmony as a collective community dissolved in a relatively short period of time, but not before it left its indelible mark on America.

Many of the same things can be said in evaluating other secular utopian settlements in America. In the case of Charles Fourier, it was not he, but his enthusiastic supporters who brought his message to America. Among the most famous of his followers were Prosper Considerant, Albert Brisbane, and Horace Greeley. Through the decade extending from 1843 to 1853, as many as forty phalanstéres were created in America. Though Brook Farm was the most famous, the most successful was established at Red Bank, New York. The Fourier settlements suffered the same internal decline, stemming from unadulterated individualism.

America, providing the perfect climate for utopia, was also the setting for many religious utopian attempts. Many of these proved to be much more successful than their secular counterparts because they did provide a force to unify individuals. The religious principles that acted as a unifying force, however, also acted as a restriction upon the free expression of individuals. Without the opportunity to participate individually in the decision making related to the community, these communities often did not contribute substantially to the tradition of workplace democracy in America.

There were other attempts at cooperative producing, but these were related to the trade-union movement. The earliest known producer cooperative was created in 1791, when a group of striking carpenters in Philadelphia organized their own cooperative. In the 1860s the National Labor Union established a successful stove foundry at Troy, New York. Another major attempt at cooperative producing was made by the Knights of Labor in 1883. They invested a relatively large amount of money in a cooperative coal mine in Cannelburg, Indiana, but their efforts came to nothing, as the railroad refused to create a link from the mine to their line. When syndicalism came to America, the organization most responsible for its transformation into industrial unionism was the Industrial Workers of the World. They, too, entertained notions of producer cooperatives, but since their ultimate goal was a complete overthrow of capitalism, much more of their attention was directed toward the revolutionary effort. The best sources of description for this group are the writings of and about Daniel De Leon, who lectured at Columbia University in international law and became the leader of the Socialist Party soon after he joined it in 1890. In a much less radical manner, unions are related to worker participation in America by the attempts government instituted to foster management and labor cooperation during periods of world war. These joint consultation efforts experienced the same life cycles as those in Britain, with interest waning quickly after the close of war.

The link between workplace democracy and industrial unionism is important because of the American tendency to associate workplace democracy with unions. In fact, it might be very useful and rewarding to contrast the previous description of cooperative producing with the American *usage* of the general term, "industrial democracy," or its equivalent. The source for many of the references will be Milton Derber's work, *The American Idea of Industrial Democracy*.[19]

The American history of the term "industrial democracy" began with the January, 1887 edition of the unsuccessful journal, *Work and Wages*.[20] In that issue a condemnation of organized labor's coercion of unorganized labor appeared in a short article entitled "Industrial Democracy." In the same year, N. O. Nelson addressed the American Association of Social Science concerning his plan for profit sharing, a plan Nelson considered to be a form of industrial democracy.[21] Though these examples represent the first time that the actual phrase, *industrial democracy*, appeared in American print, they were not the first time that an equivalent reference was recorded. Fully a century prior to Nelson, Albert Gallatin introduced a system of profit-sharing into his American glasswares enterprise, claiming that the "democratic principle on which this nation was founded should not be restricted to the political process but should be applied to the industrial operations as well." [22]

Sporadic references to industrial democracy continued to appear prior to the turn of the century. In 1893 Henry D. Lloyd, an economist and journalist with legal training, addressed the annual convention of the American Federation of Labor. Lloyd predicted that industrial democracy would follow inevitably from the existence of "political democracy," and proclaimed that it was the right of those who do the work to determine "the hours of labour, the conditions of employment, the division of the produce." [23] The same economic theme is echoed by the Reverend Lyman Abbott. In his article, "Industrial Democracy," which appeared in *The Forum*, Abbott insisted that workers deserve the entire value of their produce. [24] For the workers to receive their fair share, however, Henry C. Adams averred that workers must have a form of property rights, and, as he announced in his presidential address to the American Economic Association in December, 1896, Adams foresaw property rights evolving through collective bargaining and the formal labor contract. [25] In this way industrial democracy became linked with the growth of unions.

Many of the American writings that interpreted industrial democracy as trade unionism centered upon the English work of Sidney and Beatrice Webb, *Industrial Democracy* (1897). [26] This is not in the least bit surprising, given the fact that American and English thought and action are closely tied regarding the workplace and forms of decision making within that community. In the years immediately following its publication, Milton Derber was able to count at least three extensive American reviews and no less than five minor ones. [27] The Webbs continued the linkage between unionism and industrial democracy within the theoretical fabric of a functional representational system in which consumers determined what was to be produced, management determined how production was to occur, and unions determined the conditions of work production. The general fusion of industrial democracy with unionism was nearly complete by the turn of the century. Derber stated that by "1902 the U. S. Industrial Commission was treating industrial democracy as a term well imbedded in the jargon of industrial relations." [28] This commission's final report stated that "by the organization of labor, and by no other means, it is possible to introduce an element of democracy in the government of industry." [29] The conception of industrial democracy, which links it to unions, so predominates that Milton Derber's history of the American idea of industrial democracy is almost exclusively a history of trade unionism in America.

There emerge from this examination three conceptions of industrial democracy in early American usage: industrial democracy as profit-sharing, as functional representation, and most clearly as trade unionism, with its accompanying collective bargaining. It is interesting to note that each of these usages has linkages to liberal thought and its view of democracy. Given the rather strict division between the public and private in liberal thought, the standard liberal position would not have us apply "political" democracy to the workplace. Indeed, that was and still is the dominant position in America and Britain. But if one were to entertain notions of applying democracy to the industrial sphere, it should be a liberal-democratic form. Thus it is not surprising to find each of the forms in early American usage tied strongly to each other and to liberal doctrines. Captured well within the American usage is the liberal and utilitarian principle of maximizing benefits, while minimizing costs, or more specifically, maximizing the interests of the workers (and other groups), while minimizing the costs of participation. This is accomplished by having workers engage in the minimal exercise of electing representatives, union leaders, who then negotiate on behalf of the workers with other representatives, representing still other interests. In such a manner, trade unionism and functional representation are neatly tied within the embrace of liberalism. More modern writings in the English-American tradition highlight the connection. Hugh Clegg's *A New Approach to Industrial Democracy* is anything but new. It is a perfect application of liberal democracy to the workplace, complete with individual rights and liberties, parties of competing interest, and representative government. The Collective contract is the mechanism by which various interests are synthesized in industrial democracy. As Clegg states unambiguously, "industrial democracy must for the most part confine itself to protecting rights and interests."[30] He does not accept the proposition that the rights of workers must be secured so that workers may participate in workplace decisions, for in Clegg's view, it "is impossible for workers to share directly in management."[31]

Given the emphasis on maximizing interests, it is easy for liberalism to lapse into labelling as democratic those measures which enhance interest. This accounts for the confusion in the American and also the English usage of profit-sharing as a form of industrial democracy.

The view of democracy essentially as government *for* the people can lead to much more disturbing confusion. In the history of writings on workplace decision making, there has probably never been a less democratic system than Frederick Taylor's scientific management. Yet Frederick Taylor himself refers to scientific management as industrial democracy, on the basis that the rules that govern the workplace would be codified, and all, including the workers, will benefit. What is even worse, Milton Derber includes scientific management in his historical survey of the American idea of industrial democracy, without even a comment to the contrary.[32]

Though the protection of workers' rights and the enhancement of their interests are important, and in fact, are related to workplace democracy (the former as a precondition, the latter as a result), they are not themselves the defining characteristics of democracy in the workplace. Workplace democracy is more faithfully captured in the American tradition of producer cooperatives, as previously surveyed. Fortunately, there is recognition of this more bona fide tradition in early American usage, but seldom were references to a participatory conception of democracy part of systematic bodies of political thought. Richard T. Ely, whom many consider to be the dean of labor historians, defined industrial democracy in 1889 as "self-rule, self-control, the self-direction of the masses in their efforts to gain a livelihood . . . industrial self-government."[33] An equally clear expression is offered by Louis Brandeis. In his testimony before the United States Commission on Industrial Relations, Brandeis presents a very sophisticated discussion of workplace democracy. He distinguishes workplace democracy very clearly from trade unionism and collective bargaining, as it existed in his time. To have workplace democracy, there "must be a division not only of profits, but a division also of responsibilities. The employees must have the opportunity of participating in the decisions as to what shall be their condition and how the business shall be run."[34] It is a participatory conception of workplace decision making which deserves to be called workplace democracy.

Theoretical Development and Application

The difficulties that exist in conceptualizing workplace democracy are more related to the term *democracy*, than *workplace*. Democracy is a system of community rule, and workplace merely specifies the community. As such, *workplace democracy* is much more desirable than many other phrases intended to capture the same phenomenon. Certainly, it is much more sensible than the unfortunate liberal phraseology, *economic democracy*, which unsuccessfully attempts to transcend its own conceptual barriers. *Workplace democracy* is more meaningful than the more-often-used phrase *industrial democracy*, for industrial democracy does not specify the community in which democracy occurs. It is possible to take "industrial" to mean industrial workplace, but to do so is to restrict the phenomenon unnecessarily. Though industrial workplaces are important to our analysis, commercial, service, craft, and many other varieties of workplaces ought not be excluded. Democracy is appropriate to all places of work, and so *workplace democracy* is a much more useful expression. To appreciate fully this conclusion, it is necessary to examine the notion of democracy. Though the most substantial problem in conceptualizing workplace democracy lies in the effort to bring clarity to the befuddling concept of democracy, the effort already has been expended. It would serve us to return to the previous theoretical discussion of democracy.

The second chapter began with a literal translation of democracy as that system in which the people rule and offered a process conceptualization as the most appropriate elaboration of that literal translation. Democracy does not necessarily depend on a particular institutional configuration, nor is it simply the embodiment of a particular set of values. It does not relate directly to the content of decisions. This is a very important point, for there is a tendency to proclaim as democratic whatever accords with our values. What distinguishes a system as democratic is the way in which decisions are reached. To be considered democratic, a system's method of decision making must entail widespread and effective participation—in no other way can the people be said to rule. On the basis of these assertions, the following definition of democracy was advanced: democracy is a type of community rule in which the process of decision making generally entails widespread and effective participation of community members.

The definition places particular emphasis upon the concepts of community and participation. *Community* refers to a group of people bound into self-conscious units by common interests, concerns, and problems. Though the most readily identifiable communities are the neighborhood, city, county, state and nation, not all communities are formally political or geographically discrete—not all communities are governmental. By direct implication, democracy may be a system of decision making not only of governments (formally political and geo-graphically discrete communities), but also of religious, fraternal, ethnic, and professional groups as well (not formally political or geo-graphically discrete communities). Democracy may apply to the work-place, if consciousness of community is present among the workers. This consciousness of community may apply as well to communities that exist within the overarching workplace community. By definition, workplace democracy would be that type of workplace rule in which the process of decision making generally entails widespread and effective participation of workplace members. It is most important to stress that democracy in the workplace is as much democracy as de-mocracy in government or any other community.

The definition openly acknowledges that participation in decision making is the essential element of democracy. The two concepts are interwoven in such a manner that as participation within a commu-nity increases, so does the degree of democracy. The definitional asso-ciation between the two puts so much emphasis on participation that a more sophisticated conceptualization of it is required. This, of course, is achieved by conceiving of participation as a multidimensional, rather than unidimensional phenomenon. Participation in the work-place may be assessed along the following dimensions: extensity, scope, mode, intensity, and quality. Each of these will be discussed in terms of the workplace community.

The *extensity* of participation refers to the proportion as well as the absolute number of community members who participate in the deci-sions of their workplace. Since extensity is based on community mem-bership, it is important to specify who belongs to the community of any particular workplace. Everyone who is employed by the work-place should be considered members of that community. This means that secretaries and part-time help, as well as the managers and con-sultants, are members of the community and must be taken into consideration when measuring the extensity of participation. The di-mension of extensity is of particular significance to the workplace community, for historically, the proportion of all workers who partici-pate in the workplace decisions has been restricted severely. Such re-strictions in participation cannot be justified in terms of democracy, even though some have made the attempt by claiming that those re-stricted from participation were not really community members. Workplace democracy is curtailed to the degree that extensity is limited.

The *scope* of participation refers to the number and type of issues available for the members of the workplace community to determine. Since issues vary in a number of important ways, including how many people are affected and the ways that they are affected, it is advisable not to lump them all together. Taking a single tier corporate structure as an example, scope can be viewed in terms of the level at which decisions are made. Scope varies from the individual level, through the shopfloor and work community levels, to the corporate level, and even beyond, to extracorporate level decisions.

The *mode* of participation pertains to the actual form that participation assumes. As ideal abstractions, there are a limited number of conventional forms of participation relevant to the workplace. They would include minimal forms of input, face-to-face discussion, voting for representatives who make the decisions, actually making decisions oneself, and the like. The concept of mode takes on substance when put in relationship with decision making at a particular level of the enterprise. At any particular level of workplace decision making, it is possible to distinguish modes of participation with a negligible relationship to decision making, modes with an indirect relationship with decision making, and modes with a direct relationship.

A fourth dimension to be considered is the *intensity* of participation. Intensity relates to the psychological involvement of individuals in the act of participation. Intensity is closely associated with the mode of participation in such a way that, as the mode of participation becomes more direct, intensity is likely to increase. Despite the close connection, it is important to keep the two dimensions separate. Sometimes participation that is direct, and should be intense, is not. This could spell disaster for worker participation schemes reliant upon intense participation on the part of workers. At other times, participation that is very indirect may be accompanied by an intense involvement on the part of workers. This situation could result in a number of different outcomes, including a high level of frustration among workers who believe that their efforts are for naught, or possibly the exploitation of workers who believe that their energetic efforts make a difference when they in fact do not. Discussion of the next dimension will make apparent how this can happen.

The last dimension of participation is the *quality* of participation; it relates to whether the activity on the part of workers actually has an impact upon decisions made within the workplace. If the activity does not have such an impact, regardless of the way the workers feel, the activity is pseudoparticipation. Therein lies the potential for manipulation. There are benefits to be derived from worker participation, benefits that may result if workers feel they are involved in the decision-making process. Managers often are tempted to extend the illusion of participation to workers, thereby benefiting from the workers' involvement, without relinquishing any managerial prerogatives. There must be an objective, as well as subjective, content for participation to be genuine.

These five dimensions—extensity, scope, mode, intensity and quality—provide the basis by which the degree of democracy in any community, including the workplace community, can be assessed. When gauging the degree of democracy in a workplace, it is most useful to survey first the range of issues available for worker participation (scope), and then, in reference to those issues, inquire as to which workers participate (extensity), in what manner they participate (mode), to what degree of involvement (intensity), and with what impact upon the decisions (quality). The most democratic of all *imaginable* workplaces would be one in which all of the workers participate in the most direct fashion, with full intensity, in all of the workplace decisions, having a full impact upon those decisions. This situation, however, would be no more possible than it would be desirable. It illustrates clearly why democracy cannot be equated with what is good; no matter how desirable democracy may appear, there are always other values to consider.

On a practical level, it is very difficult to specify precisely the degree of democracy in the workplace, or any other community. The measurement of the various dimensions of participation cannot be that exact, and even when it is, the levels of participation are in constant flux. Each unit of a particular dimension cannot be taken as equivalent in importance to every other unit. For example, it is probably more important to democracy to increase a dimension when it is very low than to increase the same dimension by the same number of units when it is relatively high. It also is unlikely that one unit of a particular dimension can be taken as the equivalent of one unit of another dimension; thus an analyst must be very careful when compiling the scores of various dimensions to achieve an overall assessment of democracy in a workplace. The situation is complicated further by the fact that there tends to be a significant amount of interaction and trade-off among the various dimensions. In large communities, for example, the more extensity increases, the more likely the mode and intensity will decrease. Nevertheless, the five dimensions of participation do provide the basis by which some accurate assessment of democracy in a workplace can be offered. Moreover, democracy qua participation does create the potential for a comparative democratic study of workplaces and an evaluation of competing claims to workplace democracy. At the very least the dimensions direct our attention to various aspects of workplace participation, and we can maintain that as any dimension of participation increases in a workplace, with all other dimensions remaining the same, democracy can be said to have increased in that workplace.

Though it is participation along the five dimensions, not worker rights and liberties, which earmarks democracy, such phenomena should be considered in a discussion of workplace democracy. The various conditions of democracy do not constitute democracy, but it is rather impossible to achieve democracy without them. The breakdown of the barriers between what is public and what is private makes obvious the necessity of applying what had been considered "political" or "civil" rights to the workplace. Workers will not be able to participate in the decisions that affect their lives in the workplace unless they have the freedom to speak, to assemble, and to oppose management without the fear of reprisal. The issue of worker rights and liberties has become current under the titles of "corporate constitutionalism" and "industrial citizenship" and has attracted a number of American advocates. To truly encourage participation, however, simply removing the formal restraints to participation is not enough. Workers must be provided with all the information necessary to participate intelligently, they must be educated to understand the dimensions of the issues they are deciding, and they must be trained in the skills that will allow them to participate effectively. Only then will they have the freedom to participate as well as the freedom from restraints on participation.

Contemporary Forms of Worker Participation

Workplace democracy requires worker participation that is both widespread and effective. Though such extensive participation is seldom achieved in our world, there are numerous efforts to at least extend the boundaries of worker participation. Since this section will provide a panoramic view of worker participation forms, a guide to the discussion should be offered. Of the remarkably varied participation schemes on the international scene, three forms dominate: collective bargaining, joint consultation, and codetermination. These forms are not mutually exclusive, but it is best at first to treat them as if they were. In other words, each will be discussed as an ideal type. After each of the forms is analyzed at the *corporate* level in terms of the five dimensions of participation, the focus will shift to *subcorporate* levels of participation. This discussion, which relies heavily upon the various international expressions of worker participation, will indicate that the major forms do combine with each other in actual experience. The three major forms and their combinations, however, do not provide individual workers or working groups with sufficient opportunity to participate at the shopfloor level, and so other forms of participation must be entertained. They include: job enlargement, job enrichment, and autonomous working groups. To achieve workplace democracy, participation at all levels of the workplace must be achieved. The international scene again will be surveyed for examples which best express extensive and effective forms of worker participation. The entire discussion will close with a mention of other international examples, and a brief examination of worker participation forms in the United States.

Though there is considerable debate on the issue, collective bargaining is viewed by many as a form of worker participation. Collective bargaining generally is predicated on a sharp division between labor and management, their interests, and the roles they should assume. The natural antagonism ascribed to management and labor is institutionalized. Management is granted the right to manage, and labor, organized into unions that represent its interest, is granted the right to respond to that management. The two sides meet periodically to discuss the terms and conditions of work. Since management and labor are forever divorced by contrary and irreconcilable interests, the mode of participation available to workers is one of conflict. The negotiations between the two adversary parties is constantly subject to breakdown; thus strikes and lockouts remain an integral part of the collective bargaining system.

The actual range of issues over which collective bargaining occurs varies to an extraordinary degree. On the international scene, there is a strong emphasis on union activity and collective bargaining at high levels of decision making related to work. It is common to find the focus of a union's attention to be at the corporate level, the industry-wide level, or even at the national level. Collective bargaining is usually a force wherever nations have well-developed union organizations. Collective bargaining thus has been very important in England, Israel, Sweden and Germany. Collective bargaining has developed in less likely places such as Japan, however, where collective bargaining matured side-by-side with joint consultation in the present form of quality circles. Collective bargaining as a conflict mode of participation is particularly hostile in nations where the distinctions between labor and management are most sharply drawn, such as France and Italy.

A common form of worker participation is joint consultation between employers and employees. The assumption behind joint consultation is relatively simple: there is no necessary and all-pervasive antagonism between employers and employees. If management (or its representatives) could explain to workers (or their representatives) what they were thinking of doing, and if workers could react to those plans and inform employers of their interests and problems, then work might be conducted in a more cooperative manner to the mutual satisfaction and benefit of all. Probably the greatest impetus to joint consultation was war. When the strains of war placed severe demands on the economy of those countries involved, and on the productive capacity of their workplaces, joint consultation represented a possible remedy. Numerous committees of joint consultation were formed before and during World Wars I and II in England and other nations. After the Second World War, there was a veritable explosion of attempts at joint consultation. Part of the reason for this was the widely held belief that joint consultation was a near necessity in the effort to make nationalized industries work properly. Joint consultation was established in Norway in 1945, Finland in 1946, Denmark in 1947, Belgium in 1947, Japan in 1948, and the Netherlands in 1950. By 1951 thirty nations had established formal and permanent structures of joint consultation.

Joint consultation is widely in operation today and seems to be spreading even to nations which do not require it by law. In England, which has no national provisions for joint consultation (although there are some remnants remaining from previous world wars), there is renewed interest in the idea; some harmony must be sought between labor and management in that very shaky economy. One example of a move in that direction has occurred at British Leyland, where a system of joint consultation was instituted at the corporate level, as well as at levels within the workplace.

Codetermination is most clearly associated with corporate level decision making, especially the decision making of the corporation's board of directors. Codetermination is a system whereby worker representatives are granted voting privileges at the board level. The proportion of board members chosen by workers, how those representatives are selected, and what range of issues are decided within the board vary somewhat from nation to nation.

The most notable example of codetermination is the system in West Germany. The German system of *Mitbestimmung* (translated "having a voice") was initiated in the coal, iron, and steel industries not long after the close of World War II (1950–51). Within these industries parity was achieved between worker representatives and stockholder representatives to the supervisory board (*Aufsichtsrat*). When the provisions for codetermination were not soon extended to the rest of German industry, a general strike was threatened. To ameliorate the situation, the German legislature passed the Works Constitution Act, which provided for one-third workers' representatives at board levels. In 1976 this was extended, and by law all companies with more than 2,000 employees must arrange for the election of as many worker directors as stockholder representatives. This does not threaten the board with deadlock, however, for the stockholders retain the right to appoint the chairman of the board, who in the case of a tie may cast a double vote.

Because of the general success of the German economy and its remarkable recovery since World War II, the German model has been the subject of emulation. Since 1973, Swedish companies employing over 100 people have had two worker directors on their boards. This was altered in 1976 to include every Swedish company employing more than 25 people. In Austrian companies with more than 300 workers, one third of their board is elected by workers. There are worker representatives on corporate boards in Norway, Denmark, and Luxembourg as well. Though the Netherlands do not have worker representatives as such, the workers do have a veto power over the appointees to the board. The German idea has spread beyond Europe. Venezuela, for example, provides for workers' representation on the board of directors in all state-owned companies.

Having briefly described the operation of the three major forms of worker participation at the corporate level of workplace issues, it is possible to consider each form in light of the participatory dimensions of workplace democracy. Thus collective bargaining, joint consultation, and codetermination will be viewed in terms of the scope, extensity, mode, intensity, and the quality of participation which they provide.

In many ways, collective bargaining is the least participatory form of worker participation examined. A major problem with the system of collective bargaining is its limitation on the scope of participation. The very fact that unions grant management the ability and right to make all decisions necessary to manage means that workers are not being given the opportunity to participate in the large set of issues that belong to the province of management. Given the emphasis on the adversary relationship between management and unions, the issues that demand cooperation rather than conflict settlement likewise are denied workers. Scope is further limited through the operation of union leaders designating which issues are worthy of collective bargaining. Since collective bargaining on the international scene tends to operate from the top of the unions down to the rank and file union members, this filtering of issues can be a very significant limitation upon scope.

An even more severe problem is indicated by the last evaluative statement: collective bargaining often does not provide for high levels of the extensity of participation. Since collective bargaining operates through unions, the average worker is already once removed from decision making. This situation is aggravated by the fact that union leaders tend to dominate participation within unions. This threat is very real. As the shop-steward revolt in England indicated, there is a real potential for unions to operate without workers providing input to union leaders and there is far less chance of making the actual decisions. This generally is an accurate description of what was the case in Sweden prior to recent changes in their collective bargaining system. Collective bargaining was characterized by economy-wide negotiations between central federations of employers' associations and groups of trade union associations. The results usually entailed the superimposition of bargaining on the whole industry, with very little bargaining, and thus participation, occurring at the plant level.

The other dimensions of participation are similarly limited. With collective bargaining occurring at the upper levels of corporate decision making (if not industry or national levels), the mode of the average worker's participation is bound to be restricted to input to the union leadership and voting on the contracts arranged by the union. Such an arrangement is likely to produce intense participation only among the few union leaders close to decision making. Since there is usually little pretense related to participation within collective-bargaining systems, the quality of worker participation that is apparent tends also to be real. If unions are not at least minimally receptive to the input of their members, however, they do run the risk of wild-cat strikes and other forms of revolt. Overall, collective bargaining, especially when it is directed to high corporate levels, is a better system of promoting what is perceived by the union leadership to be in the best interest of the workers, than it is a system to promote worker participation. In this regard it is very apparent that collective bargaining and liberal-democratic thought are connected historically. Liberal democracy provided the perfect foundation for a system that attempted to represent workers' interest through the operation of elites (union leaders), who compete for the votes of the rank-and-file workers. The "market analogy," so characteristic of liberal democracy, applies as well to collective bargaining. As far as workplace democracy is concerned, collective bargaining cannot take us very far. This is most emphatically the case when the unions themselves are not internally democratic and thus do not achieve high levels of participation.

At upper levels of decision making concerning work, joint consultation does improve the quality of communication, but as a form of worker participation, it can be as limited, or even more limited, than collective bargaining. The scope of participation under systems of joint consultation is subject to considerable variation, with joint consultation in some nations restricted to matters of efficient production and those few issues upon which workers are likely to be the most sensitive. Joint consultation is invariably a representational system and thus only the representatives of workers, whether they be union representative or not, are clearly involved in participation. For the average worker to have much of an impact upon joint consultation at high levels of decision making, there must exist strong links between the workers are even less direct in their relationship to decision making. Intensity is seldom high among the rank-and-file workers, even if it is ticipation. Since the worker representatives themselves are not able to make decisions, or vote as part of the decision making, their mode is restricted to face-to-face discussions. The modes for all the rest of the workers are even less direct in their relationship to decision making.

Intensity is seldom high among the rank-and-file workers, even if it is sometimes high among those who represent workers in consultation with management. The consideration of quality of participation is crucial when dealing with joint consultation. Since there are no voting privileges extended to the representatives of workers, the risk is always present that workers will think that they are participating in the decision making of the workplace, when all they are doing is legitimizing the decisions of management. Joint consultation perpetually threatens to degenerate into pseudoparticipation, and only active and vigilant worker representatives can prevent it from doing so.

Systems of codetermination do remedy some of the problems confronting joint consultation by providing worker representatives with the right to vote on issues raised at meetings of the board of directors, but they do not resolve all of the problems related to achieving extensive and effective worker participation. One may question whether anything less than a fifty/fifty split between worker representatives and stockholder representatives merits the title of codetermination. Beyond this consideration, codetermination encounters some of the same problems in the scope of participation as joint consultation, and occasionally even more. Since workers are actually voting on the board, serious attention must be paid to the scope of issues considered by the boards. In Germany and in most other nations that have forms of codetermination, the board is divided into two tiers, with workers clearly represented only on one. The first tier, often called the supervisory board, generally has three main responsibilities: to establish an investment policy, to approve plans of the management board, and to appoint at least the director of the management board. The second tier, the management board, is entrusted with the responsibility of executing the general policies of the supervisory board. Worker representation is directed to the supervisory board, but not the board of management. This represents a curtailment of the scope of participation, since it is often in the administration of policy that policy is given shape and substance. Another indication of the limited scope of issues addressed by the supervisory board is that in Germany, and most of the other nations with such a system, the supervisory board only meets four or five times a year. Though there are real limitations to the scope of participation when considering worker representation on the board of directors, the point should not be pushed too far. Boardroom representation does bring the workers into contact with a set of issues to which they might not otherwise gain exposure, the supervisory board can hold the management board accountable for its actions in the execution of supervisory board policy, and at least in the German case, the personnel director of the management board is nominated by the union.

In most European cases, codetermination arose out of national legislation promoted by unions and sponsored by political parties aligned with labor. Thus a large part of the credit for codetermination belongs to the unions. The dominant presence of unions in codetermination, however, can effect adversely the participation of workers within the workplace. By the provisions of the 1976 German legislation, a large portion of the worker representatives to the supervisory board will be proposed by the union from among their own professionals, and in most cases will not be employees of the company on whose board they will serve. The movement of codetermination is toward greater union representation rather than worker representation as such. Even if the union representatives do an admirable job of representing the interests of the companies' workers, which is subject to some question given the close relationship between participation and quality interest representation, worker participation within the workplace community may be affected by a system that removes a large portion of worker representatives from the workers. Certainly the mode and intensity will be weakened for the relationship to decision making has been made less direct. There is also the possibility that the quality of worker participation will be undermined, given the less direct relationship it has to decision making at the corporate level. Nevertheless, codetermination is a considerably more democratic system than either collective bargaining or joint consultation.

Though each of these forms have clear weaknesses in terms of increasing worker participation, and a more elaborate form of workplace democracy can be imagined, part of the problem in assessing collective bargaining, joint consultation, and codetermination in terms of workplace democracy has been the level of the decision making analyzed. It is difficult to avoid the conclusion of Sturmthal in his assessment of German codetermination: "There is no point denying that high-level forms of industrial democracy do little to bring about genuine workers' participation and may, in fact, widen the gap between the worker and his union."[35] By the conceptualization that has been adopted, workplace democracy cannot be achieved without worker participation, and it is difficult to achieve high levels of effective participation at high levels of decision making related to work.

Achieving participatory democracy in any community will be related to devolving decision making to the lowest level at which issues can be resolved. Let us then consider the international forms of worker participation that deal with issues within the workplace and on the shop-floor level.

Since the same set of forms tend to dominate the participation of workers within the workplace, there is no need to deal again with basic definitions. It is advisable to consider at this point, however, that the forms of collective bargaining, joint consultation, and codetermination are not mutually exclusive. Collective bargaining can and often does combine with the other forms of worker participation by specifying spheres in which cooperation is possible and spheres in which it is best for management to make the decisions and representatives of workers to react to those decisions. The greatest trouble in combining collective bargaining with more cooperative forms of participation relates to adversary mentality, which sometimes pervades collective bargaining. When the lines between management and labor are drawn very distinctly any cooperation between the two may appear to be collaboration with the enemy. It is also possible for joint consultation and codetermination to combine at the same level of decision making, but in practice, one form or the other tends to dominate. At the same level of decision making, the net tends to be cast wide, and either workers are granted the right to vote on various issues, or they are only allowed to discuss and influence those decisions. This is not as true at different levels of decision making. It is very possible for one of the three forms of worker participation to dominate at one level of decision making, and to have another prevail at a different level. As we investigate the various forms of decision making within the workplace community, it is worth remembering that the difference among the three forms is often slight, with one form blending into another.

Collective bargaining within the workplace community occurs within many nations, but nowhere is it more clear and sophisticated than in England and Sweden, two nations in which trade unionism is well developed and historically entrenched. As previous discussions have indicated, the focus of collective bargaining in England once was at the corporate and industry level, if not even higher. This created a vacuum at the workplace level and encouraged the shop steward movement as a rebellion against that fact. Britain now has more than a third of a million shop stewards and other groups of people in the process of employee representation, which probably means that it leads the rest of Europe in the number of people involved. This does not mean that worker representation is best accomplished in Britain. The dominance of collective bargaining and the adversary mentality has made it very difficult to achieve cooperative forms of participation, such as joint consultation and codetermination. It was as late as 1973 that the Trade Union Congress began to switch its position in favor of codetermination à la West Germany, and then only with dissension in its ranks. The TUC has not been able to convince many other unions of the desirability of this position. This is a crucial factor since English workplaces have multiple union representation. Sometimes as many as two dozen unions are involved in the collective bargaining process within the largest of corporations. The struggle that the Bullock report encountered (a system of codetermination in which labor would choose one third of the directors, shareholders would choose one third, and the remaining one third would be chosen jointly), when it made its recommendations provides another indication of the difficulty of leaving behind a pure conflict mode. Collective bargaining may be an appropriate way to determine who gets what share of the pie, but it often requires a more cooperative mode to increase the actual size of the pie. Without a more cooperative form added to collective bargaining, it will be difficult for Britain to remain economically competitive with the rest of Europe. Given the disjointed nature of collective bargaining, and the tendency for each to protect his own, it will be very difficult to revamp the system.

Sweden has been much more successful at integrating various forms of worker participation. Its system of joint consultation, which had 2,650 firms participating by 1950,[36] and its system of having two worker representatives on the board of every company employing more than 100 people, is complemented within the workplace community with works councils. Swedish works councils, representative groups elected by employees to deal with shop-floor matters, are used to augment the collective-bargaining system. In reaction to the renown of Article 32 of the Swedish Employers Confederation statutes, which granted employers exclusive rights to "direct and distribute the work,"[37] Swedish workers have been nibbling away at such absolute managerial prerogatives. It should be stressed, however, that the occurring changes relate explicitly to the unions, not generally to workers. The unions retain the right to strike over codetermination, even when there are no-strike provisions in the contract. By a 1975 agreement, employers are obligated to provide the unions, not the rank and file workers, with information concerning the finances of the company, and if the union representatives of the workers cannot understand the information they are given, the company is further obligated to train the representatives or hire consultants to help them understand. Though management still retains the right to make final decisions within the workplace in most areas, the local union may negotiate with management such things as its investments, marketing, and the like. Through the unions, employees may refuse to perform work that they feel is outside their job classification, and may refuse to perform work that they feel is unsafe. As a matter of fact, Swedish firms have safety ombudsmen who can halt production entirely when they judge the situation to be unsafe. Furthermore, unions may resist a company's decision to contract out portions of work, which the union feels rightly belongs to the company's own employees. With the recent national legislation and agreements between Swedish labor and management, the thrust of workplace reform is clear: strengthen collective bargaining at the long neglected level of the shopfloor.

The limited amount of worker participation in France is actually a hybrid form of collective bargaining. The emphasis in France is on her *comités d'entreprise* (works councils of sorts), and "reform of the enterprise" is the phrase that currently carries the most meaning. Since 1946 it has been compulsory for industrial concerns employing more than fifty workers to establish a works committee that represents the manual workers as well as the technical grades. Major managerial acts must be submitted to these committees for concurrence, and if it is not obtained, compulsory arbitration is evoked. The committees may send nonvoting members to attend meetings of the board of directors, they may ask management to provide information, and they have the additional right of appeal to the board, if questions asked management are not clearly answered. Despite some talk of *autogestion*, opportunities for workers to participate in French workplaces are quite limited. It was only after the events of May, 1968, that unions bothered to place representatives in each workplace. This is very significant, for trade unions play an important part in French society. The opposition of many unions has placed severe limitations on forms of cooperative exchange between labor and management.

Since joint consultation is perceived as a rather innocuous form of worker participation, numerous examples of joint consultation operate within workplace communities of most industrialized nations of the world. When joint consultation is not established by national legislation, it occurs at the initiative of individual enterprises. Though joint consultation is associated with industrialized nations, it has been emulated by less developed nations. In its first year of independence (1947), India passed an act prescribing works committees, and by 1959, there were 3,133 such works committees in existence.[38]

The Germans use their institution of works councils for an extension of codetermination. By the law of 1952, works councils (*Betriebsräte*), representing both wage and salaried employees, must be elected in all establishments employing five full-time workers or more. The powers of the works councils are concentrated in codetermination rights regarding specific aspects of personnel management. The Works Constitution Act of 1972 substantially added to the powers of the councils. Most of the new provisions deal with matters that relate to the day-to-day operation of companies. The newly expanded scope of issues include working hours, use of devices to monitor workers, and some instances of wage-rate setting, to the degree not precluded by collective-bargaining agreements. Hiring, firing, promotion, allocation of work assignments, and transfers require consent in advance by the works councils. The councils have an equal say in regard to such issues as job evaluation, wage structures, training, discipline, recruitment, and holidays. In areas in which the councils have been granted codetermination rights with management, but no agreement is reached with management, the issue is resolved by German labor courts. The works councils may be influential even beyond this range of issues. Though they have no explicit powers with regard to many of the business aspects of the enterprise, in companies that employee more than 100 people the councils appoint economic committees, which are entitled to information on production programs and company finances. Employers still have the final say regarding investment, but if investments result in massive lay-offs, then the council can go to court and force employers to retrain and place displaced workers. The councils cannot call strikes, but issues emerging from the councils can be picked up by the unions and possibly become subjects for future strikes. All things considered, the legal provisions accorded the works councils in Germany may exceed those provided similar institutions in other countries.

These forms of worker participation do provide a useful addition to the varieties of participation that address upper levels of decision making by having worker representatives address issues within the workplace. Taken collectively, however, they fall short of achieving high levels of participation for the rank-and-file workers. Despite the large number of shop stewards involved in the British system of collective bargaining, it does not provide for adequate opportunity for collective bargaining at the level where all workers can participate in the process—the shopfloor. The Swedes have a more elaborate structure in their works council, but only recently has it addressed the problem of participation at the shopfloor level. Since all of the participation is carefully filtered through the union structure, there are real limitations on the participation of the average worker. The German variety of works councils is probably more effective, and certainly is a substantial improvement over what existed before 1972, but the system does not provide many opportunities for participation beyond that of voting for members of the works council. The council itself seldom meets more than four or five times a year with the assembly of plant workers. Actually, the most energetic activity involving the works council concerns its meetings with management, for they must occur by law at least once every four weeks.

To achieve, or even approach achieving workplace democracy, the opportunity to make decisions must be brought to the level of the individual and his immediate work group. This is reflected in the various dimensions of workplace participation. Only with direct participation at the individual and work-group level—along with quality indirect participation at higher levels—can the scope of participation be truly expansive. It is only with the opportunity to do more than vote for those who represent the workers that full extensity of participation is likely to be achieved. Quite obviously, participation modes will be enhanced only when workers themselves are given the opportunity to directly participate in matters that concern them in their immediate work environment, the work group. Intensity of participation cannot be achieved without direct participation opportunities. Finally, the only sure way to achieve participation of high quality is for workers to participate directly in decisions to the greatest degree obtainable. Workplace democracy cannot be achieved without allowing workers to participate to the greatest extent possible at all levels of decision making related to the workplace.

Though it is a very underdeveloped form, job enlargement may be seen as the first very small step toward increasing the decision-making ability of the individual in his immediate work environment. Job enlargement, as its name would indicate, is an effort to reverse the trend toward an ever-greater fragmentation of work into ever less meaning-ful parts.[39] Division of labor and specialization are necessary ingre-dients of modern industrial production, but they have proceeded un-encumbered beyond their point of utility. Job enlargement attempts to create jobs that encompass a larger portion of the complete process. The assumption is that if a worker is allowed, for example, to assemble an entire automotive transmission rather than just a small part, then benefits will follow. Though many analysts are not enamored with job enlargement, others such as Carole Pateman correctly see it as a "rudi-mentary form of . . . participation in the workplace." She goes on to content that "the larger job enlargement experiments are almost in-distinguishable in form from the more minor examples of experi-ments that are explicitly labelled 'participation' experiments."[40] Job enlargement by definition increases to a small degree the individual's scope of participation, makes more direct his mode of participation, and creates the possibility of enhancing by a small measure his inten-sity and quality of participation.

Since job enlargement is part of the more encompassing phenome-non known as job enrichment, the same case, but in a more persuasive manner, can be made for it. Job enrichment is an effort to create jobs that encompass not only a larger portion of the whole process, but that allow the worker to exercise more of his autonomy, creativity, and inward direction.[41] This effectively means relaxing the authoritarian bureaucratic structure to allow some open space within which the workers can operate. Job enrichment entails more self-supervision on the part of individuals and groups, as for example when work groups conduct their own quality control. Together, the twin reforms of providing larger tasks and more freedom to exercise control address the dual sources of work alienation: monotonous work and bureau-cratic authoritarianism. The importance of job enrichment and other similar efforts to reform work is again well stated by Carole Pateman. In "A Contribution to the Political Theory of Organizational Democ-racy," she maintains that "seen in the right way, they might provide a basis for 'encroaching control' in present nondemocratic organiza-tions, and they also provide valuable experience and information for the democratized organization itself. Participation in the running of the day-to-day work process is just as important as participation in wider management decisions for the development of skills and capac-ities required in a self-managing democracy."[42] Job enrichment ex-pands the scope of participation beyond that of job enlargement alone and creates the possibility of further enhancing the other dimensions of participation.

At a higher level of participation is the autonomous work group. In this system the work enterprise is divided into functional units that can, to a large extent, operate independently of one another. Each unit becomes a separate workplace in a sense—one sufficiently small to allow high levels of participation. Within the general work structure, as many decisions as possible are devolved to the functional unit where individuals exercise complete control over such intra-unit policies as the hiring and firing of unit members, the enforcement of rules, disciplinary action, quality control, and the like. The unit cannot have complete control over such decisions as shift scheduling, production pace and timing, and unit output levels, for such things affect other autonomous work groups in the same work community and thus require at least a modicum of coordination. The system's requirement for coordination among the various functional units could be fulfilled by unit representatives, meeting together in a coordinating committee to determine inter-unit policy.

Each of these forms of worker participation at the level of the individual and the work group can be witnessed on the international scene. Examples of job enlargement and job enrichment flourish throughout Great Britain and the continent. There are fewer examples of autonomous work groups. Norway has experimented with semiautonomous work groups, but the notion of autonomous work groups is as closely associated with Sweden. The most notable Swedish example is the oft-cited Volvo experiments.[43] In 1972 Volvo engaged in a major reorganizational effort designed to decentralize decision making. At the very top, the staff at Volvo's headquarters was cut from 1,800 to a mere 100 people, and each major producing group became an independent unit within the division. This same impulse to decentralize was present at the plant level. Volvo constructed its Kalmar plant so that groups of 20 people could work together in units to build their cars. The work was organized so that each group was responsible for a particular component of the automobile and eventually assumed responsibility for its own supervision and inspection. The assembly line was replaced and in effect employees were given the opportunity to design and organize their own work. The effort proved sufficiently successful that Volvo has built at least four other plants along these nontraditional lines, each designed to operate with 600 employees. Volvo also has indicated that it is possible to do things to change plants already in existence. The Volvo mother plant at Torslanda was built in 1964 when big was considered beautiful. The first major conversion move was to divide the four main departments (pressing, body work, painting and assembly), and make them as autonomous as possible. Within these four departments individual working groups were delineated. Then through a plan of job rotation developed by the employees themselves, the working groups moved from job rotation, to job enlargement and enrichment, and finally approached autonomy at the point where the group takes over supervision, control, and planning. Volvo is now in the process of applying these same principles to Volvo plants outside of Sweden, such as the Dutch DAF plant. Volvo president, Pehr G. Gyllenhammer, does not anticipate many difficulties transcending the obviously participation-conducive culture of Sweden.

Participation at the level of the individual and the work group adds an important dimension to worker participation, without which any such scheme would be woefully incomplete. Participation limited to the level of the work group, however, simply is insufficient. The objective is to integrate fully worker participation at all levels of decision making. The closer we come to realizing that objective, the closer we come to workplace democracy. There are important international attempts at achieving this goal. Such attempts exist at the level of individual enterprises, regions of the country, portions of the nation's economy, and even within entire nations. An examination of such worker-participation attempts is central to the argument.

The Porst Group, West Germany's second largest photo retailing and film processing company, provides a good example of integrated worker participation within a single enterprise.[44] As many issues as possible are presented for determination to the assembly of all workers. Some issues, such as those that require immediate attention, have a decision proposed by management and approved by the assembly. Much of the work is done through committees. For example, the salaries of all employees, including top management, are determined by an evaluation committee, which publishes a listing of all positions and the salaries that accompany them. To assure consistent representation when assemblies are uncalled for, a works council also is provided.

The notion of worker participation extended to a regional basis receives some embodiment in the Basque region of Spain.[45] In the middle of the 1950s a Catholic priest, Fr. José María Arizmendi came to Mondragon. Production began in a cooperative fashion when five graduates of his technical school formed the nucleus of the first industrial cooperative. Presently there are approximately fifty-five producer cooperatives, of which nearly fifty are industrial. In fact, Mondragon is Spain's leading producer of refrigerators. This is rather remarkable, for cooperatives tend to shy away from manufacturing, especially when it entails capital-intensive, high technologies. Success is indicated by the fact that sales of the cooperatives have increased at an average annual rate of 30 percent since 1966. The cooperatives are controlled by the general assembly of all workers, which meets to elect boards of directors and decide basic policy. The entire assembly, which operates on a one-person, one-vote basis, is sometimes called into session to handle emergency issues. Since the cooperatives are generally small, most of the average workers' participation is directed to the assembly meeting. This does create the possibility, however, of deficient participation opportunities at the shopfloor level.

A much more complete and integrated system of participation exists in Israel.[46] Collective bargaining has always been an important part of worker participation in Israel, as one might expect given the incredible strength of the General Federation of Labor, the Histadrut. Since the union itself is a major employer, however, and is in fact the largest industrial concern in the country, employing about 23 percent of all employees in Israel, many forms of worker participation, beyond collective bargaining, have been attempted. Most of the innovations beyond collective bargaining were tried first in the Histadrut's Labor Economy. In the mid-1940s, joint productivity councils were begun with the objective of raising output and providing some medium for participation, for they did consist of equal numbers of workers' representatives and management representatives. There joint consultation efforts proved fairly successful, and approximately 400 are in existence today. In the late 1950s a more radical form of worker participation within the workplace was tried, but failed. These plant councils were designed to instill the sense of community and fraternity, which was ebbing. The second part of the scheme, joint-management boards, were to give workers the opportunity to participate in decisions at the higher levels of the enterprise and corporation. At the same time, there has been a strong movement to increase worker participation in workplaces that are not part of the Histadrut's Labor Economy.

The most radical form of worker participation is achieved in an entirely different setting, namely that of the moshavim (agricultural co-

operatives) and the kibbutzim (collective communities). For the sake
of brevity, I will concentrate upon the kibbutzim. Kibbutzim were begun as rural-agricultural settlements, which only later moved to manufacturing endeavors. With about one-fourth of the economically active population of Israel, kibbutzim produce about one-third of the
agricultural output and slightly less than one-tenth of the industrial
output. The collective communities vary in size from about fifty members to 1,000. Kibbutzim indeed may represent the most complete examples of worker democracy. All members participate in decision
making. Factory members elect their supervisors, who are limited in
tenure. Indeed, a supervisor in one year may be a worker the next,
and vice versa. There are no special material rewards for occupying
the position of supervisor. The material goods of the collectivity are
distributed according to need. There is an amazingly extensive system
of committees, which supplements the electoral process. At any one
time, 40 percent of the membership belongs to one committee or
another.

The most radical attempt to integrate worker participation at all
levels of workplace decision making throughout an entire nation exists in Yugoslavia. Though extensive coverage cannot be offered (it is
readily available elsewhere), a brief exposition of the Yugoslavian system certainly is in order. The worker-participation system has its origins in the National Liberation War of 1941–45. By 1945 legal representatives of workers, known as worker commissioners, were in
existence. After the process of nationalization was completed in 1948,
joint consultation began without governmental direction. At the very
end of 1949 the government and trade unions issued joint instructions for the formation of advisory workers' councils, and by the middle of 1950, 520 councils were in operation. In June of 1950 the National Assembly proclaimed the councils to be managing bodies of
Yugoslavian enterprises.

In the full belief that workers should manage their own affairs, employees of each enterprise collectively elect a workers council, which
determines general policies, appoints people to key posts, and over-
sees the management of the enterprise. One of the critical tasks of the
council is to select a management board and a director for the enterprise. When it was found that the workers council could not handle all
of the issues brought before it, a series of commissions and committees were created to prepare decisions for the workers council. The
movement toward decentralization continued. At first only large

functional units were given the right to be self-managing, but eventually self-management rights were extended to smaller "economic units," and finally to the smallest units discernible according to financial accounting. These units, known as Basic Organizations of Associated Labor (BOALs), are granted the opportunity to determine the full range of issues that can be decided at that level. As a matter of fact, the BOALs are considered the basic units of the enterprise: the BOALs come together to form the enterprise, rather than the enterprise being divided into these basic units. In an effort to resist the tendency for technological elites to dominate the participatory system (and perhaps to bring the entire operation under more effective control of the party), the Law on Associated Labor was enacted. Formally the law expands the scope of participation by bringing health and social-service issues also within the decision-making range of workers. Further, it compels workplaces to write enterprise statutes and the BOALs to draft their own regulations and negotiate business transactions with other BOALs. In addition, other groups such as trade unions, local authorities, and commerce chambers must be incorporated into the negotiating network. It is difficult to determine what effects this formalization will have on actual participation. All that can be said is that the worker participation scheme in Yugoslavia has not fulfilled every expectation, but it has worked well.

The survey of international examples of worker participation has concentrated only upon the major European experiments. There is so much more that could have been said. Bolivia made decrees concerning worker control (*control obrereo*) after the 1963 revolution. Prior to the military coup in 1973, the Chilean government financially encouraged the development of agricultural settlements (*asentamientos*), which bear some resemblance to Israeli moshavim, and allow workers to assume production in over one hundred workplaces abandoned by their owners (*empresas de trabajadores*). The Peruvian military government, which seized control in 1968, attempted to establish its own version of *democracia social de participación plena* through junta fiat regarding worker representation and forced sharing of corporate profits with the *comunidad laboral*. At about the same time, Venezuela instituted worker representation on the board of directors in all state companies. The list of additional nations experimenting with worker participation in some form or another would include Costa Rica, Hungary, Czechoslovakia, and Trinidad, among many others. Of course, not every nation has embraced the idea. In the spring of 1976, the

Swiss electorate rejected by wide margins two referenda that would have increased worker participation. Nevertheless, the idea of worker participation clearly has arrived on the international scene.

It is an idea whose time also has come to the United States. Though the topic of worker participation in the United States will receive much more attention in my other volume examining the feasibility of worker participation and workplace democracy in the United States, something should be said now about the forms of workplace participation in this country. Since much American thought related to worker participation was inherited from Europe in general and Britain in particular, it might be assumed that the same basic forms of worker participation are available to the United States. This is true only in a formal sense; in practice, the United States has gone its own route regarding worker participation. As in Great Britain, worker participation in the United States is most often viewed in terms of collective bargaining, but unlike that of Great Britain, union attention in the United States is often focused within the workplace. It is an American labor tradition to have strong union presence at the shopfloor level. This emphasis on lower levels of decision making has been reinforced by historical and technological changes.

Specialization in American factories increased efficiency and productivity, but also created serious problems related to coordination. Part of the most-current solution to this problem is to increase authority and responsibility among the rank-and-file workers. Thus job enlargement, job enrichment, and even some experimentation in autonomous work groups is common in the United States. These factors also explain the greater willingness of American workplaces to entertain such experiments as the Scalon plan; that system of rewarding workers collectively for successful innovations operates on the shopfloor level.

The focus on the lower levels of decision making does not necessarily mean that participation at that level is fully developed. The emphasis on collective bargaining in America has led to an attempt to maintain rather strict divisions between management and labor, divisions which many view as necessary for the operation of collective bargaining. Since extensive worker participation in workplace decisions would have the effect of blurring distinctions between management and labor, the forms of participation even at the lower levels often remain rudimentary. The dominance of collective bargaining as the American form of worker participation has impeded the develop-

ment of worker participation, especially at higher levels of workplace
decision making. It is there that the distinctions between management and labor can be blurred most easily. The passive role assumed
by the United States government regarding worker participation constitutes another impediment toward achieving workplace democracy.
On the international scene, the major advances in worker participation within recent years have been the result of national legislation.
American ideology does not support the involvement of government
in decisions related to workplace ownership and management—
at least not in such overt forms as nationalization and mandatory
worker participation policies. Securing the rights of collective bargaining through legislation such as the National Labor Relations Act
constituted a major victory. No, the American form of worker participation is likely to evolve from the lowest levels of decision making
upwards, with the national government supporting the effort only
through such indirect means as extending the civil rights of citizens to
the workers in their workplaces.

The Contemporary Advocates

Workplace democracy has been defined as that type of workplace rule
in which the process of decision making generally entails widespread
and effective participation of workplace members. By this standard,
there have been very few examples of workplace democracy. If we
view as democratic any measure that increases the participation of
workers beyond present levels, however, there are numerous democratic attempts to reorganize workplace decision making. The participatory standard of democracy, which was originally developed in
the second chapter, may be applied also to those who support a more
democratic workplace. This is particularly important because the cho-
rus of advocates has grown to such an immense size in recent years.
What is more remarkable than the size of the advocate group is the
composition of the advocate group. The political right as well as the
political left lend support to the notion that workers ought to participate more in the activities related to work. Intellectuals as well as in-
dustrialists praise the effects of worker participation. In a world divided, even the representatives of the first, second, and third worlds
(if there are not more) come to apparent agreement on this vital issue,
which penetrates to the core of the age in which we life. When consen-

sus is reached among groups that diverge as radically as those who say they support worker participation and workplace democracy, however, one must be suspicious that the consensus is more apparent than real. Further investigation is warranted.

The literature addressing the issue of worker participation is now so bountiful with supporters that meaningful subdivisions are necessary to examine it thoroughly. Edward Greenberg is particularly helpful in this regard, for he has recommended that the advocates of worker participation be divided quaternarily into management, humanist psychologist, the participatory political left, and the democratic theorists.[47] By analyzing each of the advocate claims by the participatory dimensions of democracy, we may learn much about their advocacy position.

Chapter five's discussion of the importance of work served to introduce us to the managerial literature that addresses worker participation. There is widespread recognition in the managerial literature that worker participation may be a critical variable in determining the success of contemporary workplaces. Though the terminology varies, each of the following managerial thinkers offers an expression for worker participation: Likert (Participatory Group—System 4), Argyris (Adult Role, and Reality-centered), Barnes (Open System), Bennis (Problem-solving, Democratic), Blake-Mouton (Concern for People), Leavitt (People Solutions), McGregor (Theory Y), Blau (Democratic), Burns-Stalker (Organic), Shepard (Organic), Lowin (Participatory Decision Making), and Bovard (Group-centered).[48] A crucial point to emphasize in the discussion of the managerial literature recommending workplace participation is that it does not vary substantially in its objectives from the literature that does not recommend participation. Both bodies of thought seek to maximize efficiency, productivity and profit, but each employs different means of doing so. Those who elect a more participatory workplace are convinced that the best way to reverse steadily declining economic conditions is to involve workers in the enterprise. Our present economic situation is characterized by inordinately high levels of absenteeism, job turnover, sabotage, and wildcat strikes, coupled with inordinately low levels of productivity increases, work quality, and morale; the very fact that this situation exists is seen by those who would involve workers as clear repudiation of the old ways of organizing work. Since the group that recommends worker participation does not renounce the objectives of management (and they cannot, for it defines their position), some critics have denounced their interest in worker participation as false. Greenberg himself has commented, obviously referring to the managerial writings, that "the widespread support for worker participation is illusionary once we get behind the label."[49] This is not really true. The managerial interest in worker participation generally is real and sincere, but it is linked to the ability of participation to improve efficiency, productivity, and, of course, profit. Management is unlikely to recommend worker participation beyond the point at which they perceive it as yielding the greatest marginal utility in terms of their own objectives. Thus those who write from the perspective of management certainly do not advocate workplace democracy; such a measure would completely undermine the managerial role of leadership. But in extending worker participation, they do seek a workplace that is more democratic than contemporary ones.

It would be useful to apply the various participatory dimensions of democracy to the managerial advocacy. Management is keenly interested in augmenting the extensity and intensity of participation; only in a system in which all workers possible participate, and do so with some level of involvement, will the benefits of participation be maximized. On the other hand, management would not be interested in making the mode very direct, except perhaps at the lowest level of decision making. There is certainly little interest in having workers participate in the decisions that have been reserved for middle and upper management; and there is virtually no interest in having workers make corporate-level decisions. This situation of seeking high levels of extensity and intensity of worker participation along with a restricted scope and mode of participation does lead to questions concerning the quality of participation. Any time managers move very far from job enlargement and job enrichment, they may be tempted to resort to pseudoparticipation.

Many of the same points of discussion apply to humanist psychology.[50] The overlap extends beyond outlook to actual membership; many of those who were listed as managerial writers considering workplace participation also may be classified as humanist psychologists. The membership lines are blurred further because many humanist psychologists have been in managerial roles and have participated in the restructuring of work. In terms of belief, there is little value discord between the two groups concerning the premium placed upon economically viable work organizations, for humanist psychologists also grant it high priority. As with the managerial group, the school of humanist psychology generally ascribes to the values of our economic ideology, and more than occasionally produces stinging attacks on socialism and communism.[51] Like their managerial companions who adopt the participatory perspective, but even more strongly, the humanist psychologists believe that the present structure of work is needlessly injurious to individuals and the enterprises of which they are a part. Where the two groups differ is in their stress upon the value of human development. Fulfilling the developmental needs of human beings is not simply a means to achieve greater levels of efficiency, productivity, and profit for the humanist psychologist, but as an end in itself, it is at least of equal importance to the economic values. Economic and developmental values coexist, for the humanist psychologists operate on the assumption that there is little or no contradiction between the two. Whether adopting Arygris' dynamic personality model, Maslow's hierarchy of human needs, or some other program of human development, humanist psychologists envision an economically vital workplace in which people can grow. This requires restructuring, the kind of restructuring that allows individuals to operate autonomously, to exercise judgement and choice, and to take responsibility—in short, to contribute the best they can offer. This can only exist in a workplace that embraces worker participation.

Humanist psychologists are more democratic in their workplace participation recommendations than are their managerial counterparts, but in some ways, not much more democratic. The emphasis humanist psychologists place on individual development means that they are concerned that everyone participate intensely in the decisions affecting their lives. Since special developmental benefits derive from direct participation, humanist psychologists stress direct modes of participation and thus high-quality participation. But, since it is the issues that most directly affect the lives of individuals that are most important, and since humanist psychologist tend to be wedded to the traditional capitalist economic order, there is a real tendency to restrict participation to lower-level issues. In doing so, humanist psychologists, like the management, group restrict the democratic nature of their prescriptions to a level below that which should be termed workplace democracy.

A third group that advocates worker participation is the participatory left. They base much of their thought on the early writings of Marx, especially those stressing the subjugation and alienation that follows from work designed within the industrial-capitalist order. To remedy the situation, the participatory left calls for effective worker participation. Evoking such models as the Paris Commune, the post-revolutionary soviets, and the Italian worker councils of the early 1920s, socialist thinkers such as Antonio Gramsci and Andre Gorz developed the theoretical perspective of the participatory left.[52] This perspective may be found in such American writings as Tom Hayden's "Port Huron Statement."[53]

The thought of Leo Panitch may be used as a representative example of current expressions of the participatory left.[54] One of Panitch's primary concerns is to find the terminology that captures the goals of the participatory left. He rejects "worker participation," for it has been co-opted by the capitalists, who have perverted its meaning for their own ends. Similarly, he rejects "self-management"; it is subject to revisionism and, more importantly, idle utopianism. He settles upon the phrase *workers' control*, which states unambiguously the objectives of the participatory left. The participatory left largely pursues worker participation as a means to another end, namely revolution. According to the left, participation within the workplace will socialize the workers to a new consciousness—one fervently anticapitalist and revolutionary. The participatory left therefore recommends high levels of participation along all of the dimensions. Their dedication to revolution, however, can lead to limitations on worker participation. If it were found, for example, that participation in the workplace at some point moved workers to be satisfied with reform rather than revolution, the participatory left would be less enthusiastic in its endorsement. The emphasis on revolutionary workers' control, rather than participatory democracy in the workplace, can lead to ignoring worker participation at lower-level workplace decision making. After all, workers' control is achieved at the highest levels of workplace decision making. The stress upon revolution and workers' control can focus so much attention on upper-level decision making that the participatory left might restrict not only the scope of participation, but also the extensity, intensity, and mode of participation and thus not achieve workplace democracy. It is no accident that there is a strong tension between the urge to centralize and the urge to decentralize in socialist thought.

The last school to be distinguished by Greenberg relates to that group of democratic theorists who emphasize participation. Very little need be said in description of participatory democracy applied to the workplace, for this very book belongs most firmly in the tradition.

What distinguishes the participatory democrats from the other schools is their desire pursuant to other ends. Management wishes to increase efficiency, production and profits and limits participation, making it merely a means to those ends; humanist psychologists, wishing to enhance the development of individuals, concern themselves primarily with participatory attempts that are at the shopfloor level; the participatory left pursues revolution through worker participation, and in doing so, can limit worker participation.

Though the participatory democrats realize that participation will potentially lead to a plethora of benefits, they, more than the other groups, pursue workplace participation as an end in itself. Participatory democrats, by and large, want little more of participation than more participation. Democracy conceived in terms of participation comes close to defining the good life. Those who recommend workplace participation from the perspective of democratic theory seldom place effective boundaries or restrictions upon it.

The call for worker participation certainly is not unanimous. Minds as vital and diverse as Hayek,[55] Marcuse,[56] and even Arendt,[57] for one reason or another, express reservations about it. Yet it is a call that echoes from points all along the political spectrum, from groups as diverse as managers and Marxists. The call is not lightly uttered; each group has weighed its advantages and disadvantages. Since the interests of the groups vary, so will the nature of their participatory reforms. Some recommend little participatory change from the status quo, others a great deal. The cry for bona fide workplace democracy is made much less often.

7

Participatory and Workplace Democracy

Review of the Argument as a Critique of Liberalism

MUCH DISTANCE HAS BEEN COVERED OVER EXCEEDINGLY RUGGED terrain to reach this point. It would be wise to reflect upon what has been developed. Rather than simply review the argument, for which the summary within the preface might suffice, I will survey the argument placing it within the context of its inherent critique of liberalism. It is safest to begin with a reconsideration of liberalism in its classical expression.

Classical liberalism does not form a coherent philosophical statement, but it does provide a theoretical perspective that has imbued our outlook on the world. A series of positions are inherent in the liberal point of view, the most critical of which is the division of the world into social and political spheres. With the world so divided, classical liberalism generates its positions. Liberalism stresses the individual, and the importance of individual life, liberty, and property. Since these values lie in the social sphere, liberalism values the social sphere. The political sphere exists to protect those values. Liberalism's stress upon the individual indicates clearly that it values little the political sphere. Though liberalism emphasizes the individual, it describes the political as a sphere divorced from the life of most individuals, thus according it little value. The political is what is public, and what is public is captured forthrightly by government. Government should be capable of protecting individual life, liberty, and property, but beyond that it should be restricted. After all, the government that governs least, governs best. The contemporary view that politics is corrupt, while taking over the family business is honorable, is an undeniable inheritance of liberalism. Given the contention that life's true values are in the social sphere and politics is somehow sordid, the rational liberal man (and liberal man is rational in an instrumental

183

sense of rationality) would seek to limit his political activity. What is important is that his interests be represented in government and that he have the formal opportunity to participate, if it is necessary to participate to have his interests represented. Generally, it is unnecessary to involve himself in politics beyond merely voting for representatives who will insure that his life, liberty, and property are not endangered. Not only is participation limited, but it takes on a particular nature in liberal thought. Liberal views of participation emphasize *conflict* among competing interests and generally ignore the full range of cooperative participation. The objective is to solidify power among competing interests.

The emphasis on interests allows contemporary versions of liberalism to shift occasionally from individual to group-regarding interests; the most predominant of the contemporary versions is known as pluralism. This shift is but one illustration of the imperialistic nature of liberalism. There are many different statements of the ideas of liberalism, and in a fair number the individual continues to be the focus. The ideas of Thomas Hobbes, John Locke, Thomas Paine and the like do reappear in the writings of Milton Friedman, Hayek and Nozick.[1] One should not, however, become fascinated with the more lofty expressions of contemporary liberalism; the liberal perspective is most successful in coloring less philosophical efforts. Take Schonfeld's article as just one example.[2] His stress on the costs of participation, his perception that the people want a government that is distant from them and one that provides for safety but does not interfere, and his stress on the people desiring to control representatives but not to directly control the political process itself is a rather perfect expression of the liberal perspective.

This work attempts to surmount the classical liberal perspective, but it is not easy, for liberalism colors all that we see. It was certainly present in our discussion of democracy. If we are not to accept a tautological relationship between what is good and what is democratic, then we must pierce through to the core of democracy and provide a coherent translation of democracy as a system in which the people rule.

Only after we abandon the classical liberal perspective is it possible to construct a viable version of democracy as a participatory form of community rule. Such a view of democracy is distinctively different from the classical liberal formulation of democracy as representative civil government in which the interests of citizens are protected. This nonliberal (but certainly not totalitarian) form of democracy stresses the involvement of men and women in the making of community decisions that affect their lives. Liberal democracy offers a marketplace analogy. As the consumer spends his dollar for the product of his choice, liberal man spends his vote (the only rational form of participation) for the party of his choice. Unlike liberal democracy, which directs attention to the state, participatory democracy broadens the perspective to include all communities as settings for political interaction and the possible existence of democratic rule. Like liberal democracy, participatory democracy can stress the idea that democracy is a process, but unlike liberal democrats, participatory democrats reject the notion that it is a process of interest representation; instead they see it as a process of participatory decision making. Yet even in view of representation, the participatory version of democracy may be seen as preferable. After all, no one is generally in a position to consistently represent our interests better than ourselves. The more participation, the more effectively interests will be represented.

Participatory democracy is much more than another version of interest representation. It is the form of community rule that seeks to maximize the development of individuals. Through participation, participatory democrats contend, individuals will develop their special capacities. And it is through political action that the benefits will be greatest, for the quality of a man's life is determined by the nature of his activity. Though more will be said about the benefits of participation in the next section, it should be stated that a long tradition links participation to self-realization. The tradition includes the likes of Carl Friedrick (*Transcendental Justice*), Harold Laski (*Dangers of Obedience*), T. V. Smith (*The Promise of American Politics*), and Hans Kelsen (*General Theory of Law and State*).[3]

Democracy relates to the process of decision making, not to its content. This may be illustrated convincingly by the fact that a democracy and a dictatorship may pursue the same specific policy. Process, however, will influence content. Through the connection between a participatory process and content, participation not only benefits individual development, but also creates community benefits as well. Participatory democracy produces better decisions.

The community benefits of participation do not mean the democracy cannot make bad decisions; it can. Moreover, there may be points beyond which the benefits of participation in a particular community may decline; that is, the relationship between participation and benefits at some point may be curvilinear. Given the five participatory dimensions to democracy, the purest imaginable form of democracy would entail everyone (extensity), participating directly (mode), and effectively (quality), in all issues affecting them (scope), with a great amount of personal involvement (intensity). Though this will never occur, it is possible in rare moments for participation to slip beyond the ideal in the amount of participation. In almost all situations, however, any advancement of participation is likely to be a movement toward the ideal.

One advantage of the participatory conception is that it establishes a clear standard of what should be considered democratic and what should not. Using the present as a reference, a proposal to increase democracy can be considered truly democratic only if it increases participation in the focal community. Even if the proposal is very desirable, it cannot be considered democratic unless it increases participation. Attention must dwell on participation. It is easy to be lured into thinking that the cause of democracy is being served by proposals that speak of rights and privileges, of individual and common good. In American thought, however, any movement *from* the participatory standard is likely to be a drift back into classical liberalism. The participatory standard of democracy must remain unambiguous. Otherwise there is the frightful image in which people proclaim democracy to exist everywhere, but nowhere do men and women participate in the decisions that affect their lives.

Given the desirability of participatory democracy, how can we increase participation? On the basis of research literature, it is possible to claim that a general social origin underlies participation. But to make that claim, we are merely perpetuating the fundamental liberal division between the social and the political worlds. Rejecting the liberal distinctions, it becomes clear that participation is a learned response derived from previous participatory experiences. Participation can be learned anywhere, and, of course, there is a certain advantage to having participation learned early in life. If participation is not learned early in life, however, that does not put an end to the possibility. Adult socialization is just beginning to be recognized for its true importance.

This point becomes especially critical when we focus our attention on participation in government. Participation learned in one community is most easily transferred to other communities that approximate it. Participation in government is an adult activity; childhood participatory experiences temporally lie far from participation in government and can only influence participation in government through the complex of intervening experiences and communities. Of all the adult participatory experiences, the Proximity Hypothesis would indicate that participation in the workplace most clearly approximates participation in government. The connection between the workplace and government is recognized by Abraham Maslow:

In a still larger sense it can be said this way: that democracy needs absolutely for its very existence people who can think for themselves, make their own judgements, and, finally who can vote for themselves—that is, who can rule themselves and help rule their country. . . . Therefore, any man who really wants to help his country, who is devoted to it, and who would sacrifice for it and take upon his shoulder the responsibility for its improvement, must, if he is to be logical, carry this whole philosophy into his work life.[1]

To offer participatory training, all workplaces should be made more participatory. Intervention in the decision-making patterns of the workplace can initiate the process by which participation will be transferred to other communities and challenge traditional structures.

The workplace connection places great emphasis upon establishing participatory patterns of decision making within the workplace, but the connection between participation in the workplace and participation in government is not the only compelling reason to increase participation in the workplace. Work has been established as a fundamentally important element in our daily lives. It is the way we identify ourselves, the way we extend ourselves creatively into the world, and in doing so, one of the ways we expand our potentiality. In our contemporary world, work is reduced to *labor*; the intrinsic value of work is not appreciated even though intrinsic values are tied to individual health, growth and development. In large part this is a result of liberalism. From the liberal perspective, it is very difficult to accord work any intrinsic value. In classical economics, which fits hand-in-glove with liberal views of politics, work is nothing more than *labor*, a commodity, the necessary—and unfortunate—means by which we live. Not only does liberalism not attribute intrinsic value to work, it has difficulty attributing intrinsic value to anything. Since liberalism has no theory relating to human development, it cannot recognize any claims to intrinsic value. Without a theory of human development, liberalism provides no room for man's development as a moral agent.

Work can never be of intrinsic value until we break from liberal precepts and arrange for workers to participate in the basic decisions that govern their lives in the workplace. Without participation in the workplace, we threaten to alienate a value as important as work. With participation in the workplace, we bring the importance of political action to the significant community of work.

Allowing the intrinsic value of work to predominate, in itself, may lead to some welcome changes in our society. The emphasis on the intrinsic value of work may shift emphasis away from concentration upon the extrinsic values of work. As things stand now, it is only in terms of extrinsic values that most workers can justify their worklife. This leads to extreme demands for greater extrinsic values. Such demands may even become a form of rebellion based on alienation, which can produce unwanted forms of participation; work alienation can produce excessive material and monetary demands. The ability to realize the intrinsic value of work can create a situation in which there is less emphasis upon consumption. Emphasis upon the extrinsic value of work and emphasis upon consumption go together. A liberal system in which work has only extrinsic value can only produce a materialistic culture.

If emphasis is placed on participation within the workplace, then it is possible for that participation to become sufficiently extensive and effective for workplace democracy to exist. It is no accident that those who tend to make the workplace connection, and those who attach intrinsic value to work, also tend to be those who recommend consideration of workplace democracy.

Not only does workplace democracy come by a number of different expressions (e.g. industrial democracy), it also relates to a number of competing conceptual forms. Some see workplace democracy in the form of organized unions, another group as job-enlargement and job-enrichment plans, others as a vehicle for having workers elect representatives who participate with management, and still others see workplace democracy as workers owning the workplace. Democracy is best seen in the form of participation, and thus workplace democracy would be a type of workplace rule in which workers participate extensively and effectively in the decisions that affect them in the workplace. In this light, the previously listed claims to workplace democracy may be judged; each is in some degree related to workplace democracy, but is not the same thing at all. Workplace democracy is not collective bargaining between unions and management. As a matter of fact, collective bargaining conflicts with many of the underlying assumptions of cooperative forms of participation: notions of trust, flexibility, cooperation, and the like. Job enlargement and job enrichment do not carry participation anywhere near the threshold of workplace democracy. Having workers represented by other workers on governing boards may be seen as a step in the right direction, but it does not create a situation in which worker participation is both widespread and effective. Such an arrangement may turn out to be little more than another collective bargaining arrangement. Finally, there is an important distinction to be made between who controls through participation in decision making and who formally owns the workplace. Worker ownership does not guarantee that worker participation will be any greater than in typical workplaces, for the owners (in this case the workers) can still hire management to act in the traditional role of managers. Nor does a situation in which workers do not own their workplaces necessarily preclude the possibility that workers nevertheless will control the workplace through participation in widespread and effective decision making.

The whole notion of workplace democracy is antithetical to the liberal perspective. With the world divided into social and political spheres, classical liberals would not advocate the application of democracy, a political concept meant for description of the state (government), to the workplace, an important part of the social sphere. The closest liberalism would come to the idea is in the form of collective bargaining. Collective bargaining, a conflict form of participation between rival interests, does rest on liberal assumptions. It is interesting to note, however, that once the idea of workplace democracy is raised, liberalism can offer a co-opting suggestion. If we must adapt democracy to the workplace, why not adopt a form of liberal democracy? We can have representatives chosen in relatively free elections in which enfranchised workers vote to decide among themselves who will meet with management. To complete the picture, we might even have competing parties vie for the votes of workers. Naturally, there would be the appropriate set of liberal-democratic rights, which would assure that universal suffrage of the workers becomes a reality. Liberalism could again show its imperialistic nature.

Workplace democracy is heir to a number of theoretical traditions. Utopian socialism, guild socialism, syndicalism, and even anarchism have made their various contributions to workplace democracy. Not only is there a history to the idea, but there is some historical development to the practice. Robert Owen, 160 years ago, broke ground by creating New Harmony. Since the utopian efforts, there has been historical progress from collective bargaining, and from joint consultation through codetermination, and finally from forms that actually approximate workplace democracy.

Workplace democracy may not be appropriate for all nations in the world. There is a necessary set of preconditions for its existence (economic, cultural, etc.). Yet the nation meeting those preconditions the best, the United States, is lagging behind some other nations in the development of workplace democracy. The United States, the embodiment of the liberal state, has found it most difficult to shed its liberal skin. England, where liberalism originated, also lags far behind the rest of the continent. There are possible driving forces to change, however; as the United States lags behind in the development of workplace democracy, so does it lose its economic advantages in the world community. Though no one can claim that there is an isomorphic relationship, it is very likely that there is a connection. From the point of view of rationality, efficiency, productivity, and profit, we cannot afford to keep our workers passive. Even if America were resolved not to increase worker participation, there would still be the influence of European systems into America through American-based multinational corporations. It was no accident, for example, that Chrysler was the first major American company to extend worker representation to their corporate board. Just before Chrysler was forced to sell its European holdings to Peugeot, it attempted salvation through worker-participation plans. In some countries, forms of worker participation are required by law, and American-based companies will gain experience with worker participation whether they originally sought it or not. That does not mean that the United States should simply import European plans for worker participation. We can learn from experience, but each nation must develop and internalize its own appropriate forms.

It is important to make all communities more democratic, but the foregoing argument makes a compelling case for beginning with the workplace and making it more democratic. There is, of course, the workplace connection, and the fact that participation in the workplace will carry participation to the critical community of government. There is also the importance of work to consider. If work is the means by which we create ourselves, and we cannot do that in our work unless we participate in the decision making related to our work, then workplace democracy is the appropriate solution. Workplace democracy, it should be remembered, is as much democracy as democracy in any other community, including government. Workplace democracy creates the possibility of applying action to the important area of work, which in turn may eliminate the most important source of alienation. None of what has been described, however, is possible without moving beyond the confines of liberalism.

The Participatory Society

Participation is a learned response to the environment and as such, can be learned in any community. It is sad to relate, however, that most people do not learn how to participate and thus are rendered nonparticipants throughout their lives. If changes are going to lead to participatory communities, it is reasonable to question where the process of change will begin. There are those, in fact, who argue that it is not possible to change any fundamental part of our world without changing all parts of it. In short, this is an argument for revolution. Yet it is difficult to have faith in the outcome of revolutions, making the logic of this solution appear completely untenable. Nothing fundamental can change without everything fundamental changing, but since we cannot have faith in changing everything at once, then nothing can change. There is an interaction between the whole and parts, and this interaction must be recognized, yet it is possible to escape being trapped in this inextricable argument. Amitai Etzioni, for example, finds areas within the whole that can change without all changing first: "There seems to be one exception to this sociological iron law: participation in 'private governments' of corporate units as distinct from ecological-residential ones. Universities, churches, hospitals and some places of work can be made more participatory without first transforming the national structures."[5]

Of course, there are those who will make the same basic argument about the workplace. Some claim that it makes no sense, that it may well be impossible to attempt to achieve workplace democracy while the rest of the socio-economic order remains the same. Yet the following scenario is possible: Because of the impact of participation in the place of work, we will not have an island of democracy in the workplace surrounded by a nonparticipatory sea. Or if we have it, it will not last long. Participatory communities will lie in contradiction with nonparticipatory communities, and the contradiction can only be resolved safely in favor of greater participation. Participation in the workplace itself will generate demand for participation in other communities. Gramsci was correct to see workers' democracy (in this case in the form of factory councils) as "a magnificent school of political and administrative experience."[6] Participation in the workplace, which can be justified along grounds other than democracy, will give impetus to a flow of participation that will travel; the Proximity Hypothesis will show its route. The first step of participation may be related very closely to the workplace. The community that is the foundation of any particular workplace may be seen in expanded form. Residents of the geographical community in which the workplace exists, as well as consumers of the product or service of the workplace, may be included in the workplace decision making. Participation in the workplace will extend, as previous discussions have indicated, to participation in government, and to other communities that are approximate to participation in the workplace. Workers, newly socialized into participatory patterns, may take that mode of decision making home and allow family decisions to be more participatory. Such parents are certainly likely to take advantage of present opportunities to participate and insist that the decision making in schools be increased to allow them even greater participatory opportunities; they also will demand a more participatory environment for their children. After all, if schools are doing their job in preparing young men and women for productive and meaningful work, then they certainly should be preparing young adults for the new participatory workplaces. All institutions and communities will come under pressure for greater participation, and eventually, all communities will become more participatory. The major sources of control in our world, organizations, institutions, and communities of all sorts will become more democratic. Widespread and effective participation in all of the various communities which touch our lives is the embodiment of the ideal of participatory democracy.

Of course, there is bound to be a time lag. Participation in the workplace will not lead immediately to an outcry for participation, but it will come. In many ways this systematic, progressive movement fits the pragmatic nature of the American culture, which looks very skeptically on abrupt change. Yet basic change is possible within our political culture, and with it a virtual revolution in our communal existence (revolutionary meaning a fundamental change), achieved through an evolutionary manner. It begins with participation in the workplace.

Again, the critical first link is between participation in the workplace and participation in government. Although opportunities to participate in government may be seen as good, with a participatory persuasion developed in the workplace, those opportunities will be made actual, and the demand for more participation will become greater. Since the demand for increased participation cannot be handled by present governmental structures, we will probably have to create a new set of structures, which decentralize decision making as much as possible. To the degree we cannot further decentralize, we will have to rely on unambiguous rules and faithful administration.

Through the experience of participation in the workplace, the least participatory members of our society will receive training in participation, training they do not receive elsewhere. As a consequence, they will be mobilized to participate and send a message to government different from the one it is accustomed to hearing. Since the actions of government in many ways reflect those who participate, presumably, governmental policies will come to represent more closely the interests of the newcomers to politics. There will be a systematic change in who gets what, when, and how. It would be accurate to say that the changes in policy will reflect the interests of a broader class. Liberal democracy is notorious for the indulgence of upper-class rather than lower-class interests. In part this is a result of people in a high economic class knowing how to accrue advantage within "liberal democracy." Given the class nature of the situation, there is likely to be resistance to the demands of the new participants. As those who resisted the demands (articulated through participation) of immigrant groups and blacks learned the hard way, however, elected governmental officials must be responsive to those who participate. After a period of time, the new demands will not only be seen as legitimate, but they will actually be anticipated by government officials.

In discussing governmental participation, it must remain clear that more is being said than that more people will be voting in elections and the like. It also is being claimed that more people will be involved in the entire governmental process, including the administration of governmental programs. Based on the Administrative Procedures Act of 1946 and renwed efforts on the part of recent presidents, a serious attempt is being made to offer the public opportunities to par-

194 Participatory and Workplace Democracy

ticipate in the administration of government. Of course few governmental agencies (the Corps of Engineers may be one of those exceptions)[7] are interested in promoting actual participation. For them, imbued as they are with liberal beliefs, the opportunity to participate is more than sufficient. With substantial training in participation and a well-developed participatory persuasion, actual participation will meet present opportunities and overflow in the form of demand for yet greater participation. Thus the major change that will result is that the working class will become more politically active, and with that will come a change in governmental policy.

As the chapter on democracy affirmed, participation will result in community benefits that extend beyond public policy conforming with public opinion, when public opinion is more representative of the actual public. Participation, for example, will also create stability. There is no mere coincidence that the most stable nations of the world, the western European nations, tend to be the more participatory. Theorists of different schools recognize this possibility. We would expect Rousseau to make the claim, but so too does de Tocqueville. Though he is often portrayed as an opponent of mass participation, he realized that stability may very well be the product of participation: "When I am told that the laws are weak and the population wild, that passions are excited and virtue is paralyzed, and that in this situation it would be madness to think of increasing the rights of people, I reply that it is for these very reasons that they should be increased."[8]

Naturally, this position assumes a particular type of participation. Given that participation itself is a socializing agent, participation in truly democratic processes will produce participation generally supportive of the democratic institutions. There is no need to resort to disruptive forms of participation when it is possible to participate meaningfully and effectively through conventional channels. It is true that many individuals could not handle participation if it were *suddenly* forced upon them, but this is not likely to happen. What could happen is instability *if* individuals do develop a participatory persuasion but are denied the opportunity to participate. Once the process of participation begins in workplace experiences, it would be unwise to attempt to thwart it.

Many other community benefits should follow from participation, but rather than list them and repeat many of chapter two's arguments, it would be more wise to remind the reader that counterpart to the community benefits are the individual benefits that arise from participation. Through the process of participation, individuals will develop their uniquely human capacities. The process of self-realization, whether in the hands of Maslow or Marx (*selbstbetatigung*), is a participatory one.

What begins in the workplace will spread, and the nonparticipatory cycle of despair will be broken. Though the most radical changes are likely to affect the working class, society in general will benefit. Everyone will have the opportunity to participate and the training to do so. Under a situation in which all communities are democratic, benefits of participation will be maximized.

None of the promised benefits are guaranteed. It is worth repeating that there are many possible pitfalls, not the least of which is man himself. Men are fallible, and therefore democratic government can make bad decisions, decisions that adversely affect the community and the individuals within it. Once again, it is important to avoid the trap of considering everything democratic as good. Even if democracy is the prime value of our times, it is not the only value. We may elect to limit participation, at least temporarily, to secure other values. Yet let us not underestimate the value of democracy. Because, and not in spite of man's fallibility, it must be argued that democratic government is more likely than other forms to achieve favorable decisions. And no other form of community decision making can rival democracy in the extent of individual benefits.

Participationism, the Philosophy of Participation

The development of major theoretical alternatives does rest on the rejection of liberalism, but that is truly easier said than done. Much has been said about liberalism, and this is not the only work that attacks it. Judith Shklar's *Legalism* offers a very solid critique of liberalism, especially when it identifies values such as freedom and privacy with the social sphere and links costs such as sanctions and force with government. Kenneth Hoover rightfully indicts liberalism for moral bankruptcy and indicates its responsibility for a massive crisis in identity. To these could be added a spate of books, including McWilliam's *Idea of Fraternity in America*, Ferkiss's *The Future of Technological Civilization*, and Abbott's *The Shotgun Behind the Door*, all of which criticize liberalism.[9] For decades the general critique has pronounced the end of liberalism, yet liberalism survives. It is part of the imperialistic nature of liberalism that it can absorb such attacks and actually incorporate them into the liberal dogma.

This is what has been said. What has *not* been done by contemporary critics is to offer a positive alternative to liberalism, once liberalism has been rejected. That is not to say that there are no alternatives to liberalism. In dichotomizing the world, liberalism has offered totalitarianism as the only distinct alternative. Thus from this perspective, when an alternative to liberalism is raised (let's take Marxism, for example), it gets pushed into a totalitarian category and all the purely nontotalitarian features of Marxism are ignored, or perverted. The movement away from liberalism must be characterized and then defended in a manner that is not reduced to totalitarianism.

Ironically, generating alternatives to liberalism can begin within the circle of what hitherto had been considered liberal writing. Though they were certainly liberal theorists, much of the writing of men such as John Stuart Mill and John Dewey moves beyond the traditional boundaries of liberalism. John Stuart Mill departed from liberal democracy when he recommended a cooperative work arrangement, "not that which can exist between a capitalist as chief, and the workpeople without a voice in the management, but the association of the labourers themselves on terms of equality, collectively owning the capital with which they carry on their operations, and working under managers elected and removable by themselves."[10]

John Dewey was on the threshold of something different from liberal democracy when he indicated that democracy rests on faith in the capacities of human nature, faith in human intelligence and faith in the power of collective experiences. These things need not yet be realized; it is only necessary to believe that if given the opportunity, they will grow and be able to generate progressively the knowledge and wisdom needed to guide collective action.[11] These valuable departures from conventional liberal thinking represent a transition to a non-totalitarian alternative to liberalism.

It is my claim that a philosophy of participation can provide the nontotalitarian alternative to liberalism. At the risk of committing the sin of coining a neologism, such an alternative, because it is based on a strong belief in participation (just as liberalism originally was based on a strong belief in liberty), justifiably could be called *participationism*. As liberalism can produce concordant versions of other phenomena based on its perspective, so can participationism. The most obvious example is democracy. In contrasting participatory democracy with liberal democracy, the outstanding characteristics of participationism will emerge. In participatory democracy there is no split between the social and political worlds. There is, however, recognition of differences among communities; government is not confused with the academy, but what is political is not equated with what is governmental. Thus participatory democracy truly does move beyond John Locke's view of the political as equivalent to civil government.

Participatory democracy is not predicated on class division, whereas liberalism, in terms of its thought as well as its historical development, is contingent upon class distinctions. Liberal democracy enfranchised people to participate by granting them certain necessary rights, but the clear emphasis is on the *opportunity* to participate. If anything, actual participation beyond the civil ritual of voting is discouraged. Liberalism does not have a theory of individual development; thus liberal democracy cannot recognize that individual development and self-realization are dependent upon participation. The participatory view, as an alternative, is most clearly captured in opposition to these last two ideas.

Though both views of democracy deal with participation, there is a world of difference between them. Liberal democracy sees participation as an instrumental activity, one that advances an individual's interests, protects his rights, and legitimizes his position. To accomplish this, the individual influences elites. Since this pits individual against individual, group against group, and interest against interest, the emphasis is upon conflict and the power to prevail amid conflict. Though participatory democracy is dependent upon many of the same civil libertarian rights, it depicts participation in terms of cooperation as well as conflict. Viewing participation as intimately connected with self-development, political virtue, and the like, participatory democracy does not emphasize power. In liberal democracy, interest and self-development depend little upon participation. Even limited participation is considered the *cost* that must be paid to insure that one's interest is not ignored and that government will not expand too greatly. This raises the question of why some people participate more than others. Within the liberal model, it is easy to view the activist as someone who is psychologically twisted and seeking to sublimate feelings of inadequacy through the pursuit of power. With individuals within the liberal system, there may be some truth to the claim. From the view of participatory democracy and its view of participation, the activists are more likely to be mature human beings seeking to develop themselves and their sense of the community good.

It is important to emphasize again that this whole movement of thought is predicated on the important first distinction, that of the description of the political. The break from liberalism is accomplished by a break from the liberal view of politics. Liberalism described the political as a sphere consonant with government, and in doing so, deprecated the value of the political. Participationism, on the other hand, sees the political as activity related to group decision making. Thus there is politics and always will be politics whenever people gather together to make decisions. Politics cannot be done away with as long as we live in groups and make decisions governing those groups. Nor would we want to. Unlike liberalism, participationism sees politics as a potential good, not simply as a necessary evil.

This leads to a most interesting observation concerning totalitarianism. From the liberal point of view, totalitarianism is evil because it is a system in which the political invades all of the areas of our life (the valued social sphere). This representation is only true from the liberal perspective, which relates politics to that which is government. From the participatory point of view totalitarianism is indeed evil, but totalitarianism is the wanton spread of nonparticipatory government, not the spread of politics. As a matter of fact, totalitarianism does not permit much participation in decision making of genuine quality. Because totalitarianism does not allow individuals to participate in the decisions that govern their lives, and because it attempts to destroy the multiplicity of communities in which the opportunity to participate could exist, totalitarianism is not the spread of the political, but exactly the opposite. Democracy encourages the spread of the political, for democracy is a system of community rule in which participation is both widespread and effective. It is interesting to entertain the notion that there is more political life in a democratic community and less political life in a totalitarian system. Hannah Arendt is not wrong when she claims that

Tyranny . . . was a form of government in which the ruler, even though he ruled according to the laws of the realm, had monopolized for himself the right of action, banished the citizens from the public realm into the privacy of their households, and demanded of them that they mind their own, private business. Tyranny, in other words, deprived of public happiness, though not necessarily of private well-being, while a republic granted to every citizen the right to become a "participator in the government of affairs," the right to be seen in action.[12]

An important part of participationism, the identification of the political and rights related to the political with participation, is not entirely new. It begins with the Greeks and continues, albeit in interrupted fashion, throughout much of history. Aristotle defined the citizen as "one who has the right of sharing in deliberative or judicial office."[13] In a very real sense, participationism is neo-Hellenic.

It is not possible to develop the tenets of participationism very far beyond what was revealed in the discussion of participatory democracy versus liberal democracy, but it is possible to say a bit more about the values and phenomena with which participationism accords, and those things with which it conflicts. Participationism is tied closely to community. In fact it is participation within a group that helps establish community. One of the places at which participationism breaks cleanly from liberalism is in placing emphasis on the expressive aspects of participation, the true sense of belonging to a community (*gemeinshaft*).

From the point of view of participationism, other values will be put in contrast. Whereas liberalism heralded representation as the hallmark of democracy, participationism makes clear that it is no such thing. At best, representation is a necessary evil, one to be overcome in time if technological progress and the like can pave the way. If democracy is the reflection of participation, then representation is a curtailment of democracy. It may be true that we must rely on representation when the numbers in a community rise to unmanageable proportions, but it is not something we should accept passively.

In much the same way participationism, far more than liberalism, is likely to be a foe of bureaucracy, which limits participation. If bureaucracies attempt to operate in a classical sense, then rules will specify actions as far as possible. Participationism is antithetical to that kind of codification. Of course, participation can occur within bureaucracies, and that is the direction in which we should be moving. It will be easier to convert bureaucracies to a participatory mode than do away with them. As Max Weber states "Once it is fully established, bureaucracy is among those social structures which are hardest to destroy."[14]

More could be said about the perspective and views of participationism, including that although participationism partially rests on the rights and liberties of liberalism, it offers a positive view of liberty, while liberalism stresses the negative view. Participationism, however, does more than assume perspective and positions different from those of liberalism; it adds whole new dimensions to the activity of political theory. From the perspective of extending the political to all communities and not just the community of government, it can be understood just how much a critique of liberalism workplace democracy is. There is politics in the workplace, and if the decision making in the workplace is both widespread and effective, the workplace may be considered democratic. It is with the identification of the political as part of other communities that interesting new possibilities in political theory emerge. If politics is not confined to the state, then the concepts important to politics need not be limited to the state, either. Not only will democracy be discussed without necessarily referring to the state, but so will the full range of theoretical politics. Concepts such as equality and justice can be examined in reference to the workplace or any other community. Liberalism made theories of politics theories of the state. Participationism opens whole new vistas for theoretical elaboration.

Conclusion

There is always the possibility of a new political order. In this case the dream is of an order in which men and women participate in the decisions that affect their lives. What is desired is a new variety of participant (homo participans), one who is aware of himself (liberal man), and at the same time, is aware of himself and others as part of an organic community. What is sought is political action tempered with community awareness. Human liberation may depend upon it.

The change in the political order may have a specific place of focus. Though there is a general trend toward democracy, the next battleground may be in the workplace. The attention that workplace democracy is receiving worldwide indicates this. It is unclear whether the United States will keep pace with other nations or fall behind the movement toward democracy. The question is sufficiently important to be the subject of the companion volume, "The Feasibility of Workplace Democracy in The United States."

I cannot say that there will be a new order. I can only say that it is possible, and that if it is to occur, it very well may take the democratic form discussed. Workplace democracy contains the seeds of a new world order that is neither socialist nor capitalist in nature. What I do believe is that the whole thing becomes more of a possibility once we break from liberal thought. A shift in what is seen as political could make the entire difference.

In a passage within Plato's *Protagoras*, Hermes asks Zeus whether he should distribute consciousness and justice to the few or the many. Zeus replies that unlike practical crafts, all must share in these qualities, or else a well-run polity cannot be established or maintained.[15]

Notes
Bibliographic Essay
Index

Notes

1. Theoretical Background

1. Robert Dahl, *Modern Political Analysis*, 3d ed. (Englewood Cliffs, NJ: Prentice-Hall, 1976).

   David Easton, *The Political System*, 2d ed. (New York: Knopf, 1971).

   Fred M. Frohock, "Notes on the Concept of Politics: Weber, Easton, Strauss," *Journal of Politics* 36 (May 1974): 379–408.

   Giovanni Sartori, "What is 'Politics,'" *Political Theory* 1 (February 1973): 5–26.

   Carl Schmitt, *The Concept of the Political*, trans. George Schwab (New Brunswick, NJ: Rutgers Univ. Press, 1976).

   Leo Strauss, *Natural Right and History* (Chicago: Univ. of Chicago Press, 1953).

   ————, *What is Political Philosophy?* (Glencoe, IL: Free Press, 1959).
2. John Locke, *The Second Treatise of Government*, ed. J. W. Gough (New York: Macmillan, 1956), sec. 127.
3. Ibid., sec. 128.
4. Hannah Arendt, *The Human Condition* (Chicago: Univ. of Chicago Press, 1958).

   Giovanni Sartori, "What is 'Politics'."

   Richard Sennett, *The Fall of Public Man* (New York: Vintage Books, 1978).
5. Sheldon Wolin, *Politics and Vision* (Boston: Little, Brown, 1960).
6. Ibid., p. 2.
7. Ibid., p. 10.
8. Ibid., p. 61.
9. "Sublimation and Reification: Locke, Wolin and the Liberal Democratic Conception of the Political," *Politics and Society* 5, no. 4 (1975): 441–68.
10. *The Political System*, p. 134.
11. *Modern Political Analysis*, p. 3.
12. Ibid., p. 3.
13. *The Theory of Democratic Elitism: A Critique* (Boston: Little, Brown, 1967), p. 73.
14. *Political Science: A Philosophical Analysis* (Stanford: Stanford Univ. Press, 1960), p. 131.
15. Robert Dahl, *Modern Political Analysis*, pp. 29–32.
16. Sheldon Wolin, *Politics and Vision*.

    Donald Keim, "Participation in Contemporary Democratic Theories," in

Participation in Politics, ed. J. Roland Pennock and John W. Chapman (New York: Lieber-Atherton, NOMOS XVI, 1975), pp. 1–38.

17. John Dewey, *The Public and Its Problems* (New York: Henry Holt, 1927).
18. *The Concept of Community: Readings with Interpretations* (Chicago: Aldine Publishing, 1969).
19. Grant McConnell, *Private Power and American Democracy* (New York: Knopf, 1966). See also Robert Dahl, *Who Governs? Democracy and Power* (New Haven: Yale Univ. Press, 1961). In *After the Revolution* (New Haven: Yale Univ. Press, 1970), Dahl amends his position, claiming that it is absurd to view the contemporary economic corporation as "private." He still reveals a tendency, however, to extend the category of government rather than extending the category of politics.
20. George E. Berkley and Douglas M. Fox, *80,000 Governments: The Politics of Subnational Governments* (Boston: Allyn and Bacon, 1978), pp. 3–4.
21. James Madison, Alexander Hamilton, and John Jay, *The Federalist Papers* (New Rochelle, NY: Arlington House, nd). Benjamin Franklin, "A Treatise on Liberty and Necessity, Pleasure and Pain," *Selected Works* (Boston: Phillips and Sampson, 1857), pp. 125–126, 147 and 167. See also *Writings*, ed. A. H. Smyth (New York: Macmillan, 1905–07): 3, iv.
22. Sheldon Wolin, *Politics and Vision*, p. 315.

2. Participatory Democracy as a Political Ideal

1. *Principles of Social and Political Theory* (London: Clarendon Press of Oxford Univ., 1951), p. 207.
2. Carl Cohen, *Democracy* (New York: Free Press, 1973).
   Garaint Parry, "The Idea of Political Participation," in *Participation in Politics*, ed. Garaint Parry (Manchester: Manchester Univ. Press, 1972), pp. 3–38.
   Robert Salisbury, "Research on Political Participation," *American Journal of Political Science* 14 (May 1975): 323–41.
3. *Small Groups and Political Behavior: A Study in Leadership* (Princeton: Princeton Univ. Press, 1961).
4. "Some Issues in the Community Development Corporation Proposal," in *The Case for Participatory Democracy*, ed. C. George Benello and Dimitrios Roussopoulis (New York: Grossman, 1971), p. 66.
5. *Political Theory* (London: Methuen, 1956), p. 87.
6. "A Day in the Life of a Socialist Citizen," in *Obligations: Essays on Disobedience, War and Citizenship*, ed. Michael Walzer (Cambridge: Harvard Univ. Press, 1970), pp. 229–38.
7. This definition of democracy is a modified version of Carl Cohen's definition in *Democracy*, p. 7. Though there are important points of dif-

ference, not the least of which concerns the evaluation of opportunity to participate, Cohen's *Democracy* has had a strong influence on the general view of democracy expressed in this work.

8. Those who stress the participatory nature of democracy include such diverse personages as James Feminore Cooper, quoted in Arne Naess, et al., *Democracy, Ideology and Objectivity* (Oslo: Oslo Univ. Press, 1956), p. 283; Francis Coker, *Recent Political Thought* (New York: Appleton-Century, 1934), p. 300; T. D. Weldon, *States and Morals* (New York: Whittlesey House, 1947), p. 186; H. E. Barnes, "History of Democracy," *The Encyclopedia Americana* (New York: Americana Corporation), 8:639; Ricardo Pascual, contributor to the UNESCO democracy project, quoted in Naess, p. 328; Stuart Gerry Brown, contributor to the UNESCO democracy project, ibid., p. 335; Carole Pateman, *Participation and Democratic Theory* (Cambridge: The Cambridge Univ. Press, 1970), ch. 2; Robert Fluno, *The Democratic Community* (New York: Dodd, Mead, 1971), ch. 3; Terrance Cook and Patrick Morgan, *Participatory Democracy* (San Francisco: Canfield Press, 1971), ch. 1; C. George Benello and Dimitrios Roussopoulos, eds., *The Case for Participatory Democracy*, "Introduction"; David Kramer, *Participatory Democracy* (Cambridge, MA: Schenkman Publishing, 1972).

9. *Democracy and the American Party System* (New York: Harcourt, Brace, 1956), p. 11.

10. *The Education of Free Men in American Democracy* (Washington, D.C.: The Educational Policies Commission of the National Education Association, 1941).

11. *What is Democracy?* (Chicago: Univ. of Chicago Press, 1941), p. 92.

12. *The Democratic Way of Life*, rev. ed. (Chicago: Univ. of Chicago Press, 1939), p. 12.

13. *Encyclopedia of the Social Sciences*, 1934 ed., s.v. "Democracy," p. 76.

14. Although the formulation is attributed to Abraham Lincoln, it was not part of his "Gettysburg Address," as is commonly believed. It was instead part of his speech delivered in Bloomington, Illinois, September 26, 1854.

15. *The Real World of Democracy: The Massay Lectures* (London: Oxford Univ. Press, 1966).

16. Ibid., p. 37.

17. Thoman Landon Thorson, *The Logic of Democracy* (New York: Holt, Rinehart and Winston, 1962), p. 152.

18. *The Democratic Citizen* (Cambridge: Cambridge Univ. Press, 1970).

19. *The Modern Democratic State* (London: Oxford Univ. Press, 1942), p. 270.

20. Aristotle, *The Politics of Aristotle*, ed. and trans., Ernest Barker (New York: Galaxy, 1962), p. 123.

21. M. E. A. Shaw, "A Comparison of Individuals and Small Groups in the

Rational Solution of Complex Problems," *American Journal of Psychology* 44 (October 1932): 491–504.

22. D. W. Taylor, P. C. Berry and C. H. Block, "Does Group Participation When Using Brainstorming Facilitate or Inhibit Creative Thinking?" *Administrative Science Quarterly* 3 (June 1958): 23–47. For a more complete development of the literature that addresses this question see Victor H. Vroom, "Industrial Social Psychology," in *The Handbook of Social Psychology*, ed. Gardner Lindzey, 2d ed. (Reading, MA: Addison-Wesley Publishing, 1969), 5: 196–268.

23. *Participatory Democracy*, p. 12.

24. For example, D. W. Taylor and W. L. Faust, "Twenty Questions: Efficiency in Problem Solving as a Function of Size of Group," *Journal of Experimental Psychology* 44 (November 1952): 360–68.

25. Carole Pateman provides an excellent discussion of Rousseau and participatory democracy. See *Participation and Democratic Theory*, ch. 2.

26. The notion that participation in decision making increases the enforceability of those decisions is supported by A. Bevelas, "Communication Patterns in Task-oriented Groups," *Journal of the Acoustical Society of America* 22 (November 1950): 725–30; J. R. R. French, Jr., J. Israel, and D. As, "An Experiment on Participation in a Norwegian Factory," *Human Relations* 13 (February 1960): 3–19; N. R. F. Maier, *Problem Solving Discussions and Conferences: Leadership Methods and Skills* (New York: McGraw-Hill, 1963), and B. M. Bass and H. J. Leavitt, "Some Experiments in Planning and Operating," *Management Science* 9 (July 1963): 574–85.

27. *Representative Government* (London: J. M. Dent and Sons, Everyman Library, 1951), p. 375.

28. *The Political Writings of Thomas Jefferson* ed. Edward Dumbauld (New York: Bobbs-Merrill, 1955), pp. 99, 117.

29. Gabriel Almond and Sidney Verba, *The Civic Culture* (Boston: Little, Brown, 1965), p. 198.

30. Some examples of studies conducted at the local level which examine the relationship between participation and legitimacy include: Robert Agger and Vincent Ostrom, "Political Participation in a Small Community," in *Political Behavior*, eds. Heinz Eulau et al. (Glencoe, IL: The Free Press, 1956), pp. 139–140, 144; Alice S. Kett and David B. Gleicher, "Determinants of Voting Behavior," *Public Opinion Quarterly* 14 (Fall 1950): 393–412; Morris Rosenberg, "Some Determinants of Political Apathy," *Public Opinion Quarterly* 18 (Winter 1954–55): 349–66.

31. *Representative Government*, p. 291.

32. Herbert McCloskey, "Consensus and Ideology in American Politics," *American Political Science Review* 58 (June 1964): 361–82; see also James Prothro and Charles Grigg, "Fundamental Principles of Democracy:

Bases of Argument and Disagreement," *Journal of Politics* 22 (May 1960): 276–94.

33. *Representative Government*, p. 373. The emphasis on *sentiments* is supplied.
34. Bernard Bosanquet, *The Philosophical Theory of the State*, 4th ed. (London: Macmillan & Co., 1923).
   Jay W. Hudson, *Why Democracy?* (New York: Appleton-Century, 1936).
   Arthur Kenyan Rogers, *Theory of Ethics* (New York: Macmillan Co., 1922).
   Westel Woodbury Willoughby, *The Ethical Basis of Political Authority* (New York: Macmillan Co., 1930).
35. Although this theme is present in many of her writings, it is most clearly expressed in *The Human Condition* (Chicago: Univ. of Chicago Press, 1958).
36. Implicit in broadening cognitive horizons is the assumption that participation will increase political knowledge. Students of political science invariably construct the hypothesis in the opposite direction: that political knowledge leads to participation. It is interesting to note that at the bottom of Lester Milbrath's hierarchical ranking of participation lies "exposing oneself to political stimuli"; Lester Milbrath, *Political Participation* (Chicago: Rand McNally, 1965), p. 18. If the exposure itself is an act of political participation, then participation precedes accumulation of knowledge. Given the temporal sequence, the most correct construction is participation augmenting political knowledge. The actual relationship between participation and political knowledge is obviously reciprocal, with participation resulting in political knowledge and higher levels of knowledge fostering more participation. This reciprocal relationship is another example of participation promoting itself.
37. *The Civic Culture*, pp. 206–7.
38. For a brief review of political efficacy findings, see Lester Milbrath and M. L. Goel, *Political Participation*, 2d ed. (Chicago: Rand McNally, 1977), p. 57–61.
39. Again, political scientists believe that political knowledge leads to participation, not that participation leads to knowledge.
40. *Who Governs? Democracy and Power in an American City* (New Haven: Yale Univ. Press, 1961).
41. *Political Participation*, p. 59.
42. See C. B. Macpherson, *The Theory of Possessive Individualism* (London: Oxford Univ. Press, 1962).
43. Ed. C. K. Ogden (London: Routledge and Paul, 1931).
44. James Mill, *Essays on Government, Jurisprudence, Liberty of the Press and Law of Nations* (New York: A. M. Kelley, 1967).
45. *Representative Government*.

46. *Collected Works*, ed. J. Robson, (Toronto, Canada: University of Toronto Press, 1965), bk. 4, ch. 7.
47. *Capitalism, Socialism and Democracy* (New York: Harper & Brothers, 1942), p. 269.
48. Ibid., p. 285.
49. Ibid., p. 295. First emphasis supplied.
50. Robert Dahl and Charles Lindblom, *Politics, Economics and Welfare* (New York: Harper & Row, Torchbook, 1953).
51. The label, "democratic revisionists," is widespread in its currency. It is employed consistently to refer to the same general set of political thinkers (e.g. Schumpeter, Berelson, Milbrath) by such theorists as Carole Pateman, Henry Kariel, Peter Bachrach and John Plamenatz.
52. Bernard Berelson, Paul Lazarsfeld, and William McPhee, *Voting* (Chicago: Univ. of Chicago Press, 1954).
53. Ibid., p. 314.
54. The apathetics are the roughly 40 percent who do not bother to vote.
55. Berelson, Lazarsfeld, McPhee, *Voting*, p. 314.
56. (New York: Harper & Row, 1957).
57. *Participation and Democratic Theory*, p. 17.
58. *Democracy and Illusion* (Plymouth, London: Longman Group Limited, 1973), p. 96.
59. *Essays on Politics and Culture*, ed. G. Himmelfarb, (New York: Doubleday, 1963), p. 229.
60. Examples of "elitist revisionists" would include Schumpeter, Milbrath, Sartori and McClosky, to mention a few.
61. *Political Man* (New York: Doubleday-Anchor, 1963), p. 121.
62. Sidney Verba and Norman Nie, *Participation in America: Political Democracy and Social Equality* (New York: Harper & Row, 1972).
63. The twelve political activities are: voting in presidential elections, voting in local elections, participating in at least one organization involved in community problems, working with others in trying to solve some community problems, attempting to persuade others to vote as they would, working for a party or candidate during an election, contacting local government official about some issue or problem, attending at least one political meeting or rally in the last three years, contacting a state or national government official about some issue or problem, giving money to a party or candidate during an election campaign, and being a member of a political club or organization.
64. *Participation in America*, p. 32.
65. Ibid., p. 32.
66. Ibid., p. 33.
67. Peter Bachrach, *The Theory of Democratic Elitism: A Critique* (Boston: Little, Brown, 1967).

Lane Davis, "The Cost of Realism: Contemporary Restatements of Democracy," *Western Political Quarterly* 17 (March 1964): 37–46.

Carole Pateman, *Participation and Democratic Theory*.

John Plamenatz, *Democracy and Illusion*.

68. Robert Fluno, *The Democratic Community*.

Cook and Morgan, *Participatory Democracy*.

C. George Benello and Dimitrios Roussopoulos, ed., *The Case for Participatory Democracy*.

David Kramer, *Participatory Democracy*.

69. (London: Oxford Univ. Press, 1977).

70. Ibid., p. 114.

71. P. 37.

72. *Representative Government*, pp. 291–92.

3. Liberalism and Participation Research

1. "Human Nature and Participatory Democracy," in *The Bias of Pluralism*, ed. William E. Connolly (New York: Atherton Press, 1969), p. 199.

2. *Participation in America* (New York: Harper & Row, 1972), p. 148.

3. Lester Milbrath and M. L. Goel, *Political Participation*, 2d ed. (Chicago: Rand McNally, College Publishing, 1977), p. 53. Italics mine.

4. "Social Structure and Political Participation: Developmental Relationships: Part 1," *American Political Science Review* 63 (June 1969): 365. See also "Social Structure and Political Participation: Developmental Relationship: Part II," *American Political Science Review* 63 (September 1969): 808–32.

5. Ibid., p. 364.

6. Ibid., p. 366.

7. "Social Structures and Individual Political Participation in Five Countries," *American Journal of Sociology* 77 (May 1972): 1103–4.

8. Sidney Verba, Norman Nie and Jae-on Kim, *The Modes of Democratic Participation: A Cross-National Comparison* (Beverly Hills: Sage Publications, 1971).

9. David Sallach, Nicholas Babchuk and Alan Booth, "Social Involvement and Political Activity: Another View," *Social Science Quarterly* 52 (March 1972): 888.

10. Marvin Olsen, "Social Participation and Voting Turnout: A Multivariate Analysis," *American Sociological Review*, 37 (June, 1972): 318.

11. Ibid., p. 323.

12. Ibid., p. 324.

13. Ibid., p. 331.

14. Ibid., p. 319.

15. Sallach, et al. "Social Involvement and Political Activity," p. 888.
16. "Social Participation and Voting Turnout," p. 323.
17. P. 184.
18. Ibid., p. 186.
19. At one point in *Participation in America*, Verba and Nie wrote, "affiliation with manifestly non-political organizations does increase an individual's participation rate, but only if there is some political exposure," (p. 194). This seemed so contrary to their data and previous discussion that I called Sidney Verba's attention to the statement. In personal correspondence, Verba replied, "I think we were a bit careless in the way in which we wrote up the data for the organizational effects in figure 11–5 or table 11–4. We were focusing mostly on the nature of exposures and did not say explicitly—which the data make clear—that activity within organizations by itself is a potent force."
20. Ibid., p. 187.
21. Sidney Verba, Norman Nie and Jae-on Kim, *Participation and Political Equality* (New York: Cambridge Univ. Press, 1978).
22. Angus Campbell, et al., *The American Voter* (Chicago: Univ. of Chicago Press, 1960).
    Norman Nie, Sidney Verba and John Petrocik, *The Changing American Voter* (Cambridge: Harvard Univ. Press, 1976).
23. *Participation in America*, p. 182.
24. *Political Participation* (Chicago: Rand McNally, 1965), p. 17.
25. Lester Milbrath and M. L. Goel, *Political Participation*: pp. 1–2.
26. "On Methods in the Study of Politics," *Political Science Quarterly* 38 (December 1923): 638.
27. Erik Allardt, Pentti Jartti and Finan Jyrkila, "On the Cumulative Nature of Leisure Activities," *Acta* Sociologica 3 (fasc. 4), 165–72.
    Morris Axelrod, "Urban Structures and Social Participation," *American Sociological Review* 21 (February 1956): 13–18.
    Nicholas Babchuk, et al., *The Voluntary Association in the Slum* (Lincoln: Univ. of Nebraska Press, 1962).
    Theodore Caplow and Robert Forman, "Neighborhood Interaction in a Homogenous Community," *American Sociological Review* 15 (June 1950): 357–66.
    Scott Greer, "Urbanism Reconsidered: A Comparative Study of Local Areas in Metropolis," *American Sociological Review* 21 (February 1956): 19–25.
    Arthur Jacoby, "Personal Influence and Primary Relationships: Their Effects on Associational Membership," *Sociological Quarterly* 7 (Winter 1966): 76–84.
    Bartolomeu Palisi, "Ethnic Generation and Social Participation," *Sociological Inquiry* 35 (Spring 1965): 219–26.

————, "Patterns of Social Participation in a Two Generation Sample of Italian-Americans," *The Sociological Inquiry* 7 (Spring 1966): 167–88.
John C. Scott, Jr., "Membership and Participation in Voluntary Associations," *American Sociological Review* 22 (June 1957): 315–26.
James Williams, "Close Friendship Relations of Housewives Residing in an Urban Community," *Sociological and Social Research* 47 (January 1958): 201–9.

28. Stephen J. Cutler, "Age Differences in Voluntary Association Memberships," *Social Forces* 55 (September 1976): 43–58. Cutler is a leading investigator of this phenomenon. See also his "Aging and Voluntary Association Participation," *Journal of Gerontology* 32 (1977): 470–79. David Knoke and Randall Thomson claim that this pattern is attributable to religious voluntary associations. With that exempted, the pattern returns to the familiar curvilinear relationship pattern. See their "Voluntary Association Membership Trends and the Family Life Cycle," *Social Forces* 56 (September 1977): 48–65.

29. J. C. Van Es and Daniel J. Loenig, "Social Participation, Social Status and Extremist Political Attitudes," *The Sociological Quarterly* 17 (Winter 1976): 16–26.

4. The Workplace Connection

1. "Social Participation and Voting Turnout: A Multivariate Analysis," *American Sociological Review* 37 (June 1972), 331. (Italics mine.)

2. Ruth S. Jones reports of a somewhat successful experiment in her article, "Changing Student Attitudes: The Impact of Community Participation," *Social Science Quarterly* 55 (September 1974): 439–50.

3. *Political Learning, Political Choice and Democratic Citizenship* (Englewood Cliffs, NJ: Prentice-Hall, 1974).

4. *Children and Politics* (New Haven: Yale Univ. Press, 1965), p. 56.

5. *Political Socialization* (New York: Free Press, 1959), p. 19.

6. Several works which examine the effects of the Vietnam War experience on soldiers are Loch Johnson, "Political Alienation Among Vietnam Veterans," *Western Political Quarterly* 29 (September 1976): 398–409; John Pollock et al., "When Soldiers Return: Combat and Political Alienation Among White Vietnam Vets," in *New Directions in Political Socialization*, eds. David Schwartz and Sandra Schwartz (New York: Free Press, 1975), pp. 317–33. The number of articles that consider the socialization impact of the Watergate experience is much larger. For example, see F. C. Arterton, "Impact of Watergate on Children's Attitudes Toward Political Authority," *Political Science Quarterly* 89 (June 1974): 269–88, or his "Watergate and Children's Attitudes Toward Political Authority Revisited,"

Political Science Quarterly 90 (Fall 1975): 477–96. See also G. F. Bishop, "Resolution and Tolerance of Cognitive Inconsistency in a Field Situation: Change in Attitudes and Beliefs Following the Watergate," *Psychological Reports* 36 (June 1975): 747–53.

7. M. Kent Jennings and Richard G. Niemi, "Continuity and Change in Political Orientations: A Longitudinal Study of Two Generations," *American Political Science Review* 69 (December 1975): 1335.
8. *Socialization After Childhood* (New York: Wiley, 1966).
9. Lewis Edinger and Donald Searing, "Social Background in Elite Analysis: A Methodological Inquiry," *American Political Science Review* 61 (June 1967): 445.
10. Among adult experiences, occupation was the best predictor of attitudes. In Venezuela it was significantly related to 84 percent of all attitudes. Donald Searing, "The Comparative Study of Elite Socialization," *Comparative Political Studies* 1 (January 1969): 476.
11. Ibid., p. 498.
12. Allan Kornberg and N. Thomas, "The Political Socialization of National Legislative Elites in the United States and Canada," *Journal of Politics* 27 (November 1965): 761–75. See also Allan Kornberg, Joel Smith, Mary-Jane Clarke, and Harold Clarke, "Participation in Local Party Organizations in the United States and Canada," *American Journal of Political Science* 17 (February 1973): 23–57.
13. Kenneth Prewitt et al., "Political Socialization and Political Roles," *Public Opinion Quarterly* 30 (Winter 1966–1967): 581.
14. "Political Socialization in the American Family: The Evidence Re-examined," *Public Opinion Quarterly* 36 (Fall 1972): 330.
15. Donald Searing, Joel Schwartz and Alden Lind, "The Structuring Principle: Political Socialization and Belief Systems," *American Political Science Review* 67 (June 1973): 415.
16. Ibid., p. 419.
17. Michael Hanks and Bruce Ecland, "Adult Voluntary Associations and Adolescent Socialization," *The Sociological Quarterly* 19 (Summer 1978): 481–90.
18. "Occupational Socialization," in *Handbook of Socialization Theory and Research*, ed. D. A. Goslin (Chicago: Rand McNally, 1969), p. 861.
19. *Statistical Abstract of the United States* (Washington: U.S. Department of Commerce—Bureau of the Census, 98th ed., 1977), p. 388, and *Historical Statistics of the United States: Colonial Times to 1957* (Washington, D.C.: U.S. Department of Commerce—Bureau of the Census, 1969), p. 70.
20. See Robert Owen, "Fourth Essay on the Formation of Character," "Report to the County of Lanark," and "A Further Development of the Plan for the Relief of the Poor and the Emancipation of Mankind," *A New*

View of Society and Other Writings (London: J. M. Dent and Sons, 1927), pp. 63–92, 245–98, and 224–44.

21. *Historical Revelations: Inscribed to Lord Normandy* (New York: H. Fertig, 1971), chs. 9 and 11.

22. See Pierre-Joseph Proudhon, "Seventh Study: Absorption of Government by the Economic Organism," *General Idea of Revolution in the Nineteenth Century* (London: Freeman Press, 1923), pp. 240–87. See also Proudhon's "Psychological Exposition of the Idea of Justice and Injustice, and a Determination of the Principle of Government and of Right," in *What is Property? An Inquiry into the Principle of Right and Government* (New York: Dover Publications, 1970), esp. pp. 250–80. See also "Mutualism," and "Federalism," *Selected Writings of Pierre-Joseph Proudhon*, ed. with intro. Stewart Edwards (Garden City, NY: Anchor Books, 1969), pp. 56–70 and 102–12.

23. Emile Durkheim, *The Division of Labor in Society*, trans. George Simpson (Glencoe, IL: The Free Press, 1933), p. 28.

24. Ibid.

25. Ibid., p. 27.

26. Ibid.

27. Ibid.

28. For the cross reference of the Mill citations, please see Chapter Two, "Participatory Democracy as a Political Ideal—The Benefits."

29. *Participation and Democratic Theory* (Cambridge: Cambridge Univ. Press, 1970), p. 33.

30. John Stuart Mill in J. Robson, ed., *Collected Works* (Toronto: Univ. of Toronto Press, 1965), bk. 4, ch. 7, sec. 6, p. 792. Carole Pateman isolated this and the following John Stuart Mill references.

31. *Collected Works*, bk. 2, ch. 1, sec. 3, p. 205.

32. *Collected Works*, bk. 4, ch. 7, sec. 6, p. 775.

33. The distributists asserted that the old variety of capitalism was fading as a result of socialist legislation. They therefore recommended that employers should be made responsible for the welfare of the workers by enforcement of the state. The best known "distributist" by far was Hilaire Belloc. For a discussion of the position by Belloc please see Hilaire Belloc, *The Servile State* (London: T. N. Foulis, 1912) and Hilaire Belloc, *An Essay on the Restoration of Property* (London: The Distributist League, 1936).

34. *Fors Clavigera: Letters to the Workmen and Labourers of Great Britain* (New York: Greenwood Press, 1968. Originally published in 1886).

35. For a brief survey of William Morris' beliefs, please see the following works by Morris: . . . *Chants for Socialists* (New York: New Horizon Press, 1935); *Factory Work, As It Is and Might Be: News from Nowhere* (London:

Routledge and Kegan Paul, 1970); and *The Political Writings of William Morris* (New York: International Publishers, 1973).

36. A. J. Penty, *The Restoration of Gild System*, published again under the title, *Guilds and the Social Crisis* (London: G. Allen and Unwin, 1919).

37. *National Guilds: An Inquiry into the Wage System and the Way Out* (1914) quoted in S. T. Glass, *The Responsible Society: The Ideas of Guild Socialism* (London: Longmans, Green and Co., 1966), p. 30.

38. S. T. Glass, *The Responsible Society*, p. 37.

39. *Labour in the Commonwealth* (London: Headly Bros., 1918), p. 35.

40. *Self-Government in Industry* (London: G. Bell and Sons, 1919), p. 157.

41. *Guild Socialism Re-stated* (London: Leonard Parsons, 1920), p. 12.

42. See John H. Cammet, *Antonio Gramsci and the Origins of Italian Communism* (Stanford: Stanford Univ. Press, 1967); Antonio Gramsci, *The Modern Prince* (London: Lawrence and Wishart, 1957); Antonio Gramsci, *Letters from Prison* (New York: Harper & Row, 1973); and Giuseppi Fiori, *Antonio Gramsci: Life of a Revolutionary* (New York: Schocken Books, 1970).

43. *A Strategy for Labor* (Boston: Beacon Press, 1967) and *Socialism and Revolution* (Garden City: Anchor Books, 1973).

44. Chris Argyris, *Personality and Organization* (New York: Harper Brothers, 1957) and Chris Argyris, *Integrating the Individual and the Organization* (New York: Wiley, 1964).

Peter Bachrach, *The Theory of Democratic Elitism: A Critique* (Boston: Little, Brown, 1967).

Ernest Barker, *Principles of Social and Political Theory* (London: Clarendon Press of Oxford Univ., 1951).

C. George Benello and Dimitrios Roussopoulos, *The Case for Participatory Democracy* (New York: Grossman Publishers, 1971).

T. B. Bottomore, "The Insufficiency of Elite Competition," in Henry Kariel's *Frontiers of Democratic Theory* (New York: Random House, 1970), pp. 127–39.

Terrance Cook and Patrick Morgan, *Participatory Democracy* (San Francisco: Canfield Press, 1971).

Erich Fromm, *The Sane Society* (New York: Rinehart, 1955).

G. David Garson, *On Democratic Administration and Socialist Self-Management: A Comparative Survey Emphasizing the Yugoslav Experience* (Beverly Hills: Sage Publications, 1974).

Edward Greenberg, *The American Political System: A Radical Approach* (Cambridge, MA: Winthrop Publishers, 1977).

Tom Hayden, "The 'Port Huron Statement' of the Students for a Democratic Society" in Kenneth M. Dolbeare, ed., *Directions in American Political Thought* (New York: Wiley, 1969), p. 468–86.

Workers' Control, eds. Gerry Hunnius, G. David Garson, and John Case (New York: Vintage Books, 1973).

David Jenkins, *Job Power* (New York: Doubleday, 1973).

Henry Kariel, ed., *Frontiers of Democratic Theory* (New York: Random House, 1970).

C. B. Macpherson, *Democratic Theory: Essays in Retrieval* (Oxford: Clarendon Press, 1973).

C. Wright Mills, *The Power Elite* (New York: Oxford Univ. Press, 1959), and C. Wright Mills, *White Collar: The American Middle Classes* (New York: Oxford Univ. Press, 1951).

Carole Pateman, *Participation and Democratic Theory*.

Dennis F. Thompson, *The Democratic Citizen* (Cambridge: Cambridge Univ. Press, 1970).

Tony Topham and Ken Coates, eds., *Workers' Control* (London: Panther Modern Society, 1970).

Graham Wooten, *Workers, Unions and the State* (New York: Schocken Books, 1971).

45. "The Insufficiency of Elite Competition," p. 135.
46. *The Civic Culture*, p. 271.
47. Ibid., p. 303.
48. Ibid., p. 294.
49. Ibid., ch. 10, pp. 244–65.
50. David Sallach, Nicholas Babchuk and Alan Booth, "Social Involvement and Political Activity: Another View," *Social Science Quarterly* 52 (March 1972): 879–92.
51. *American Political Science Review* 58 (December 1964): 951–62.
52. *American Sociological Review* 38 (December 1973): 697–711.
53. Robert Blauner's use of the concept, alienation, places it in direct opposition to participation. He stated that alienation "exists when workers are unable to control their immediate work process, to develop a sense of purpose and function which connects the jobs to the overall organization of production, to belong to integrated industrial communities, and when they fail to become involved in the activity of work as a mode of personal expression." Robert Blauner, *Alienation and Freedom* (Chicago: Univ. of Chicago Press, 1964), p. 15.
54. Ibid., p. viii.
55. Ibid., pp. 69–70. Carole Pateman provides this distillation in *Participation and Democratic Theory*, p. 52.
56. Ibid., p. 178.
57. Ibid., pp. 176 and 43. Summary again provided by Pateman, p. 52.
58. "Political Efficacy and Political Illusion," *Journal of Politics* 37 (May 1975): 469–87.
59. Robert Agger, Marshall Goldstein, and Stanley Pearl, "Political Cynicism: Measurement and Meaning," *Journal of Politics* 23 (August 1961): 477–506.

Gabriel Almond and Sidney Verba, *The Civic Culture*.

Bernard Berelson, Paul F. Lazarsfeld and William McPhee, *Voting* (Chicago: Univ. of Chicago Press, 1954).

Angus Campbell, Phillip Converse, Warren Miller, and Donald Stokes, *The American Voter* (New York: Wiley, 1960).

Robert Dahl, *Who Governs: Democracy and Power in an American City* (New Haven: Yale Univ. Press, 1961).

Dwight Dean, "Alienation and Political Apathy," *Social Forces* 38 (March 1960): 185–89.

Jack Dennis, "Support for the Institution of Elections by the Mass Public," *American Political Science Review* 64 (September 1970): 819–35.

Giuseppe DiPalma, *Apathy and Participation* (New York: The Free Press, 1970).

Ada Finifter, "Dimensions of Political Alienation," *American Political Science Review* 64 (June 1970): 389–410.

Howard Hamilton, "The Municipal Voter: Voting and Non-Voting in City Elections," *American Political Science Review* 65 (December 1971): 1135–40.

Edward Muller, "Cross-National Dimensions of Political Competence," *American Political Science Review* 64 (September 1970): 792–809.

Marvin Olsen, "Two Categories of Political Alienation," *Social Forces* 47 (March 1969): 288–299.

Wayne Thompson and John Horton, "Political Alienation as a Force in Political Action," *Social Forces* 38 (March 1960): 190–195.

Sidney Verba and Norman Nie, *Participation in America*.

Susan Welsh, John Comer, and Michael Steinman, "Political Participation Among Mexican Americans: An Exploratory Examination," *Social Science Quarterly* 53 (March 1973): 799–813. For a more extensive bibliography see David Easton and Jack Dennis, "The Child's Acquisition of Regime Norms: Political Efficacy," *American Political Science Review* 61 (March 1967): 25–38.

60. J. Miller McPhersen, Susan Welsh, and Cal Clarke, "The Stability and Reliability of Political Efficacy: Using Path Analysis to Test Alternative Models," *American Political Science Review* (June 1977): 509–21.

61. Lester Milbrath, *Political Participation* (Chicago: Rand McNally, 1965), p. 59. See also:

Gordon W. Allport, "The Psychology of Participation," *Psychological Review* 52 (May 1945): 117–32.

Angus Campbell, "Surge and Decline: A Study of Electoral Change," *Public Opinion Quarterly* 24 (Fall 1960): 397–418.

———, "The Passive Citizen," *Acta Sociologica* VI (fasc. 1–2), 9–12.

Robert Dahl, *Who Governs?*

Robert E. Lane, *Political Life: Why People Get Involved in Politics* (Glencoe, IL: The Free Press, 1959).

Paul Mussen and Anne Wyszynski, "Personality and Political Participation," *Human Relations* 5 (February 1952): 65–82.

62. Angus Campbell, *The Voter Decides.*

Angus Campbell, Phillip Converse, Warren Miller and Donald Stokes, *The American Voter* (New York: Wiley, 1960).

Dwaine Marvick and Charles Nixon, "Recruitment Contrasts in Rival Campaign Groups," in Dwaine Marvick, ed., *Political Decision-Makers* (Glencoe, IL: The Free Press, 1961), pp. 193–217.

63. Lester Milbrath, *Political Participation*, p. 75.

64. Ibid.

65. For example, see Roberta Sigel, "Psychological Antecedents and Political Involvement: The Utility of the Concept of Locus of Control," *Social Science Quarterly* 56 (September 1975): 315–23.

66. Robert Agger, Marshall Goldstein and Stanley Pearl, "Political Cynicism: Measurement and Meaning."

Gabriel Almond and Sidney Verba, *The Civic Culture.*

Angus Campbell, "The Passive Citizen."

Dwight Dean, "Alienation and Political Apathy."

Giuseppe DiPalma, *Apathy and Participation.*

William Erbe, "Social Involvement and Political Activity," *American Sociological Review* 29 (April 1964): 188–215.

Kenneth Janda, "A Comparative Study of Political Alienation and Voting Behavior in Three Suburban Communities," in *Studies in History and the Social Services—Studies in honor of John A. Kinneman* (Normal, IL: Illinois State Univ. Press, 1965), pp. 53–68.

Arthur Kornhauser, Albert Mayer, and Harold Sheppard, *When Labor Votes* (New York: Univ. Books, 1956).

Murray Levin, *The Alienated Voter* (New York: Holt, Rinehart and Winston, 1960).

Edgar Litt, "Political Cynicism and Political Futility," *The Journal of Politics* 25 (May 1963): 312–23.

Edward McDill and Jeanne Ridley, "Status, Anomia, Political Alienation and Political Participation," *American Journal of Sociology* 67 (September 1962): 205–17.

Morris Rosenberg, "Some Determinants of Political Apathy," *Public Opinion Quarterly* (Winter 1954–55): 349–66.

Donald Stokes, "Popular Evaluations of Government: An Empirical Assessment," in Harlan Cleveland and Harold Lasswell, eds., *Ethics and Bigness* (New York: Harper, 1962), pp. 61–72.

Frederic Templeton, "Alienation and Political Participation."

Wayne Thompson and John Horton, "Political Alienation as a Force in Political Action."

67. See Lester Milbrath's discussion of alienation and unconventional political participation in *Political Participation* (Chicago: Rand McNally, second edition, 1977), pp. 68–74.

68. See for example:
Ada Finifter, "Dimensions of Political Alienation."
David Nachmias, "Modes and Types of Political Alienation," *British Journal of Sociology* 25 (December 1974): 478–93.
James House and William Mason, "Political Alienation in America 1952–1968," *American Sociological Review* 40 (April 1975): 123–47.
Avery Guest, "Reply with Rejoinder to House/Mason, Political Alienation in America," *American Sociological Review* 41 (April 1976): 365–76.
James Wright, "Alienation and Political Negativism: New Evidence from National Surveys," *Sociological and Social Research*, 60 (January 1976): 111–34.

69. *Participation and Democratic Theory*, p. 50.

70. *Political Man* (New York: Anchor/Doubleday, 1962), p. 198.

71. Ibid.

72. *Political Participation*, 2d ed., p. 102. See also:
Robert Agger and Vincent Ostrum, "Political Participation in a Small Community," in Heinz Eulau, Sam Eldersveld, and Morris Janowitz, eds. *Political Behavior* (Glencoe, IL: The Free Press, 1956), pp. 138–48.
James David Barber, *Citizen Politics* (Chicago: Markham, 1969).
Stephen Bennett and William Klecks, "Social Status and Political Participation: A Multivariate Analysis of Predictive Power," *Midwest Journal of Political Science* 14 (August 1970): 355–82.
John Bonham, "The Middle Class Elector," *British Journal of Sociology* 3 (September 1952): 222–30.
Philip Buck, *Amateurs and Professionals in British Politics* (Chicago: Univ. of Chicago Press, 1963).
Angus Campbell and Robert L. Kahn, *The People Elect a President* (Ann Arbor: Univ. of Michigan, SRC, 1952).
Gordon Connelly and Harry Field, "The Non-Voter: Who He Is, What He Thinks," *Public Opinion Quarterly* 8 (Summer 1944): 175–87.
Robert Dahl, *Who Governs?*
Howard Hamilton, "The Municipal Voter."
Donald Mathews and James Prothro, *Negroes and the New Southern Politics* (New York: Harcourt, Brace and World, 1966).
William McPhee and William Glaser, eds., *Public Opinion and Congressional Elections* (New York: The Free Press, 1962).
Marvin Olsen, "A Model of Political Participation Stratification," *Journal of Political and Military Sociology* 1 (Fall 1973): 183–200.

73. *Political Life*, ch. 15.
74. "Workplace Alienation and the Need for Major Innovation." Report of a special task force to the secretary of Health, Education and Welfare, *Work in America* (Cambridge: MIT Press, 1973), pp. 99, 241.
75. Ibid., p. 99.
76. Neil McWhinney as quoted in David Jenkins, "Democracy in the Factory," *The Atlantic* (1973), p. 78.

5. The Importance of Work

1. *The Compact Edition of the Oxford English Dictionary*, s.v. "Work."
2. (Chicago: Chicago Univ. Press, 1958), p. 127.
3. Erich Fromm, *Marx's Conception of Man* (New York: Frederick Ungar Publishing Co., 1961).
4. Aristotle, "Nicomachean Ethics" in *Introduction to Aristotle*, ed. Richard McKeon (New York: The Modern Library, 1947), bk. 1, ch. 5, sec. 1096.
5. *Homo Faber* (New York: Harcourt, Brace, 1930).
6. Stanley Parker, *The Future of Work and Leisure* (New York: Praeger, 1971), p. 36.
7. Genesis 3:19.
8. James Gillespie, "Toward Freedom in Work," eds. C. George Benello and Dimitrios Roussopoulos, *The Case for Participatory Democracy* (New York: Grossman, 1971), p. 78.
9. Ibid.
10. Robert Beum, "From Millennium to Malaise: Reflections of Modern Work," *Modern Age* 22 (Winter 1978): 54–63.
11. *From Max Weber*, trans. and ed. H. H. Gerth and C. Wright Mills (New York: Oxford Univ. Press, 1946), p. 313.
12. David Jenkins, *Job Power* (Garden City, NY: Doubleday, 1973), p. 21.
13. Sheldon Wolin, *Politics and Vision* (Boston: Little, Brown, 1960), pp. 294–95.
14. John Locke, *The Second Treatise of Government*, ed. J. W. Gough (New York: Macmillan, 1956), sec. 35.
15. *Politics and Vision*, p. 341.
16. Jeremy Bentham, *Jeremy Bentham's Economic Writings*, ed. W. Stark (London: Allen and Unwin, 1954), 3:425. Cited in Sheldon Wolin's *Politics and Vision*, p. 341.
17. *Cyropaedia*, trans. Walter Miller (London: Heinemann, 1914): bk. 7, sec. ii.
18. *The Wealth of Nations* (London: Dent, 1910), 1:5.
19. Ibid., 2:264–65.
20. Frederick Taylor, *Shop Management* (1903) included in Frederick Taylor,

Scientific Management (New York: Harper and Row, 1947), pp. 42–46.

21. This is reported in David Jenkins, *Job Power*, p. 27. The general discussion of Frederick Taylor's scientific management is informed by Jenkins' discussion, pp. 25–31.
22. Taylor, *Scientific Management*, p. 59.
23. Ibid., pp. 61–62.
24. Eugene Zamiatin, *We* (New York: E. P. Dutton, 1952).
25. "Testimony Before the Special House Committee" in *Scientific Management*, p. 86.
26. Nikolai Lenin, "The Immediate Tasks of the Soviet Government," *Pravda* No. 83, April 28, 1918, reprinted in Nikolai Lenin, *Questions of the Socialist Organization of the Economy* (Moscow: Progress Publishers, nd.), pp. 97–135.
27. Frederick Taylor, *Shop Management*, pp. 54–55.
28. Frederick Taylor, *Testimony Before the Special House Committee*, p. 262.
29. "Work and the Changing American Scene" in *Research in Industrial Human Relations*, ed. Conrad M. Arensberg et al. (New York: Harper, 1957), p. 63.
30. Frederick Taylor, *Testimony Before the Special House Committee*, p. 49.
31. Frederick Thayer argues that perhaps the pyramidal command structure never existed. Frederick Thayer, *An End to Hierarchy, An End to Competition* (New York: New Viewpoints, 1973).
32. "The Ideal Bureaucrat," ed. Gerald D. Bell, *Organizations and Human Behavior* (Englewood Cliffs, NH: Prentice Hall, 1967), p. 86–89.
33. *Dimensions of Work: The Sociology of a Work Culture* (New York: David McKay, 1964), p. 89.
34. *Freedom, Power and Democratic Planning* (New York: Oxford, 1950), p. 267.
35. *Utopia*, trans. and ed. H. V. S. Ogden, (Northbrook, IL: AHM Publishing Corporation, 1949).
36. *Marx's Conception of Man* (New York: Frederick Ungar Publishing Co., 1961), pp. 41–42.
37. *Economic and Philosophical Manuscripts*, in *Karl Marx Early Writings*, trans. and ed. T. B. Bottomore (New York: McGraw-Hill, 1963), p. 168.
38. (Chicago: Charles H. Kerr and Co., 1906), 1:708.
39. Karl Marx and Frederick Engels, *German Ideology*, ed. R. Pascal (New York: Informational Publishers, 1939), p. 14.
40. Karl Marx, *Economic and Philosophical Manuscripts*, p. 122.
41. Ibid., p. 125.
42. Ibid., p. 129.
43. This was reported by Alasdair Clayre, *Work and Play* (London: Weidenfeld and Nicolson, 1974), p. 42.
44. Hegel as he was quoted in Erich Fromm, *Marx's Concept of Man*, p. 40.

45. Saint-Simon's announcement appeared in his Lettres d'un habitant de Genève. See: Oeuvres de Saint-Simon et d'Enfantin (Paris, 1865–1878), 15:55 as quoted in *The Utopian Vision of Charles Fourier*, trans. and ed. Jonathan Beecher and Richard Bienvenu (Boston: Beacon Press, 1971), p. 27.
46. Ibid., p. 32.
47. Ibid., p. 29.
48. Ibid., p. 27. As the previous discussion should have indicated, the qualifying adverb, *relatively*, must be stressed.
49. Martin Buber discussed the conflict between Marxism and Utopian Socialism in his work, *Paths in Utopia* (Boston: Beacon Press, 1958).
50. James Gillespie, "Toward Freedom in Work," p. 77.
51. Ibid., p. 76.
52. Ibid.
53. See Henry David Thoreau, *Walden* (New York: Holt, Rinehart and Winston, 1958).
54. *Civilization and Its Discontents* (London: The Hogarth Press, 1930), p. 68. This contention is incorporated in today's practice of work therapy.
55. *Psychology of the Unconscious* (New York: Dodd, 1963).
56. *The Function of Orgasm*, trans. T. P. Wolfe (New York: Meridian Books, 1942).
57. *The Sane Society* (New York: Holt, Rinehart and Winston, Inc., 1955), p. 159.
58. Report of a special task force to the secretary of Health, Education, and Welfare, *Work in America* (Cambridge: MIT Press, 1973), opposite title page.
59. Stanley Parker, *The Future of Work and Leisure*, p. 2.
60. See Frederick Herzberg, *Work and the Nature of Man* (New York: World Book, 1966) and *The Managerial Choice: To be Efficient and to be Human* (Homewood, IL: Dow Jones-Irwin, 1976).
61. See Douglas McGregor, "The Human Side of Enterprise," *The Management Review* 46 (Nov. 1957): 22–28, 88–92.
62. See Abraham Maslow, *Motivation and Personality* (New York: Harper Brothers, 1954) and *Eupsychian Management* (Homewood, IL: Richard D. Irwin, 1965).
63. Research on human needs supports the insertion of a need for autonomy between Maslow's needs for self-esteem and self-actualization. See L. W. Porter, *Organizational Patterns of Managerial Job Attitudes* (New York: American Foundation for Management Research, 1964) and Edward E. Lawler, *Motivation in Work Organizations* (Monterey, CA: Brooks/Cole, 1973).
64. See *Understanding Organizational Behavior* (Homewood, IL: The Dorsey Press, 1960).

65. See *The Human Organization* (New York: McGraw-Hill, 1967).
66. See *Control in Organizations* (New York: McGraw-Hill, 1967) and *Hierarchy in Organizations* (San Francisco: Josey-Bass, 1974).
67. For a brief survey of the school, see Rinehard Bendix, *Work and Authority in Industry* (New York: John Wiley, 1956); B. B. Gardner, *Human Relations in Industry* (Chicago: Irvin, 1945); W. Brown, *Explorations* in *Management* (New York: John Wiley, 1960); Amitai Etzioni, *Complex Organization* (New York: Holt, Rinehart, 1961); F. J. Roethlisberger and W. T. Dickson, *Management and the Worker* (Cambridge: Harvard Univ. Press, 1939).
68. See C. N. Cofer and M. H. Appley, *Motivation: Theory and Research* (New York: Wiley, 1964), and Edward E. Lawler and John Rhode, *Information and Control in Organizations* (Pacific Palisades, CA: Goodyear Publishing Company, Inc., 1976).
69. This seems to have been the case in the famous Lordstown auto plant strike. The Vega plant incorporated new designs that allowed the assembly line rate to be increased. All this produced, however, was a wildcat strike on the part of the rather well-paid workers. For details of the Lordstown strike and other similar events, see: D. Garson, "Luddites in Lordstown," *Harpers* 244 (June, 1972): 68–73; Martin Glaberman, "Unions vs. Workers in the Seventies: The Rise of Militancy in the Auto Industry," *Society* 10 (November, 1972): 23–28; Emma Rothschild, "G. M. in More Trouble," *New York Review of Books* 18 (March 23, 1972): 18–25.
70. Elton Mayo, *The Human Problems of an Industrial Civilization* (New York: Macmillan, 1933).
71. Derek Biddle and Geoffrey Hutton, "Toward a Tolerance Theory of Worker Adaptation," *Human Relations* 29 (September 1976): 832–62.
72. *Information and Control in Organizations*, p. 65.
73. *Economic and Philosophical Manuscripts*, p. 125.
74. *Alienation and Freedom* (Chicago: Univ. of Chicago Press, 1964), pp. 183–84.
75. Ferdynand Zweig, *The British Worker* (London: Penguin, 1952), p. 97.
76. Georges Friedmann, *Anatomy of Work* (Glencoe, IL: The Free Press, 1961), pp. 104–5.
77. *International Social Science Journal* 12 (Fall 1960): 543–560.
78. "The Long Arm of the Job: A Study of Work and Leisure," *Industrial Relations* 10 (Oct. 1971): 239–60.
79. Ibid., p. 260.
80. Erdman B. Palmore, "Predicting Longevity: A Follow-up Controlling for Age," *Gerontology* 9 (Winter 1969), 247–50.
81. Erdman B. Palmore and Virginia Stone, "Predictors of Longevity: A Fol-

low-up of the Aged in Chapel Hill," *Gerontologist* 13 (Spring 1973), 88–90.

82. Marvin Mariotti, "Worker Conditions and Manner of Aging," in *Work and Aging* (Paris: International Center of Social Gerontology, 1971), pp. 163–84.

83. C. D. Jenkins, "Psychologic and Social Precursors of Coronary Disease," *New England Journal of Medicine* 284 (1971): 244–45, and S. Sales and J. House, "Job Dissatisfaction as a Possible Risk Factor in Coronary Heart Disease," *Journal of Chronic Disease* 23 (1971): 861–73.

84. S. V. Kasl and S. Cobb, "Blood Pressure Changes in Men Undergoing Job Loss: A Preliminary Report," *Psychosomatic Medicine* 32 (January/February 1970): 19–38.

85. J. R. P. French, J. Tupper, and E. Muller, *Work Load of University Professors* (Ann Arbor: Cooperative Research Project No. 2171, U.S. Office of Education, University of Michigan, 1965).

    M. Frideman, R. H. Rosenman, and V. Carroll, "Changes in the Serum Cholesterol and Blood Clotting Time of Men Subject to Cyclic Variation of Occupational Stress," *Circulation* 17 (1957): 852–61.

    H. H. W. Miles et al., "Psychosomatic Study of 46 Young Men with Coronary Artery Disease," *Psychosomatic Medicine* 16 (November/December 1954): 455–77.

    H. J. Montoye et al., "Serum Uric Acid Concentration Among Business Executives with Observations of Other Coronary Heart Disease Risk Factors," *Annals of Internal Medicine* 66 (May 1967): 838–50.

    A. Pepitone, "Self, Social Environment and Stress," in M. H. Appley and R. Trumbull eds., *Psychological Stress* (New York: Appleton-Century-Crofts, 1967), pp. 182–208.

    H. I. Russek, "Emotional Stress and Coronary Heart Disease in North American Physicians, Dentists and Lawyers," *American Journal of the Medical Sciences* 243 (1962): 716–25.

    ———, "Stress, Tobacco, and Coronary Disease in North American Professional Groups," *Journal of the American Medical Association* 192 (1965): 189–94.

    S. M. Sales, "Organizational Roles as a Risk Factor in Coronary Heart Disease," *Administrative Science Quarterly* 14 (Sept. 1969): 325–36.

86. Thomasina Smith, "Sociocultural Incongruity and Change: A Review of Empirical Findings," *Milbank Memorial Fund Quarterly* 45, pt. 11 (1967): 23–39.

87. Stanislow Kasl and Sidney Cobb, "Physical and Mental Health Correlates of Status Incongruence," *Social Psychiatry* 6 (1971): 1–10.

88. M. Susser, "Cause of Peptic Ulcer: A Selective Epidemiologic Review," *Journal of Chronic Diseases* 20 (1967): 345–56.

Joseph V. Brady, "Ulcers in 'Executive' Monkeys," *Scientific American* 199 (Oct. 1958): 95–100.

89. S. H. King and S. Cobb, "Psychosomatic Factors in the Epidemiology of Rheumatoid Arthritis," *Journal of Chronic Diseases* 7 (1958): 466–75.
S. Cobb, *The Frequency of the Rheumatic Diseases* (Cambridge: Harvard Univ. Press, 1971).

90. For an excellent summary of this topic see Bruce L. Margolis and William Kroes, "Work and the Health of Man," in James O'Toole, ed., *Work and the Quality of Life: Resource Papers for Work in America* (Cambridge, MA: MIT Press, 1974): 133–44.

91. "Toward a Description of Mental Health," *Bulletin of the Menninger Clinic* 26 (1962): 178–88.

92. *The Quality of American Life: Perceptions, Evaluations, and Satisfactions* (New York: Russell Sage Foundation, 1976), p. 313.

93. This was cited in *Work in America*, p. 82.

94. "Technology, Alienation and Mental Health: Summary of a Social Psychological Study of Technology and the Worker," *Acta Sociologica* 19 (1976): 83–93.

95. The arguments concerning SES's relationship to occupation and participation are developed in the last section of ch. 4.

96. Cited in *Work in America*, p. 82.

97. For an excellent summary of this research, see Stanislav V. Kasl, "Work and Mental Health," in James O'Toole, ed., *Work and the Quality of Life*, pp. 171–96.

98. *Work in America* has a section entitled "Special Means of Coping," in which the widespread problem of drug abuse is discussed, pp. 85–88.

99. Ibid., p. 82.

100. Theodore D. Kemper and Melvin L. Reichler, "Work Integration, Marital Satisfaction, and Conjugal Power," *Human Relations* 29 (Oct. 1976): 929–44.

101. (New York: The Free Press, 1972).

102. Ibid., p. 90.

103. Ibid.

104. Ibid., p. 135.

105. Abraham K. Korman, "Work Experience, Socialization, and Civil Liberties," *Journal of Social Issues* 31 (Spring 1975): 139–140.

106. The following discussion is taken from the summary of *Mental Health of the Industrial Worker* appearing in *Work in America*. The HEW research team stated their synopsis in this way:

—Job satisfaction varied consistently with the skill level of jobs held. Higher-level blue-collar workers had better mental health than non-skilled workers.

—Job dissatisfaction related to the characteristics of the jobs—dull, repetitive, unchallenging, low-paying jobs rated lowest in satisfaction. Absenteeism correlated loosely with job dissatisfaction.

—Work was the most central measurable institution in the lives of the workers, above family, leisure, and social activities, but only 25 percent of the workers would choose the same kind of job if they had to do it again.

—Feelings of helplessness, withdrawal, alienation, and pessimism were widespread. For example: 50 percent of assembly-line workers felt that they had little influence over the future course of their lives (compared with only 17 percent of non-factory workers).

—Workers with the lowest mental health and job satisfaction scores were often escapist or passive in their vote; and did not participate in community organizations.

—Wages, security and physical conditions of work were not as accurate predictors of mental health as challenge of the job and intrinsic interest.

—Self-esteem correlated strongly with job satisfaction and mental health.
Work in America, pp. 83–84.

107. "The Relationship Between Perceived Job Characteristics and Job Satisfaction Among Status Groups," *Sociology of Work and Occupations* 5 (May 1978): 179–191.

108. "Work Values and Job Rewards: A Theory of Job Satisfaction," *American Sociological Review* 42 (February, 1977): 124–143.

109. *Work in America*, p. xvi.

110. "Factory Work," *The Simone Weil Reader*, ed. George A. Panichas (New York: David McKay, 1977), p. 71.

111. Jon M. Shepard, "Functional Specialization and Work Attitudes," *Industrial Relations* 8 (Feb. 1969): 184–95.

112. E. Jacobson, "Foreman-Steward Participation Practices and Worker Attitudes in a Unionized Factory," (Ph.D. diss., University of Michigan 1951).

113. Nancy Morse and E. Reimer, "The Experimental Change of a Major Organizational Variable," *Journal of Abnormal Social Psychology* 52 (Jan. 1956): 120–29.

114. Alfred J. Marrow, David G. Bowers, and Stanley E. Seashore, *Management by Participation* (New York: Harper & Row, 1967).

115. Rosabeth Moss Kanter, "Work in a New America," *Daedalus* 107 (Winter 1978): 47–78.

116. *Capitalism and Freedom* (Chicago: Univ. of Chicago Press, 1962), p. 133.

117. Herbert Marcuse, *Eros and Civilization* (Boston: Beacon, 1966), p. 142.

118. *Work and Play* (London: Weidenfeld & Nicolson, 1974).

119. *The Need for Roots*, trans. A. F. Wills (London: Routledge Press, 1952), pp. 91–92.

6. Workplace Democracy

1. Philippe Buchez quoted in *Self-Management: Economic Liberation of Man*, ed. Jaroslav Vanek (Baltimore: Penquin Books, 1975), p. 17.
2. *Karl Marx and Friedrich Engels: Writings on Politics and Philosophy*, ed. Lewis Feuer (Garden City, NY: Anchor Books, Doubleday, 1959), p. 70.
3. Louis Blanc, *Organisation du travail* (Paris: Prévot, 1840).
4. *Marx and Engels Writings*, p. 390.
5. Ibid., pp. 366–67. Italics mine.
6. Karl Marx, *Capital* (Chicago: C. H. Kerr, 1906–1909), vol. 3, ch. 48, sec. 2.
7. Karl Marx and Friedrich Engels, "The German Ideology," in *Marx and Engels Writings*, p. 254.
8. (Baltimore: Penguin Books, 1976).
9. *Selected Writings of Pierre Joseph Proudhon*, ed. Steward Edwards (London: Macmillan, 1970).
10. (New York: Knopf, 1917).
11. (London: Allen and Unwin, 1974).
12. *Guild Socialism Re-stated*, (London: Leonard Parsons, 1920), p. 13.
13. Ibid., pp. 48–49.
14. "Introduction to The Civil War in France," in *Marx and Engels Writings*, p. 356.
15. "The Civil War in France," in *Marx and Engels Writings*, p. 369.
16. Nikolai Lenin quoted in E. S. Mason, *The Paris Commune* (New York: Howard Fertig, first published by Macmillan Co., 1967), p. ix.
17. See, for example, Harvie Ramsay, "Cycles of Control: Worker Participation in Sociological and Historical Perspective," *Sociology* 11 (September 1977): 481–506.
18. Don Blair, *The New Harmony Story* (New Harmony, IN: New Harmony Publications Committee, n.d.), p. 50.
19. *The American Idea of Industrial Democracy, 1865–1965* (Urbana: Univ. of Illinois Press, 1970).
20. Ibid., p. 7.
21. N. O. Nelson, as quoted in Milton Derber, p. 7.
22. *Profit Sharing Trends* (Chicago: Council of Profit Sharing Industries, March–April, 1959), p. 3.
23. *Men, the Workers* (New York: Doubleday, Page, 1909), p. 91.
24. Lyman Abbott, as quoted in Milton Derber, p. 8.
25. Henry C. Adams, as quoted in Milton Derber, p. 9.
26. (London: Longmans, Green, 1897).
27. *The American Idea of Industrial Democracy*, pp. 9–10.
28. Ibid., p. 10.

29. *Report of the U.S. Industrial Commission*, 14 (Washington, DC: Government Printing Office, 1901), p. 306.
30. Hugh Clegg, *A New Approach to Industrial Democracy* (Oxford: Basil Blackwell, 1960), p. 119.
31. Ibid.
32. *The American Idea of Industrial Democracy*, pp. 208–10.
33. *An Introduction to Political Economy* (New York: Eaton and Mains, 1889), pp. 236–39.
34. Louis Brandeis quoted in Volkomer, *The Liberal Tradition in American Thought* (New York: Putnam, 1969).
35. Adolf F. Sturmthal, "Unions and Industrial Democracy," *The Annals of the American Academy of Political and Social Science* 431 (May 1977), 18.
36. Branko Horvat, "A New Social System in the Making: Historical Origins and Development of Self-governing Socialism," in *Self-Governing Socialism*, eds. Branko Horvat, Mihailo Markovic and Rudi Supek, 2 vols. (White Plains, NY: International Arts and Science Press, 1975), 1:45.
37. Brent Schiller, "Industrial Democracy in Scandinavia," *The Annals*, p. 68.
38. Branko Horvat, "A New Social System in the Making," 1:45.
39. Examples of job enlargement will be provided in the next volume. For a brief introduction to the literature on job enlargement, see: R. C. Bishop and J. W. Hill, "Job Enlargement vs. Job Change and Their Effects on Contiguous but Non-manipulated Work Groups," *Journal of Applied Psychology* 55 (1971): 175–81; Charles L. Hulin and Milton R. Blood, "Job Enlargement, Individual Differences and Worker Responses," *Psychological Bulletin* (January 1968); T. P. Pauling, "Job Enlargement—an Experience at Philips Telecommunication of Australia, Ltd., *Personnel Practice Bulletin* 24 (September 1968): 194–96; Irwin A. Rose, "How to Increase Productivity Through Job Enlargement," *Plant Executive's Bulletin*, Report 191 (October 15, 1963): 1; and P. P. Schoderbek, "Uses of Job Enlargement in Industry," *Personnel Journal* 47 (November 1968): 796–801.
40. *Participation and Democratic Theory* (Cambridge: The Cambridge Univ. Press, 1970), p. 58.
41. Examples of job enrichment will be provided in the next chapter. For a brief introduction to the literature on job enrichment, see: William Dettleback, W. William, and Philip Kraft, "Organization Change Through Job Enrichment," *Training and Development Journal* 25 (August 1971): 2–6; Robert Janson, "Job Enrichment: Challenge of the 70s," *Training and Development Journal* 24 (June 1970): 7–9; Frederick Herzberg, *The Managerial Choice: To Be Efficient and To Be Human* (Homewood, IL: Dow Jones-Irwin, 1976); Roy Kaplan, Curt Tausky, and Bolaria Bhopinder, "Job Enrichment," *Personnel Journal* 48 (October 1969): 791–98; J. R.

Maher, ed., *New Perspectives in Job Enrichment* (New York: Van Nostrand, Reinhold, 1971); and Scott M. Myers, "Overcoming Union Opposition to Job Enrichment," *Harvard Business Review* 49 (May–June 1971): 37–49.

42. *Administration and Society* 7 (May 1975): 20–21.

43. This description of Volvo based on Pehr G. Gyllenhammer, "How Volvo Adapts Work to People," *Harvard Business Review* 55 (July–August 1977): 106.

44. Description of the Porst Group reported in *Business Week* (December 11, 1978), pp. 72, 74.

45. This description of Mondragon based on R. Oakeshott, "Mondragon: Spain's Oasis of Democracy," in *Self-Management*: 290–96.

46. This description of Israel is based primarily upon Eliezer Rosenstein, "Worker Participation in Israel: Experience and Lessons," *The Annals*, pp. 113–22.

47. "The Consequences of Worker Participation: A Clarification of the Theoretical Literature," *Social Science Quarterly* 56 (September 1975): 191–209.

48. See G. Dale Meyer, *Participative Decision Making: An Analysis and Review* (Iowa City: Center for Labor and Management Monograph #15, September 1970).

49. "The Consequences of Worker Participation," p. 191.

50. Some classics in the field of humanist psychology are: Chris Argyris, *Organization and Innovation* (Homewood, IL: Dorsey Press, 1962); Arthur Kornhauser, *The Mental Health of the Industrial Worker* (New York: Wiley, 1965); Abraham Maslow, *Eupsychian Management* (Homewood, IL: Irwin, 1965); Maslow, "A Theory of Human Motivation," *Psychological Research* 50 (July 1943): 370–96; Maslow, *Motivation and Personality* (New York: Harper and Row, 1957); and Carl Rogers, *Client-Centered Therapy* (Boston: Houghton-Mifflin, 1951).

51. For example, see Abraham Maslow, *Eupsychian Management*.

52. Two major members of the "participatory left" are Antonio Gramsci and Andre Gorz. Some of the important works by and about them listed by Greenberg are: John M. Cammett, *Antonio Gramsci and the Origins of Italian Communism* (Stanford: Stanford Univ. Press, 1967); Andre Gorz, *A Strategy for Labor* (Boston: Beacon Press, 1967); Gorz, *Socialism and Revolution* (Garden City: Anchor/Doubleday, 1973); Antonio Gramsci, *The Modern Prince* (London: Lawrence and Wishart, 1957); Gramsci, *Letters from Prison* (New York: Harper and Row, 1973); Giuseppe Fiori, *Antonio Gramsci; Life of a Revolutionary* (New York: Schocken Books, 1970).

53. "The 'Port Huron Statement' of Students for a Democratic Society," in *Directions in American Political Thought*, ed., Kenneth M. Dolbeare (New York: Wiley, 1969), pp. 468–86.

54. Leo Panitch, "The Importance of Workers' Control for Revolutionary Change," *Monthly Review* 29 (March 1978): 37–48.

55. F. A. Hayek, *Studies in Philosophy, Politics and Economics* (New York: Simon and Schuster, A Clarion Book, 1967), esp. ch. 22.

56. Herbert Marcuse, "The Obsolescence of Marxism," in *Marx and the Western World*, ed. N. Lobkowicz (South Bend, IN: The University of Notre Dame Press, 1967), p. 415.

57. Hannah Arendt, *On Revolution* (New York: The Viking Press, 1963), esp. pages 277–79.

7. Participatory and Workplace Democracy

1. Milton Friedman, *Capitalism and Freedom* (Chicago: Univ. of Chicago Press, 1962).
   F. A. Hayek, *Studies in Philosophy, Politics and Economics* (New York: Simon and Schuster, A Clarion Book, 1967).
   Robert Nozick, *Anarchy, State, and Utopia* (New York: Basic Books, 1974).

2. William R. Schonfeld, "The Meaning of Democratic Participation," *World Politics* 28 (1975): 134–58.

3. T. V. Smith, *The Promise of American Politics* (Chicago: The University of Chicago Press, 1936), p. 84.
   C. J. Friedrich, *Transcendental Justice: The Religious Dimension of Constitutionalism* (Durham, NC: Duke Univ. Press, 1964), pp. 95–96.
   H. J. Laski, *The Dangers of Obedience and Other Essays* (New York: Harper and Brothers, 1930).
   Hans Kelsen, *General Theory of Law and State* trans. Anders Wedberg, (Cambridge: Harvard Univ. Press, 1945).

4. *Eupsychian Management* (Homewood, IL: Irwin, 1965), pp. 61–62.

5. "The Fallacy of Decentralization," *The Nation* (August 25, 1969), p. 147.

6. Antonio Gramsci, "Soviets in Italy," *New Left Review* 51 (September–October, 1968): 22–58.

7. See Daniel A. Mazmanian and Jeanne Nienaber, *Can Organizations Change?* (Washington: The Brookings Institution, 1979).

8. Quoted in Jack Lively, *The Social and Political Thought of Alexis de Tocqueville*, (New York: Clarendon Press of Oxford Univ., 1962), p. 111.

9. Judith N. Shklar, *Legalism* (Cambridge: Harvard Univ. Press, 1964).
   Kenneth R. Hoover, *A Politics of Identity: Liberation and the Natural Community*, (Urbana: Univ. of Illinois Press, 1975).
   Wilson Carey McWilliams, *The Idea of Fraternity in America* (Berkeley, CA: University of California Press, 1973).
   Victor C. Ferkiss, *The Future of Technological Civilization* (New York: G. Braziller, 1974).

Phillip Abbott, *The Shotgun Behind the Door: Liberalism and the Problem of Political Obligation* (Athens: Univ. of Georgia Press, 1976).
10. John Stuart Mill in J. Robson, ed., *Collected Works* (Toronto: Univ. of Toronto Press, 1965), bk. 4, ch. 7, sec. 6, p. 775.
11. See *The Public and Its Problems* (New York: Holt, 1927).
12. *On Revolution* (New York: Viking Press, 1965), p. 127.
13. Aristotle, *The Politics of Aristotle*, ed. and trans. Ernest Barker (New York: Oxford Univ. Press, 1958), p. 95.
14. *From Max Weber*, ed. and trans. by H. H. Gerth and C. Wright Mills (New York: Oxford Univ. Press, 1946), p. 228.
15. Plato, *Protagoras*, trans., with notes by C. C. W. Taylor, (New York: Clarendon Press of Oxford Univ., 1976), 322–23, pp. 14–15.

Bibliographic Essay

THE FIRST GREAT WORK IN THE AREA OF PARTICIPATORY DEMOC-
racy, without a doubt, belongs to Carole Pateman. *Participation and
Democratic Theory* sets the stage for most of the important arguments
on the subject that were to follow. Pateman's attack on the revisionist
"democratic" theorists and her explication of the participatory theory
of democracy remain as valid today as when she wrote them. Among
her many contributions, the most important, certainly, would have to
be the emphasis she places upon the workplace, and the role, within
participatory democracy, she ascribes to it. It is difficult to compete
with the originality of her work; she was first. After a decade of reflection on the various propositions relative to participatory democracy,
however, it is possible to elaborate, update, and perhaps improve
upon some of those contentions. It is also possible to offer a few observations that are new.

In at least the following ways the thrust of my work carries beyond
the boundaries of *Participation and Democratic Theory*. *Participatory and
Workplace Democracy* forthrightly positions participatory democracy in
opposition to liberal democracy. Participatory democracy rests on a
different philosophical basis, and this breech must be maintained to
prevent liberal democracy from consuming participatory democracy
as just another liberal model. That is why at each step of the argument
it is necessary to reveal the untoward effects of liberal conceptualizations. This work develops the tenets of participatory democracy, especially in terms of the various dimensions of participation. In doing so, it
resists the liberal temptation to measure democracy in terms of *opportunity* to participate, civil rights, and civil liberties as measures of democracy. Liberalism divided the world into social and political parts
and made analysis of participation very difficult. The view of the political had to be reconceptualized to a nonliberal version before the patterns of participation as a learned response could be revealed. The
strength of the workplace connection could not have been understood
without also understanding that participation in the workplace was
political participation, and not "social" or "economic" participation.

In working with the connection between participation in the workplace and participation in government, it is possible to identify some

of the main processes through which those experiences take place. Pateman discusses efficacy, but more than a decade later there is more to say about efficacy than what Almond and Verba offer, and more than efficacy to what I call the participatory persuasion. In fact, contemporary analysts must be very careful of their use of efficacy. The compelling case for workplace participation is also articulated through the association of workplace participation with the intrinsic value of work. There is no way for work to be meaningful and valuable without allowing workers to participate in the decisions related to that work. In developing these themes, I hope that *Participatory and Workplace Democracy* is seen as more than a footnote to Pateman's excellent work.

It is possible to consider each of the contributions listed above (and more) in light of some other works related to the same endeavors. Take for example C. B. Macpherson's work, *The Life and Times of Liberal Democracy*. At the base of all that is examined within the various dimensions of this work lies the system of thought and belief known as liberalism. Since the most immediate concern is with the notion of democracy that was laid upon the liberal base, the reader might be well-advised to skip the general treatments of liberalism, such as the excellent volume of de Ruggiero, and the less excellent work of Manning's, *Liberalism*, and go directly to the succinct presentation offered by Macpherson. Within the span of little more than one-hundred pages, he captured most of the major thrusts of liberalism, especially as it accommodated the notion of democracy. That does not mean, however, that Macpherson's presentation ought not be challenged. There is some justification for the various models of liberal democracy Macpherson offers; the only trouble with them is that they are not all true models of liberal democracy. Though there is clear and direct linkage between the protective (the first) and the equilibrium (the third) models of liberal democracy, Macpherson has tapped something different in the developmental (the second) and the participatory (the fourth) models. In many of its aspects, the developmental model stands in direct contradiction to what came before (the protective model) and what came after (the equilibrium model). There are certainly sufficient common ties between liberal thought and "developmental" thinkers such as John Stuart Mill and John Dewey to warrant considering them "liberal." But when they emphasize individual development, rather than the representation of interests, they begin to move beyond the boundaries of conventional liberal thought.

It is from the exceptions to liberal thought, and not from the corpus of liberal thought, that Macpherson forms the fourth model of "liberal" democracy, that is, participatory democracy. It is worth repeating that there are ties between participatory democracy and what Macpherson calls developmental democracy, but the ties are to the parts in which developmental democracy breaks from its liberal ancestry. By viewing the individual developments of participation as part of the liberal tradition, Macpherson erroneously concludes that participatory democracy must be part of the liberal tradition.

There also is an interesting contradiction between what Macpherson is willing to consider liberal democracy and what he rejects as utopian. In the early part of the work, Macpherson eliminates from the analysis all works not based on class distinctions because they are by his definition, utopian. Yet in the final pages of the work, Macpherson advocates a society that is not cleaved by classes, thus making his own recommendations, by definition, utopian.

It was not Carl Cohen's intention in *Democracy* to place a participatory conception of democracy in the light of other versions of democracy and to discuss extensively its philosophical heritage. Instead, Cohen elaborates upon the various considerations that impinge upon a participatory conception of democracy, and he does so in a comprehensive manner. Cohen covers just about all of the ground concerning democracy: its nature, the presuppositions on which is rests, its various instrumentations, the conditions related to democracy, a defense of democracy, and the prospects for achieving it in the future.

Despite the impressive quality of the work, there are difficulties with his conception of democracy. It may be easiest to refer to the definition. Cohen defines democracy in a manner that allows restrictions—which do not affect the extent of democracy in the community—on who belongs to the community. This very consideration has been used historically to eliminate the participation of groups the power structure deemed undesirable: blacks, women, Catholics, and others. In fairness to Cohen, he does say that the burden of proof for such restrictions rests on those who wish to limit participation rights of others. But this loophole has been used so often that it seems as if what is considered acceptable proof for a particular time and circumstance is easily found (witness the Dred Scott case).

Cohen opens Pandora's Box a second time when he accepts *opportunity* to participate as the functional equivalent to *actual* participation in the assessment of democracy. It is through this hole that liberalism can pass and have its way. Liberalism is always happy to substitute amorphous rights for the concrete participation by members in community decision making. It is imperative that actual participation rates be the basis upon which democracy in a community is judged. In that regard, there is one more problem with Cohen's conceptualization. Cohen is among the number of theorists who offer various dimensions of participation in the discussion of democracy. Though there is no problem with his breadth and range dimensions, his discussion of depth is confused and should be amended.

If democracy turns on the extent of effective participation in a community, then it is important to come to a better understanding of participation. In terms of available research, this means consideration of survey research. Large-scale survey-research efforts on the subject of participation became prevalent in the 1950s and included Angus Campbell's *The People Elect a President*; Bernard Berelson, Paul Lazarsfeld, and William McPhee's *Voting*; and the first true classic in the field, Angus Campbell, Paul Lazarsfeld, Warren Miller and Donald Stokes's *The American Voter*, published in 1960. Gabriel Almond and Sidney Verba's *The Civil Culture*, the first classic in cross-national comparisons, soon was to follow.

Survey research is exceedingly expensive, and the flurry of activity that began in the 1950s soon subsided. Since the emphasis could not be on quantity, it had to be on quality. The attempt to improve on the previous classics was richly rewarded. Norman Nie, Sidney Verba and John Petrocik's *The Changing American Voter*, which appeared in 1976, amends the findings of *The American Voter* by placing it in temporal perspective; while Verba, Nie, and Kim's *Participation and Political Equality* (1978) offers many meaningful improvements upon *The Civic Culture*.

In many ways, however, the first true qualitative break from the past came with Verba and Nie's *Participation in America*, which won the American Political Science Association's Kammerer Award for the best book on American national politics in 1972. It is with this work that the importance of social class emerges and the whole notion of social participation comes to the fore. Verba and Nie identify the "social" basis to participation. This assumes meaningful proportions in light of the discovery that community leaders are likely to be more

responsive to the problem priorities of participants than nonparticipants. It is indeed unfortunate that *Participation in America* does not
offer a reconceptualization of the political. Couched uncomfortably
in the old liberal views of what is political, Verba and Nie do not make
the substantive contributions to the understanding of politics that
they could have.

What is even more unfortunate is that the works that follow do not
do any better. *The Changing American Voter's* increase in theoretical sen-
sitivity and awareness of its own limitations (viv-à-vis *The American
Voter*) is truly praiseworthy, but dedicated as it is to the liberal value of
voting at the national level, the scope of the work does not permit the
identification of important movements related to the reconceptualization of the political. In the same manner, Verba, Nie and Kim improve on *The Civic Culture* by adapting the constructions of *Participation in America* and applying them cross-nationally in their work,
Participation and Political Equality, but there are real limitations to their
contributions, for they unbudgingly restrict their definition of political participation to governmental participation. Without a reconceptualized view of the political, it is difficult to appreciate the effects of
things such as worker participation in Yugoslavia. It is difficult to
transcend the limitations of liberalism.

Since so much of participation research is published in journal
form, there is a need to summarize findings that are important and
generalizable. This function is performed by Lester Milbrath in his
first edition of *Political Participation* and by Milbrath and Goel in the
second edition of that work. It is here that the presence of liberal influences dominates, and here that it becomes clear how crippling
those influences are. With the need to categorize the participation research, the authors quickly resort to liberal categories, neatly dividing
the world into social and political groupings and hiding some of the
most important relationships in doing so. It is distressing to see research findings pushed into inappropriate categories and conceptions
of the political perverted to suit liberal imperatives.

Few contemporary works address the critical topic of work in a theoretically systematic fashion, and most of those that do, do not offer a
meaningful explication. A good example of the lack of significant
contribution is Yves Simon's *Work, Society and Culture*. Simon does
nothing more than attempt to raise the most simplistic distinctions to
the status of philosophy. The effort is woefully inadequate in nearly
every respect.

A real exception to the rule is Hannah Arendt's *The Human Condition*. Hannah Arendt is one of a handful of true theorists in our time, and *The Human Condition* may be her finest work. She is cognizant of so many things of importance: the decline of political action in our world, the establishment of labor as the predominant activity in modern life, the loss of the sense of work, among many other things. Though my own view of work and labor differs considerably from Arendt's, *The Human Condition*, nevertheless, has had considerable impact upon my thinking.

Arendt's work is so impressive that it is difficult to criticize it, but criticized it must be. I cannot help but feel that the transference of Greek ideals to our age is only possible if one remains sensitive to the absolute changes that have occurred, not the least of which relates to the fact that we live in nation-states, not city-states. Political action must look somewhat different under different circumstances. Workplace participation is likely to energize participation in other communities (including government), not enervate it, as Arendt might have us believe. Her opposition to things such as workers' councils is based on a belief that workplaces are part of the private sphere, and there, but not in the public sphere, does the role of professionalism (nonparticipation) belong.

Thus my most important criticism of Arendt is that the freedom she treasures and believes is produced by the actions of men among other men will not be achieved in some public space, unless the experience of participation is also present in what she considers private space. Here above all, the reconceptualization of the political is necessary, although Arendt's frame of reference is not liberal but ancient Greek. Her fight against society subsuming politics will only perpetuate society subsuming politics because of the basic liberal distinctions of society and politics under which most people (but not Arendt) operate. With the political attached to the nation-state, and only society intimately tied to most lives, liberal distinctions will dominate. It is simply the case that the relegation of labor and work to the private sphere, and action to the public sphere, is inappropriate and undesirable in the American context. Although brilliant, I do not believe that we can or ought to follow Arendt's path into the future.

There have been less philosophical treatments of work that ought to be reported. Early in the 1970s, Elliot Richardson, then the Secretary of the Department of Health, Education and Welfare, appointed a special task force to examine the status of work in this country. The ensuing report, *Work in America*, attempted to deal with some of the central problems confronting work in this country during the last decade. In some ways, *Work in America* represented the social-scientific treatment of the phenomenon captured so well by Studs Terkel in his classic, *Workiing*. The scope of the project was terrifically broad. The researchers not only wrestled with a basic definition of work; they also confronted empirical contentions such as that workers were severely discontent and this condition led to negative associations with worker health. They also considered alternative working life environments.

Overall, the report is a good one, although the reliability of some of the basic claims is questionable. It is quite possible that the report overestimates some of the ills associated with meaningless work; among the most important, of course, would be the amount and depth of worker discontent. Perhaps more than anything else, the report is worthy of attention because it is the result of the realization on the part of government that work in America is troubled.

Within socialist thought, there has always been a tension between those who would have us centralize and those who would have us decentralize decision making. It is within the movement to decentralize that socialist thought makes its contribution to the idea of workplace democracy. The origin of the contribution begins with utopian socialist thought and is carried in the writings of Marx, manifesting most clearly in the early writing such as the *Economic and Philosophical Manuscripts of 1844* and *The German Ideology*, but continuing in *Capital, The Critique of the Gotha Program*, and *The Civil War in France*. It would take considerable time to trace the relevant vein as it runs through socialist thought, but fortunately, that already has been done in the two volume work, *Self-Governing Socialism*, edited by Branko Horvat, Mihailo Markovic, and Rudi Supek. Volume one of the impressive work traces the historical development of self-governing socialism (also labelled self-management when the focus is on the workplace) beginning with the visionaries, extending through the movements and revolutions that took place in its name, and ending with a country-by-country analysis of the development. Given the role social and political philosophy plays in the development of the idea of self-management, it is understandable that considerable attention is paid also to those topics in the first volume. The second volume considers some of the social, political, and economic factors in the socialist tradition, which impinge upon the notion of self-management.

In many ways the strength of this work is also its weakness. The socialist perspective heightens the analysis of certain phenomena such as alienation, but weakens the analysis of many others. The weakness is evident in the very search for conceptualization. The authors cannot agree among themselves on many important points, and the usage of *self-management* is a poor term on which to find agreement. "To manage," coupled with "the self" is to fuse two antipodal ideas; thus the term, *self-management* must endlessly fight self-contradiction. Applying the notion of democracy as a participatory system of community rule is theoretically more powerful.

Workplace democracy is not socialist or capitalist, but an entirely different idea blended of the two traditions. Though the authors of *Self-Governing Socialism* occasionally seem to realize this, they are captured too well by socialist thought and terminology. They still speak of the socialist revolution and the system of self-management as the withering away of the state after the revolution and the dictatorship of the proletariat. The authors are set on the idea that it is impossible to move beyond codetermination to anything approaching the idea of self-management unless the prevailing political system is socialistic. For them, without the revolution and socialism, you never change the relationship between capital and labor. These ideas, when applied to the United States, are particularly enfeebled. There is no accident that the discussion of the United States is held to a minimum.

There are a handful of books that attempt to synthesize social science research literature with a view toward answering some fundamental questions. One that does this with worker participation is Michael Poole's *Workers' Participation in Industry*. Poole attempts to make worker participation the dependent variable. He questions what conditions lead to various forms of worker participation, and his answer is largely two-fold: what occurs is a function of who has power and what values those in power have. Thus the forms, which are a result of management initiative, reflect the power of management vis-à-vis other groups and the values they hold. So far so good. It is important to realize that perspectives influence what is seen and that values reflect interest, and that more powerful segments of society are more successful in getting what they want; however, Poole goes on to see the same two factors accounting for virtually everything, and thus produces an overly simplified view. His concentration on the independent variables, those that produce systems of worker participation, lead him to leave insufficiently analyzed the critical dependent variable, worker participation. Ironically, Poole does not even allow sufficient time to consider the factors that influence his independent variables. If he had, he might have realized more fully that the belief and practice of worker participation can act as an independent variable affecting factors such as power and, more clearly, values. It is through exposing workers to even limited experience with participation that the latent powers of workers may develop. Because the Poole analysis is conducted at the level of power and values, it does not reveal factors as basic to the understanding of worker participation as the participatory persuasion or the workplace connection. The crux of the problem lies in looking at worker participation as an index of industrial life. Poole's explicit focus on Europe, especially Great Britain, interferes with applying much of his work to our circumstances.

A number of works, which attempt to deal with the European experience of worker participation, should be considered. Although it would be unwise to attempt to simply import a European scheme, there is much we can learn from Europe's experience. If the emphasis is on description, then premium should be placed on locating recent works; after all, the circumstances are constantly changing. On the other hand, if the reader is seeking the meaning of events, as well as their description, then it is important to locate works that offer a theoretical perspective. Many of the contemporary works on the European experience fail in this very regard. They most often seize on a label, say workers' control, and mutilate the topic. A real exception to this trend is G. David Garson's *Worker Self-Management in Industry: The West European Experience.* Garson's work is especially praiseworthy in that it manages to maintain a coherent theoretical base, despite the fact that it is a collection of pieces by different authors.

Having retraced the argument in this bibliographic essay, it is only fitting to close on the notion of liberalism, and its alternative, participationism. Though it would be possible to recreate the battlefield, with the neoliberals on one side and the liberal critics on the other, it would be more informative to deal with those theorists who are attempting to go beyond liberal perspectives, rather than simply criticizing them. There are not many to choose from, but one who may fit the category is Robert Pranger.

In his books, *The Eclipse of Citizenship* and *Action, Symbolism and Order,* Pranger recognizes that there is a difference between the politics of power and the politics of participation. Pranger sees power as hierarchical dominance, and participation as group undertakings. From this perspective, it is not difficult to link liberalism's representative democracy with the politics of power and the search for extensive group undertakings with something nonliberal. In other words, it is possible to see in Pranger's work, the seeds of alternatives. This is made even more apparent when Pranger discusses existentialism and social science, as they focus on the interrelationships between action and existence, projecting, as they do, a complimentary view of human nature in political action. Pranger's concentration on participation is unmistakable. Although he does have some trouble with his use of public space, at least he does better than Arendt and Wolin in recognizing that politics extends well beyond the most encompassing of communities, and thus so must the public.

Index

243